WHO IS A BRAHMIN?

The Politics of Identity in India

WHO IS A BRAHMIN?

The Politics of Identity in India

GILLES CHUYEN

MANOHAR

CENTRE DE SCIENCES HUMAINES
2025

First published 2004
Reprinted 2020, 2021, 2022, 2023, 2024, 2025

ISBN 978-81-7304-603-2

Published by

Ajay Kumar Jain for
Manohar Publishers & Distributors
4753/23 Ansari Road, Daryaganj
New Delhi 110 002

Printed at

Replika Press Pvt. Ltd.

Contents

Preface 7

Introduction 9

1. Classification of the Relationship between Middle-class Brahmins and Politics 33

PART I: BRAHMIN IDENTITY AND THE PROFESSIONAL VARIABLE

BRAHMINS IN THE ARMY 61

2. History of Brahmins and the Military A Long-term Analysis: From the Vedas 63

3. Brahmin Identity in the Armed Forces 93

PART II: BRAHMIN IDENTITY AND THE REGIONAL VARIABLE

TAMIL BRAHMINS 119

4. Brahminism in the History of South India Medium Period: From the Late Nineteenth Century 121

5. Portrait of Tamil Brahmins 146

PART III: DIALOGUES ON IDENTITY AND OTHERNESS IN THE 1990s

BRAHMINS AND THE UNDERPRIVILEGED 119

6. Construction of Anti-Brahmin Identities by Untouchables 191

7. Brahmins and Social Justice: Who are the Underprivileged? 228

Conclusion 259

Appendix: Information Related to the Brahmin Interviewees 267

Bibliography 275

Index 289

Preface

This book is a translation of a doctoral thesis submitted to the Institute of Political Studies at Aix-en-Provence, Aix-Marseille III University, in June 2001. The intent of this research was to work in a transversal manner, to question values through an analysis of historical and regional disparities, to make Brahmins speak about themselves, and put these discourses into perspective by examining their ideological backgrounds.

The book, therefore, has an open time and space framework. It deals with Brahminical readings of contemporary Indian society, through issues of caste, culture and politics at the national level and with reference to more specific pockets—Delhi, Agra and Chennai—where we conducted our fieldwork.

I would like to acknowledge the following persons and institutions for helping and guiding me in my research: the Centre de Sciences Humaines, New Delhi, with special thanks to its current Publications In-charge, Attreyee Roy Chowdhury; Professors Jayati and Gyaneshwar Chaturvedi from St. John's College, Agra; Professor Radhakrishnan from the Madras Institute of Development Studies; my Ph.D. guide, Dr Christophe Jaffrelot; the French Ministry of Foreign Affairs for its financial support; and Jean and Elizabeth Nandou for being my first gurus and initiators into the fascinating Indian ethos. Finally, I would like to express my love and respect to my parents for their continuous support.

New Delhi
October 2004

GILLES CHUYEN

Introduction

After more than half a century of Independence, India with its complex society and its glorious and ancient civilization finds itself facing a number of contemporary problems that provide food for reflection. Books trying to reduce India to an 'idea' and newspaper articles grappling with the meaning of 'being Indian' are presenting debates on conflicts of values. These values concern both internal and external issues such as the working of the democratic system in a society characterized by extreme cultural diversity, economic liberalization, modernization and Westernization.[1]

In view of these circumstances, it is but natural that Hinduism and, consequently, the problem of caste should be in the forefront today. Apart from its religious and philosophical content, Hinduism is also a social organization of which the notion of caste is an integral part, even though the original relationship between the Hindu religion and the caste system is still a subject of debate. Whether we look at it positively or negatively as an institution, the notion of caste continues to be at the heart of any discourse on Indian society and remains active in different kinds of environments, thus offering the various possible images of its content. After assessing the historical and ideological aspects of this notion, we will deal with the one that is of prime importance today, viz., its political dimension, the central point of our analysis of Brahmin identity.

Although the word 'caste' is of Portuguese origin dating from the first wave of colonization of the Indian subcontinent, it covers notions that go back much further in time. The true origin of caste lies in the hierarchical principle underlying the Indo-European civilization, which persists in India to this day in myriad forms reflecting the different phases of its history and especially its colonial legacy.

The division of society into castes is based on the hierarchical principle enshrined in the Vedas, India's oldest texts that define 'knowledge', especially sacred knowledge. This principle is enunciated in the *Rigveda*, in the hymn to *Purusa* (*Rigveda*, X. 90). Although this hymn is considered to be an interpolation, its approach is intrinsically linked to the foundations of the Indo-European civilization.[2]

6

When the gods performed the sacrifice
with man as the oblation,
spring served as butter (ritual),
summer as firewood, autumn as the offering. (...)

11

When they had dismembered Man,
how did they distribute the different parts?
What happened to his mouth, his arms?
His thighs, his feet, what name were they given?

12

His mouth became the Brahmin,
the Warrior was the product of his arms,
his thighs became the Artisan,
from his feet was born the Servant.[3]

First of all, the hymn explains that the organized world centred around Brahmin society was born of the sacrifice of a primeval victim. This theory of the origin of the universe describes creation as the dismemberment of a cosmic *Purusa*. This *Purusa*, who later stands for the empirical man, signifies in this case 'the Male' and the description of his different parts dismembered during the sacrifice to give birth to living beings shows that he has a human form. Thus the sacrifice of a creature that had the appearance of a man, without actually being one, gave rise to the cosmos.[4]

This myth of the dismemberment of a primitive man is also found in other Indo-European cultures. Many Persian texts describe a similar process. They say that Ahura Mazda created the world within his body and transferred it into the real world with his own body. Similarly, the *Edda*, a collection of old Scandinavian literary works, relates the dismemberment of the giant Ymir.

From Ymir's flesh was the earth created,
From his legs mountains,
The sky from the giant's skull cold as snow,
The backwash from his blood.[5]

Indian civilization has a number of triads for classifying nature. Thus the system of *gunas* consists of the three essential elements of the universe—*sattva*, pure and luminous, *rajas*, dynamic and passionate and *tamas*, a factor of darkness and inertia—expressed in three symbolic colours—white, red and black.[6]

This ternary division applied to surroundings, values and mythical themes is also reflected socially in the division of work. Just like the three 'estates' that existed in France during the Ancien Régime, Indian society is organized around three functional poles consisting of magical and religious activities, political and martial activities and economic and productive activities, according to the Indo-European principle of trifunctionality mentioned in the works of Dumézil and Benveniste. Hindu gods are classified in a similar manner with Mitra and Varuna as the supreme gods, Indra the god of war and the Ashwins, the twin patrons of farmers and cattle-breeders.[7]

Actually, it is the three higher *varnas* (colours) that constitute the real caste structure while the fourth category, viz., the Shudras or servants, certainly consisted of the aboriginal peoples of India.[8] Hindu society is thus divided into four categories, each having a specific function. So, the Brahmin is the priest, the Kshatriya the warrior, the Vaishya is involved in trade and farming while the Shudra performs menial tasks. The first three *varnas* are the *dvija*, the twice-born, because they alone have the right to undergo a second birth in the form of a ritual initiation which allows them to participate in all religious ceremonies.

This division into *varnas* represents a hierarchy of social relationships centred around sacrificial rites.[9] It is this symbolic structure that forms the basis of the hierarchy of *jatis*, or castes as they exist today, as hereditary endogamous groups separated from each other by their well-defined occupations.

The *varna* and *jati* systems are further divided according to the notions of what is pure and impure. A hierarchy of occupations is thus established according to their relationship to various substances like blood or other natural impurities that may cause pollution.[10] With the growth of population and through the various phases of Indian history, this system of watertight and conceptual categories underwent many changes.[11] However, this symbolic hierarchical system has often been applied in its original form to the functioning of Indian society, especially through the works of Western Orientalists. This approach does not take into account either the changes that the social hierarchy has undergone through the ages or the truly functional dimension of the notion of caste, especially when it is used for political purposes.

The earliest European travellers, who came looking for 'their India', do usually only refer to the *varna* system. It was after the establishment of the British colonial presence in the second half of the eighteenth century that caste came to occupy a special place in the perception of Indian society. From then on, the British colonial authorities showed a desire to acquire a more systematic knowledge of this society, as illustrated on the ideological plane by the evolution of the Orientalist approach and on a more concrete plane by a series of efforts to classify the population.

Orientalism, defined by the Petit Robert dictionary as a 'study of Oriental things' and by the Petit Larousse dictionary as 'all disciplines devoted to the study of Eastern civilizations', is a rather ponderous term associated with the colonial period. It has ideological and methodological connotations and can be associated in modern times with the works of Louis Dumont.

The term Orientalism should be handled carefully, especially because of its various ideological connotations. It is often associated with imperialism and it is therefore necessary to make a distinction between the two terms and clarify their relationship. An analysis of the career and works of Max Mueller in particular helps us to understand the issues involved in the debate. Max Mueller, who was a Professor in Oxford University and directed a monumental series of fifty-one volumes entitled *The Sacred Books of the East*, is a typical example of the difference between political and cultural imperialism. He clearly declared himself in favour of imperial authority and policies while analysing India respectfully and avoiding any tendency to treat it as an inferior civilization.[12] This distinction is not very obvious in the case of Orientalism, especially when it comes to Edward Said's work on the Middle East or Ronald Inden's work on India, where cultural imperialism and Orientalism are shown as being on at par with each other in the context of colonization.[13]

Further, a distinction must be made between the research conducted by Orientalists and its use by imperialistic colonial powers.[14] For instance, James Mill's *History of British India* written in 1817, which is a typical example of ethnocentrism, denounces and severely criticizes the autocratic monopolization of learning by the Brahmins. The colonial authorities, on the contrary, took the strategic decision of not interfering with local power-centres but of using them instead as allies and a means of penetrating Indian society. His approach is thus directly opposed to various traits considered to be characteristic of Orientalism. He is particularly critical of the use of mythological material by scholars to analyse the societies they came across.[15] Nevertheless, his work remains a product of cultural imperialism in tune with the utilitarianism that was in vogue in England at that time.

Contemporary Orientalists are fully aware of this debate. In a White Paper on French Orientalism, they admitted that 'the term Orientalism is a legacy from the past. If it is a subject of controversy today, it is so because it is sullied by western ethnocentrism'. But they reversed this reasoning by adding that 'the problem concerns only the West and does not in any way question the validity of studies on eastern civilizations (...). The accusations against Orientalism are a direct result of the western notion of human sciences and society. It is therefore this western prejudice that should be questioned'.[16] The 'validity of studies on eastern civilizations' is indisputable, but it is not at the core of the critics of Orientalism who tend to highlight problems of methodology in this field of study which could have led to a biased view of the societies under study.

The key problem is related to the systematic use of written documents, whether mythological or religious, to understand social phenomena. Developing such an approach, where textual references are often the principal material, give rise to a hackneyed view of Hinduism. It is in fact necessary, especially in the case of a country like India, to highlight the historical nature of various social phenomena. Although Edward Said and Ronald Inden criticize any stereotyped view of societies they study, they do not seem to identify themselves with this approach. In an article analysing the works of these writers, Aijaz Ahmad points out in particular that Inden, in spite of his erudite denunciation of Eurocentricism, has a tendency to reject one essential category, viz., caste, and replace it with another, viz., Royalty.[17] This same tendency of approaching fixed categories from an intellectual angle is found in Louis Dumont's works on Indian society.

Louis Dumont's works on both anthropology and Indology, though enlivened by an innovative spirit, have been widely criticized because of their ideological colonial legacy and Orientalist approach.[18] For instance, they are a fairly good example of the 'brahmanocentrism' mentioned earlier.

The theoretical basis of his reference work, *Homo Hierarchicus* published in 1966, is methodological holism, which means that hierarchy is the central principle that explains the working of the caste system in a set-up where a part has some meaning only in relation to the whole. In another book entitled *La civilisation indienne et nous*—The Indian Civilization and us—he expresses this idea by pointing out that a specific notion of the being is defined in India. Far from being an isolated unit, as in the West, 'the being is a part of the relationship and the poles of this relationship do not have an independent ontological status (...). The necessary and hierarchical coexistence of contradictory elements is the essence of the caste system.'[19]

This tendency to separate the East and the West so explicitly, and even oppose them, is characteristic of an Orientalist approach. This leads to an overestimation of the importance of religion in Eastern societies and an exaggerated attention to ancient texts in order to understand India's past. It is in this context that Dumont explains the caste system by basing himself on the essential dichotomy between the pure and the impure and repeating Célestin Bouglé's definition of the 'caste spirit' as the coming together of the three tendencies of 'repulsion, hierarchy and hereditary specialization'.[20]

However, Louis Dumont wanted to establish a balance between field studies and the use of Sanskrit texts as a reference. As a matter of fact, his work is inherently paradoxical because of the contradictory intellectual influences that characterized French Indology during the 1930s. To start with, Dumont identifies himself with René Guénon, an essayist attracted by the esoteric, who states a perfect similarity between the spiritual hierarchy of principles and the social hierarchy of castes, according to an organicist vision, thereby justifying the Brahminical theory of power. He also bases his work on Durkheim's view of sociology which, when applied to Indology, makes it possible to deconstruct the different categories of Brahminical thought, thus being in opposition with the essentialist vision of the social sphere. The sociologist, Roland Lardinois, explains how Dumont tries to reconcile these two contradictory approaches by retranslating the Brahminical model in the idiom of a value-based society and offering it as a learned model of Indian society. However, this attempt goes against the very core of Durkheim's perception which seeks to distinguish between indigenous and sociological understanding.[21]

Homo Hierarchicus is nevertheless a seminal work essential for understanding the working of caste affiliations, even though the economic and political aspects are generally rather underestimated, due to the period when the field study was carried out, as this period was not very conducive to such phenomena or at least to their extensive study. The fact remains that Louis Dumont highlighted one political dimension of caste, with the notion of substantiation. This concept led to the development of the notion of caste as an interest group, which is essential in the contemporary understanding of caste.

Apart from the orientalist perspective, colonial views gave birth to processes of classifying Indian population, which had tremendous effects on the classification itself, within the caste system. After the 1760s, the British needed very precise information about this vast new colony to promote their economic interests. The management of the East India Company in Bengal wanted to set-up an administrative system that was capable of maintaining law and order and collecting sufficient revenue to run the Company and also make a profit. The first phase of collecting information about landed property prepared the ground for a series of projects for collecting the required information and laying down a systematic procedure for this purpose. This tendency led to official surveys that were subsequently integrated into the ambitious project of taking a census of the Indian population. Thus the first attempts to assess the country's population in the 1820s were succeeded by modern census methods after the 1870s and 1880s.

From my point of view, recording the caste of the individuals questioned during census operations is of particular interest. When such an exercise is undertaken, it is necessary to find out its exact purpose and Ghurye and Srinivas worked exactly on this issue. It is possible to advance two main explanations for this action, viz., issues relating to colonial strategy and the repercussions with reference to the perception of the notion of caste.

In the first place, it appears quite legitimate from the viewpoint of the British policy of colonization to relate this process of acquiring information to the overall scheme of domination. Arjun Appadurai talks of 'enumeration strategies' when he actually means quantification policies. They may have initially been a pragmatic exercise, but they gradually acquired a crucial significance in colonial thinking wherein quantifiable abstractions created an impression of a quantifiable indigenous reality.[22]

But even in more general terms, this strategy can be associated with the overall intention to 'divide and rule'. This is one way of interpreting the tendency to use these surveys to emphasize the specific characteristics of various communities constituting the Indian population. The fact remains, as B.S. Cohn points out in his study that is now considered a classic, that the census operations had an effect on the object of their study by creating 'an awareness of caste'.[23] The ethnographic study conducted by H.H. Risley in Bengal, which served as a basis for the 1901 census, fully conforms to this approach. In the course of this survey people were asked their opinion about the results of the census before it was completed. Quite naturally, many hostile opinions were expressed on the subject. For example, the placing of Kayasths just below the Brahmins in the caste hierarchy, roused the ire not only of the former but also of the Kshatriyas and the Vaishyas who refused to be considered inferior to them. The initial reaction in the form of letters of protest, quotations from religious texts, opinions of respected Sanskrit scholars was accompanied by the formation of caste-based associations called *sabhas* to defend the group's status and specific interests.[24] These associations are very active even today in the Indian social system.

Cohn also highlights the effects of these census operations on the theoretical views of Indian administrators and the census-takers on Indian society. He points out that treatises on the caste system written between 1880 and 1950 are mostly the work of men holding important positions connected with census operations, such as various Census Commissioners. Apart from

H.H. Risley, this was also true of D. Ibbetson and J.H. Hutton. Other authors, who do not belong to this category, such as C. Bouglé, A.M. Hocart and W. Crooke, did still use census results as the main material for their studies.

In his study on the tribes and castes of north-west India, W. Crooke analyses the notion of caste. In conclusion he makes the following observations: the Vedas mention only a rough division of work; the first signs of caste as we know it today are to be found in the 'Ordinances of Manu' but the rules described are quite different from those that prevailed during his time; far from being eternal and unchanged, caste had undergone constant changes as evidenced by Hindu history and mythology. Further, the institution of caste is not peculiar to India; it is a sociological rather than a religious phenomenon; the original division into *varnas* does not coincide with social reality and these terms do not correspond to distinct ethnological groups. And from these observations, he draws the conclusion that the only reliable base for an ethnological study is anthropometry.[25]

However, there is an obvious contradiction between his awareness of a constant change in the nature of caste and his willingness to analyse it with the help of a tool as rigorous as anthropometry. As a matter of fact, this kind of analysis tends to look on caste as a 'thing', a concrete and measurable entity having definite characteristics. Hence India is perceived as a 'collection of castes' and the Brahmin as 'the preserver of an intellect superior to that of all other races'.[26]

The entire process being a mixture of strategy and uncontrolled repercussions, has led to the crystallization of the divisions within the caste system into watertight groups as well as to the crystallization of the notion of caste. This burdensome legacy exerts a strong influence on the understanding of the notion of caste, particularly in relation to the political domain. The political dimension of caste will be taken up first through theoretical discussions on the nature of caste, especially on the hesitation to assimilate politics into the notion of caste. This topic will then be addressed through the central theme of this study, viz., Brahmin identity today.

The colonial period, as we have seen, has left its mark on theoretical as well as ordinary opinions regarding caste. Some theoretical conceptions, still current, tend to minimize the importance of the political factor and go against historical facts. Others understand the notion of caste in its contemporary form by assimilating politics into it.

Orientalists had a tendency to rigidify the theoretical approach to caste by focusing only on the study of theoretical principles involved. Dumont's work illustrates this failing. The Indian sociologist, André Béteille, criticized this approach soon after the publication of *Homo Hierarchicus*. In an article written in response to this work, he pointed out that this type of study of traditional Indian culture and society contains two major distortions. It gives too much importance to caste and depicts it as a system of non-antagonistic groups. In fact, it is quite obvious that there are social relationships in Indian society that lie outside the domain of pure caste-based relations, particularly when economic and political stakes are involved. Further, he emphasizes that caste itself is a favoured channel for political and economic negotiations. He explains that Louis Dumont's work, as well as the approach adopted by E.R. Leach and F.G. Bailey, are mainly concerned with studying the structure of values without taking into account the structure of interests and offer a stereotyped and false view of the actual working of the caste system.[27]

These theoretical blocks, already a thing of the past, categorically denying the economic and political dimensions of caste, have now made way for approaches that take cognizance of these dimensions, but in a dissociated manner. It is thus possible to envisage two different phenomena that could be accommodated under the term 'caste': a structural system that is actually the element of a system and a dynamic force forming a series of autonomous groups.[28] This dichotomy does not have a concrete presence given the overlapping of the religious, economic and political spheres in contemporary Indian society and it does not account for the historical relationship between the phenomenon of caste and politics.

In fact, during the British colonial period, the dynamic progress in the representation of the Indian people in politics from the beginning of the twentieth century occurred through the efforts of communities and not through 'isolated individuals'.[29] Furthermore, as we have seen earlier, demographic classification policies pursued by British officials led to the creation of caste-based associations capable of defending the interests of a particular caste as regards its status and political representation. This latter phenomenon is the crystallization of the narrow relationship that still exists within Indian society between the caste structure and political advantages.

It should be noted, that although it rejects the conception of Indian society as a whole consisting of distinctive communities—construct of the colonial mind, post-colonial politics does not appear to break away from it as evidenced by the alliances between various castes and communities in present-day politics. Partha Chatterjee points out the present reluctance to conduct a theoretical debate, in the framework of a modern state, on the stakes of the community perceived as the 'universal prehistory of progress'. In the eyes of non-Western societies, it seems that colonized peoples are unwilling at a given point of time to belong to a civil society consisting of subjects defined by the colonizer and prefer to (re)construct their identity(ies) outside the conceptual framework of the modern state. They would rather adopt a different identity, one provided by the community that in India is related to the living cultural environment of the caste.[30] And this tendency to use sub-national links for political mobilization and representation exists even in the post-colonial period.

It thus appears that the pertinent questions concerning the relationship between the notion of caste and politics are not to be taken into account in terms of exclusion but rather in terms of interaction, as Rajni Kothari did way back in 1970 by asking, 'What form does politics assume in a society structured by caste?' and 'What form does caste assume under the influence of modern politics?'.

Firstly, it must be noted that important political stakes involved in the organization and expression of electoral support in India cannot but depend on caste constituting one of the major social networks in India. Secondly, the democratic political scene in India is often disparagingly described as 'casteist', meaning thereby that electoral campaigns depend on the solidarity between the members of the candidate's caste. But it would be more appropriate to consider this so-called 'casteism' in Indian politics as a consequence of the 'politicization of caste'.[31] This shows that in the contemporary political scene in India, there are processes at work in which different forms of caste and different types of politics come together and undergo changes in the course of their interaction.[32]

A contemporary understanding of caste should therefore distance itself from the ideology of caste which defines caste exclusively as a hierarchical system governed by rules of purity and pollution. As we have already seen, this view was encouraged by the British and served as a field of study for ethnographers trying to analyse 'traditional' Indian society. On the contrary, castes should be considered as interest-based groups that tend to act independently in relation to the overall caste system. This is exactly what Louis Dumont claimed when he talked of the 'substantiation of caste', that is to say 'the passage from a fluid structural universe where there is emphasis on interdependence (...) towards a universe of impenetrable self-sufficient blocs that are essentially identical and in competition with one another'.[33]

This substantialist affirmation of cultural distinctiveness within the caste system is at the core of contemporary Indian politics based on the solicitation of support from rival autonomous communities. The passage from ethnicity to caste described in Max Weber's model is inverted in the Indian situation. What we have instead, is the movement from an interdependent hierarchical system towards a set of autonomous groups having different interests; or dissociated ethnic groups, in a process involving the 'ethnicization of caste'.[34] This phenomenon does not refer to a narrow 'racial' conception of caste but to a wider perception that includes socio-economic and political dimensions in direct conflict. It must also take into account not only political stakes that accentuate the dividing line between different groups but also the cultural and identity stakes of each group so defined because, as the Africanist anthropologist Luc de Heusch rightly points out, 'affirming, from a general sociological viewpoint, that culture as such should be removed from the definition of the ethnic group is a dangerous position'.[35]

It is now necessary to determine at what level of segmentation caste enters the political process. André Béteille criticizes Srinivas because he says that a distinction must be made between caste at the political level, and caste at the social or ritualistic level, and that the latter aspect represents a smaller unit. As a matter of fact, Srinivas seems to consider the caste's political stakes only at the overall state level without taking into account the stakes involved in political negotiations, for example at the village level. Further, by establishing such a hierarchy, Srinivas denies the existence of a certain amount of social and ritualistic coherence at a level higher than that of the actual endogamous caste or *jati*.[36] I differ from André Béteille, however, when he sums up the contemporary evolution of caste as two related changes—emphasis on politics instead of religion and on *jati* instead of *varna*.[37] In fact, belonging to the Brahmin *varna* can have definite political implications today.

In what way does belonging to a particular caste, understood both as *jati* and *varna*, have political implications? Brahmins have enjoyed a privileged position in society for a very long time. They stand at the top of the socio-ritualistic hierarchy and, because of this, they follow practices that are different from those followed by other castes, constituting therefore a sign of their superiority. So what is the position of contemporary Brahmins caught up in issues of socio-economic status and political competition? There is a need to question this validity of a Brahmin identity and its substance, especially in relation to politics.

Rather than 'a museum where new forms are superimposed on old ones without removing the latter and thus producing a stratified mass where the contribution of successive ages is recognizable'[38], the Indian social system seems more like a game involving processes of evolution, redefinition and reconstruction within different categories that were once distinct. In this process where reality becomes more complex, what place does the Brahmin, who was originally at the top of the social hierarchy, occupy today? The Brahmin, as a theoretical category, has to give way to Brahmins with various attitudes and status.

The study of a Brahminical model, as related to the original social function, has no meaning today as far as our approach is concerned because it is crystallized and cannot fit into analysis situated in time and space. Although it is a commendable effort, especially from the philological point of view, it is biased as it tends to project a generalized description of contemporary Indian society. Developing such an approach, where textual references are often the main source of material, leads to a stereotyped conception of Hinduism. This tendency was peculiar to the

Orientalist approach centred around essentialist categories, especially caste, as was elaborated before.[39] When it is a matter of analysing the status of Brahmins in particular, such an endeavour tends to be misleading. It must be remembered that Brahmin scholars, who wrote the basic texts, managed to diffuse through their writings a normative model supporting their interests.[40]

So if we were to confine ourselves to such an approach, we would end up with a system that is closed because it is hierarchical and built upon immutable Brahminical values. There is no longer any question of a traditional model that is unitary and monolithic. It is necessary to put into proper perspective the fact that contemporary Brahmins have followed extremely heterogeneous paths of varying historical phases, geographical location and economic situation, which have given rise to numerous subcultures and world-views.

The larger framework of this study attempts to understand the cultural context of politics. Even among Brahmins, different codes and symbols may have different meanings for different groups. Each group identifies its reference points by referring to certain elements in its past and by interpreting tradition selectively. These references then sustain and legitimize the attitudes of the different groups. Each group thus defines a certain legacy of meanings made up of emblematic figures, texts and events that serve as references. Contemporary Brahmins, in relation to their origins, opt for a process of 'distance-memory' which makes some of them dream of a golden age that is long past.[41] This primary operation involving a selective memory opens the competition of rival social groups to reconstruct the past. So, supported by different reference points, each group tries to define belief systems built around values and, driven by ideological dynamics, devise new processes to rebuild tradition. These different discourses of contemporary Brahmins question the significance of caste at the present time in relation to a living democracy and the issue of belonging to an élite class, thus raising the crucial question of the validity of socio-political programmes.

These disparate parameters can be analysed with reference to the notion of identity. Initially studied and conceptualized in the field of psychology, identity was first expressed in its individual form as personal identity. This multidimensional notion can be defined as 'all the feelings and impressions that a person develops regarding him/herself' or as 'that which allows a person to remain the same, to fulfil and become him/herself in a given culture and in relation to others'.[42] Psychology emphasizes the construction process that it entwines in a dual movement of assimilation and differentiation, identification with others but also distinguishing oneself from them.

This relationship with others is also present in philosophical analysis. Paul Ricoeur, for example, shows the relationship between identity and alterity. First, he differentiates between two main meanings: identity = *idem* or sameness, i.e. identity of the same and identity = *ipse* or self, i.e. identity of self. Identity = *idem* refers to oneness, extreme resemblance, uninterrupted continuity and permanence in time. Identity = *ipse* does not presuppose an invariable nucleus in a personality. Alterity is a part of its ontological constitution. The other must imagine him/herself as being in his/her exclusive sphere; the other is obviously not one of the objects of thought but, like me a subject of thought. 'In the event that I am alone, this experience can never be summed up without the help of the other who helps me to gather myself, to assert myself and maintain myself within my identity'.[43]

This notion of alterity is more significant when one considers identity in its social dimension. Identity is then intrinsically related to the notion of culture. Culture, which has been discussed threadbare and is either a key term or taboo for various social sciences and their theoreticians, has been defined in numerous ways. In a critical approach to culturalism, culture has been analysed as a simplification based on the notion of common values, a strategic rationalization by specific social players who are most of the time members of the intellectual élite.[44] Further, Clifford Geertz has proposed a definition that avoids any reference to the idea of value and clarifies that rather than a set of complexes of concrete behavioural models involving customs, habitual practices and traditions, culture is a set of controlling mechanisms including plans, procedures, rules and instructions. And a human being who is thoroughly dependent on these controlling mechanisms, develops thoughts that, far from being simple 'events' in his/her brain, refer to a 'movement of meaningful symbols'.[45]

There is nothing new about this symbolic dimension attributed to the notion of culture. The work of Lévi-Strauss is a beautiful example.[46] But his reference to a 'movement' of symbols which sets the perspective from the domain of interpretation, and no longer from pure meaning, clarifies the relationship between culture and identity. The notion of identity, as a matter of fact, is by its very nature linked to the interpretation process and to questions of limitation, which leads us to alterity (exclusion/inclusion—who belongs to it?).[47]

There is differentiation of identity between social groups and also within each group. Culture first fashions collective identity by defining the basis of a common sense. The group's identity then impregnates individual attitudes thus giving rise to various interpretations.[48] In the course of this analysis I also question the nature of the phenomena of culture and identity with reference to flexibility and malleability. Michel Serres' contribution to aesthetic studies offers a particularly rich description of culture as a crossroads, a space open to the other that is sensitive to external influences. Culture has a meaning for him only because of the intricacy of cultures.[49]

My study fits in with this perspective by questioning 'contemporary Brahmin identity'. Being in favour of a flexible conception of identity, it attempts to determine the extent to which different types of Brahmins relate to a referential Brahmin identity and questions the existence of a hard core of contemporary Brahmin identity.

The main purpose of the study is to assess the pluralism of contemporary Brahmin identity in the context of the major socio-political debates taking place in the Indian democracy. Shifting from the individual to the collective and from the collective to the individual, identity belongs to the domain of history. It arises out of the discourse on the collective 'we' which links with variable strength individuals and groups.[50]

Contemporary Brahmin identity is thus the discourse of present-day Brahmins on Brahminism. In other words, Brahminism is often presented as a set of fixed values, which is the core of Indian civilization according to some scholars and, according to others, the source of socio-economic inequalities. However, the Brahmins themselves are now subjecting it to interpretation and reinterpretation, particularly in political terms, in the form of a discourse on identity. Contemporary Brahmin identity is thus expressed in the discourse on Brahmin culture understood as a set of values as well as mechanisms for exercising control and domination.

In order to draw up a list of the topics deemed relevant by the actors concerned, an investigation was undertaken in Delhi, Agra and Chennai (Madras). A series of around seventy non-directive interviews were conducted on the basis of an open question, viz., 'What does it mean to you to be a Brahmin in India today?'. This study is intended to highlight the internal pluralism of the Brahmin category, or, in other words, question the existence of transversal notions and central values in self-definitions that are more or less shared within this category, with special reference to the political sphere. In addition to these interviews, there were more focused interviews of both Brahmins and non-Brahmins on specific subjects to obtain precise information on particular points.

The interviewees themselves were selected from the urban middle class. This choice of milieu is related to various factors. In the first place, it involves a stratum of the population that is distinct from the large mass of poor people with reference to purchasing power. It is thus directly affected by the consequences of the opening of the country's economy since 1991 and the benefits of the modernization and Westernization of lifestyles in terms of imported goods and changes in the audio-visual scene.

This group is preoccupied with professional gains brought by the country's modernization but, at the same time, it is firmly attached to its roots and has shown itself to be acutely aware of major intellectual debates, especially those on caste.[51] In this respect, it occupies a privileged position for assessing the conflict between contemporary Indian values.

For this purpose, the perspective chosen is not to study a representative sample but to cover the widest possible range of attitudes towards the subject in question. The factors that were taken into account for this investigation included sex, age, geographical origin, educational qualifications, languages known and socio-professional category. We are not trying to reach a quantitative conclusion but to present a wide range of varied attitudes and opinions that would be used for a typology.

By analysing these interviews, we have been able to assess the perceptions of the various actors belonging to the Brahmin category, but this assessment must take into account the inner building process inherent to any object of knowledge. The information provided by the interviewees was indeed not simply recorded but it was filtered through various screens of interpretation determined by the history of the individual and his group. This meant going back to the circumstances and strategies that had conditioned the person and given rise to particular opinions on Brahmin identity or, in other words, defining the various 'habitus of *varna*' in action, to borrow a phrase from Bourdieu.

It is thus possible to talk of durable and transposable tendencies in relation to *varna*, in the dimension of identity, i.e. in relation to the discourses on *varna* without taking into account the question of birth. As a matter of fact, for some actors, belonging to a particular *varna* means much more than the birth factor, in relation to values and certain professions especially. The first division appears to be a result of the opposition of views between what I would call the 'impersonal category' and the 'personalized category'. The Brahmin category is 'impersonal' when it has no special significance of its own for the actor and is just a category imposed by society. The category is 'personalized' when the actor attributes to it a personal definition related to his public and private spheres, defined as 'objective' in relation to factors like birth, special rituals, a particular geographical origin or an appropriate profession and 'subjective' when based on reference values. We will refer to this classification between the 'impersonal' and 'personalized' categories several times in the course of this study, according to the definition of these terms I have just given.

On the basis of the sixty odd interviews conducted in Delhi, Agra and Chennai, I have established a general typology for the relationship of Brahmins to politics. The last two cities were selected after the first stage of interviews conducted in Delhi involving some twenty odd Brahmins from different parts of India. Agra was selected because I wanted to include a town in Uttar Pradesh, the state where the use of caste in politics is very evident and widespread and because of its proximity to the rural world. Chennai became almost an automatic choice because of the glaring difference in the attitudes of Brahmins in north India and south India, as we shall soon see.

The first chapter of this study deals with the typology as such and outlines the attitudes of contemporary Brahmins classified according to the degree and the type of acceptation of links between their Brahmin identity and politics. I had no reference to a representative sample and did not look at any quantitative conclusion. The object of this classification of the relationship of Brahmins to politics is to evaluate the role played by politics in the formation of the Brahmin identity in India today.

Through these interviews, I have been able to isolate three major unifying domains that make it possible to understand contemporary Brahmin identity from various complementary angles. These domains are profession, geographical origin and the issue of the assertion of underprivileged sections. They constitute the three parts of this study.

This means defining the socio-historical processes that support the affirmation of this identity with reference to professional activity, geographical origin and determining to what extent urban middle-class Brahmins appreciate the efforts of the lower castes to assert themselves. In this framework, it is extremely important to define the concept of alterity as a part of these processes in order to understand how different identities are formed.

This study is thus an analysis of types, presenting variations of the Brahmin identity according to the different lines of thinking as defined in the attitudes and opinions of the Brahmins we interviewed, but viewed in the proper perspective and context and with a critical eye. Each part is subdivided into a more historical chapter explaining the context and the game played by Brahmins as actors, as seen from the outside, while the second chapter concentrates more on analysing the attitude of the Brahmins towards the specific topic of study, as seen from inside.

My approach uses different historical scales for the three parts. The three time-scales correspond to the three levels of reference used by the actors for defining their identity. In order to define their Brahmin identity, they depend on three major types of support, viz., philological support by referring to books of a religious nature, historical support by invoking certain events between the late nineteenth century and the present, and the analysis of political debates that have taken place during the last decade. These three time-scales are paired with the three unifying domains identified earlier. After the first chapter dealing with general typology, the other three domains are addressed as the three main parts of this analysis.

First of all, I deal with the variable of profession with reference to the Hindu sacred texts or, in other words using the long period scale, through the case study of Brahmin warriors. This first part consists of the study of Brahmins employed in the army and tends to clarify the dominant discourse in this institution regarding caste and questions the links defined in ancient times between caste identity and occupation. In this first part, Chapter 2 deals with specific historical conditions characterizing this group of Brahmin warriors, while Chapter 3 analyses the domination of military culture over caste references as expressed by Brahmins of this group.

Secondly, the issue of geographical origins has been addressed on a medium period scale, from the late nineteenth century, starting with the anti-Brahmin movement in Tamil Nadu. I decided to focus on Tamil Brahmins, because they are extremely conscious of their Brahmin identity and express themselves forcefully on this subject, with reference to the origins of anti-Brahmin politics in this region. In Chapter 4 the nature of the advantages enjoyed by Brahmins in the history of south India is elucidated, in order to explain the circumstances that led to the attitudes of contemporary Tamil Brahmins described in Chapter 5.

The third and final part will deal with dialogues on identity and alterity between Brahmins and the underprivileged classes by focusing on the political scene in north India during the 1990s which have been witness to innovative political manifestations in this respect. Chapter 6 defines the anti-Brahmin identity of untouchables. Chapter 7 deals with the way Brahmins interpret social justice in a socio-political context that is perceived to be hostile.

NOTES

1. See Sunil Khilnani, *The Idea of India*, London: Hamish-Hamilton, 1997. *The Hindu*, 14/02/97; *The Times of India*, 09/12/97; *India Today*, 18/08/97.

2. R. Thapar, *Ancient Indian social history—some interpretations*, Delhi: Sangam Books, 1984, pp. 127-8.
3. From the English translation of *Hymnes spéculatifs du Véda*, French version by Louis Renou, Paris: Gallimard, 1956, pp. 97-9.
4. M. Biardeau, *L'hindouisme—anthropologie d'une civilisation*, Paris: Flammarion, 1981, p. 31.
5. J. Naudou, 'Polymorphisme du divin et monothéisme en Inde' in *Les Grandes Figures Religieuses, Lire les Polythéismes 1*, Annales littéraires de l'Université de Besançon, Paris: Les Belles Lettres, 1986, pp. 15-17.
6. J. Naudou, 'L'analyse ternaire de la nature dans la pensée indienne', *Revue de l'Histoire des Religions*, Paris, 1980, pp. 15-22.
7. L. Renou and J. Filliozat, *L'Inde classique. Manuel des Etudes indiennes*, Paris: Librairie d'Amérique et d'Orient, Jean Maisonneuve, 1985, vol. 1, pp. 315-23.
8. L. Dumont, *Homo Hierarchicus*, Paris: Gallimard, 1992, pp. 93-5.
9. M. Biardeau, *L'hindouisme—anthropologie d'une civilisation*, Paris: Flammarion, 1981, p. 27.
10. L. Dumont, *Homo Hierarchicus*, Paris: Gallimard, 1992, pp. 71-3.
11. That there is social mobility within the system is a fact as we shall see in the course of the analysis of the historical basis of the links between the Brahmin *varna* and military activity in Chapter 2.
12. D. Vidal, 'Max Müller and the theosophists, or the other half of Victorian Orientalism', *Pondy Papers in Social Sciences*, no. 24, Institut Français de Pondichéry, 1997, pp. 14-16.
13. E.W. Said, *Orientalism, western conception of the Orient*, London: Penguin Books, 1995. R.B. Inden, *Imagining India*, Oxford: Basil Blackwell, 1990.
14. It must however be kept in mind that the research work specifically related to the caste system was closely linked with colonial policies, as we shall see later.
15. He is in fact against any reference to imagination, unlike the earlier accounts of 'imaginary communities' in the late eighteenth and early nineteenth centuries, exposed in particular by the critical biblical studies of German scholars. See J. Majeed, *Ungoverned imaginings—James Mill's The History of British India and Orientalism*, New York: Clarendon Press, Oxford, 1992, pp. 123-50, 175-6, 181-3.
16. *Livre blanc de l'orientalisme*, Paris: Société Asiatique, 1993, pp. 13-14.
17. A. Ahmad, 'Between Orientalism and Historicism: Anthropological Knowledge of India', *Studies in history*, Delhi: Sage Publications, vol. 7, no. 1, 1991, pp. 156-7.
18. See C.A. Breckenridge and P. van der Veer, *Orientalism and the Postcolonial Predicament*, Delhi: Oxford University Press, 1990.

19. L. Dumont, *La civilization indienne et nous*, Paris: Armand Colin, 1975, p. 28.
20. A. Farooqui, 'Some Comments on Louis Dumont and the Orientalist Understanding of Caste', *Trends in Social Science research*, Delhi: Cambridge Press, vol. 3, no. 2, December 1996, p. 53.
21. R. Lardinois, 'Louis Dumont et la science indigène', *Actes de la Recherche en Sciences Sociales*, Paris: Seuil, nos. 106-7, March 1995.
22. A. Appadurai, 'Number in the colonial imagination' in *Orientalism and the postcolonial predicament*, ed. C.A. Breckenridge and P. van der Veer, Delhi: Oxford University Press, 1990, p. 317.
23. This is a recent process that Louis Dumont has not particularly dwelt on while presenting a 'naturally' compartmentalized caste system resulting from an ancient hierarchical order.
24. B.S. Cohn, *An anthropologist among the historians and others essays*, Delhi: Oxford University Press, 1990, pp. 241-7.
25. W. Crooke, *The Tribes and Castes of the North-Western India,* Delhi: Cosmo Publications, 1974 (1st ed. 1896), vol. 1, pp. xxv-vi.
26. B.S. Cohn, *An anthropologist among the historians and others essays*, Delhi: Oxford University Press, 1990, pp. 154-5.
27. See André Béteille's article (1966), 'The politics of "non-antagonistic" strata' in his collection of essays entitled *Society and Politics in India—Essays in a Comparative Perspective*, Delhi: Oxford University Press, 1992, pp. 122-39.
28. N. Jayaram, 'Caste and Hinduism: changing protean relationship', in *Caste—its twentieth century avatar*, ed. M.N. Srinivas, New Delhi: Viking, 1996, p. 71.
29. S. Khilnani, *The idea of India*, London: Hamish Hamilton, 1997, pp. 24-5.
30. See the extremely interesting article by Partha Chatterjee: 'The Manifold Uses of Jati', in *Social Change and Political Discourse in India: Structures of Power, Movements of Resistance*, vol. 3: *Region, Religion, Caste, Gender and Culture in Contemporary India*, ed. T.V. Sathyamurthy, New Delhi: Oxford University Press, 1996, pp. 281-92.
31. R. Kothari, ed., *Caste in Indian politics*, Delhi: Orient Longman, 1991, pp. 3-5.
32. See C. Jaffrelot, *La démocratie en Inde*, Paris: Fayard, 1998, Chapter 6, pp. 193-234.
33. L. Dumont, *Homo Hierarchicus*, Paris: Gallimard, 1992, p. 280.
34. C.J. Fuller, ed., *Caste Today*, Delhi: Oxford University Press, 1996, pp. 20-2.
35. L. de Heusch, 'L'ethnie: les Vicissitudes d'un Concept', *Archives Européennes de Sociologie*, Cambridge University Press, XXXVIII, 2, 1997, pp. 188-9.

36. A. Béteille, *Society and politics in India—essays in a comparative perspective*, Delhi: Oxford University Press, 1992, p. 87.
37. A. Béteille, 'Caste in contemporary India', in *Caste Today*, ed. C.J. Fuller, Delhi: Oxford University Press, 1996, p. 170.
38. L. Dumont, *La civilisation indienne et nous*, Paris: Armand Colin, 1975, p. 52.
39. W. Halbfass, *India and Europe—an essay in philosophical understanding*, Delhi: Motilal Banarsidass, 1990. B.S. Cohn, *An anthropologist among the historians and others essays*, Delhi: Oxford University Press, 1990. R.B. Inden, *Imagining India*, Oxford: Basil Blackwell, 1990.
40. P. van der Veer, 'The concept of the ideal Brahman as an indological construct' in *Hinduism reconsidered*, ed. H. Kulke et al., New Delhi: Manohar, 1991.
41. P. Nora, 'Entre Mémoire et Histoire' in *Les lieux de mémoire*, ed. P. Nora, Paris: Gallimard, 1993, vol. 1.
42. See interview with Pierre Tap, psychologist specializing in identity in *Sciences Humaines*, Identité–Identités, Special Issue, no. 15, Paris, p. 9.
43. P. Ricoeur, *Soi-même comme un autre*, Paris: Seuil, 1990, p. 384.
44. R. Boudon and F. Bourricaud, *Dictionnaire critique de la sociologie*, Paris: PUF, 1994, p. 143.
45. C. Geertz, *The interpretation of cultures*, London: Fontana Press, 1993, pp. 43-5.
46. Lévi-Strauss defines culture as a 'set of symbolic systems in the forefront of which are language, matrimonial rules, economic relationships, art, science and religion', in his *Introduction à l'œuvre de Marcel Mauss* (M. Mauss, *Sociologie et Anthropologie*, Paris: PUF, 1993, p. XIX).
47. Comments of Bishnu Mohapatra on 23/04/97 during the International Seminar on 'Culture, Communication and Power', Jamia Hamdard, New Delhi, 21-3/04/97, CSH-CCRSS.
48. Marc Augé's work, written earlier, emphasizes variability, for different groups and at different times, of access to these sources of knowledge or symbolic codes constituting a culture. M. Augé, *Le sens des autres—actualité de l'anthropologie*, Paris: Fayard, 1994.
49. M. Serres, *Esthétiques sur Carpaccio*, Paris: Hermann, 1975. Denis-Constant Martin's work also expresses exactly the same point of view.
50. D.C. Martin, ed., *Cartes d'identité—Comment dit-on'nous' en politique?,* Paris: Presses de la FNSP, 1994, pp. 18-23.
51. At the time of independence, the significance of caste for Indians was determined by the dialectics between colonial and national views. The colonial authorities considered the caste system as a prominent institution in Indian society and were opposed to the nationalists who

insisted that the institution was in decline. Indian intellectuals favour the second view because of their national pride—the caste system, like poverty and ignorance, is believed to be an obstacle on the path of progress—but also due to the weakening of the religious aspects of caste.

CHAPTER 1

Classification of the Relationship between Middle-class Brahmins and Politics

As explained in the introduction, caste is a complex concept and its present significance is the result of a long process of historical evolution and diverse ideological interpretations. Its political dimension, which forms the core of my study, plays a crucial role in these ideological debates. In the course of the sixty odd interviews that I conducted, it appeared that the attitude of Brahmins towards the politicization of caste is quite varied. This chapter aims to classify the relationship between Brahmins and politics on the basis of this series of interviews. The resulting typology takes into account the divisions pointed out in the introduction between private and public spheres and between personalized and impersonal categories. The first part discusses attitudes that do not fully recognize the political dimension of Brahmin identity, that is to say, its simultaneous action in the private and public spheres. I will then take up attitudes that fully accept the political dimension of Brahmin identity where Brahmins recognize the political dimension of their caste belonging, both in their private lives and in the way they look at the public space.

PARTIAL APPROACHES: THE POLYMORPHIC REJECTION OF THE TOTAL POLITICIZATION OF BRAHMIN IDENTITY

Brahmins who were interviewed on the subject of Brahmin identity tend to compartmentalize their references to this identity. In the first place, we will consider extreme cases based on the notion of a Brahmin identity totally dissociated from politics. We will then deal with discourses on identity where the Brahmin category is treated as being linked with politics, but without any real link with the private life (impersonal Brahmin category).

The Dissociation of Brahmin Identity from Politics

I will first deal with Brahmin attitudes which exclude the political dimension from their definition of Brahmin identity. I will analyse cases based on an impersonal Brahmin identity followed by cases of personalized identity, according to the meaning attributed to these terms in the introduction.

THE ABSENCE OF A LINK BETWEEN BRAHMIN IDENTITY AND POLITICS AND IMPERSONAL BRAHMIN IDENTITY

There are two types of approaches based on indifference to politics or interest in it.

Impersonal Brahmin Identity and the Absence of Involvement in Politics

This applies to Brahmins who define themselves without referring either to the fact that they are Brahmins (impersonal category), nor to any political dimension.

Let us take the case of a young theatre enthusiast who works for television. He does not think that being born a Brahmin is a part of his identity. The Brahmin category lies outside the sphere of his identity—it is defined in books and he does not connect it with political issues. It is so impersonal that he thinks that it would be good to be associated with it only if he were to make a film on the subject.[1]

This was also true of a fifty-nine-year-old Brahmin woman who admitted that she had never in her life given any thought to the significance of being a Brahmin and preferred to be considered a Kashmiri Hindu without any political implications.

I never thought about, that's a good question, but I can't think now, what do I. . . . as a Brahmin, that's a very good question, but I really can't think about it now...actually we have forgotten this type of a thing, Brahmin, Vaishya, Kshatriya, Shudra, whatever. . . .[2]

Of all the Brahmins who were interviewed, this type of attitude was more common among young middle-class urban Brahmins who shun politics either out of personal choice or because their family environment encourages such an attitude. This absence of politicization may also be seen among the less educated classes and particularly women. In the cases we came across, the ambiguousness of the relationship with caste can be explained by the low level of education or the Westernized urban environment of the interviewees.

Young Brahmins, who claim to be detached from the caste factor, have a 'modern' and 'progressive' approach to life and have not yet faced the identity debate that comes up at the time of marriage. In the case of older persons, I will not consider marriage as an ever-relevant issue when analysing the importance given to caste. Most of the Brahmins who were interviewed had, as a matter of fact, married a member of their own caste, due to parental pressure more than due to personal convictions about the importance of caste. For these older Brahmins, the minimal importance of caste in their personal lives may also, in some cases, be the result of the feeling deep down that they belong to an élite group that has existed for hundreds, if not thousands, of years, even though they may not express it consciously. We are thus closer in this case to the 'natural' variant explained later.

Impersonal Brahmin Identity and Involvement in Politics

This attitude was true of only one of the Brahmins I interviewed. He declared that politics was the very essence of his existence, but he refused to acknowledge the importance of his being a Brahmin. What mattered most in his definition of identity was being a Hindu or Indian, two terms that were synonymous in his lexicon. This amalgamation of the two terms is explained by the fact that he is an active member of the Rashtriya Swayamsevak Sangh (RSS), which tends to define the Indian nation in accordance with its religious ideology.

The interviewee also promotes the theory that belonging to a particular caste depends on action (*karma*) and not on birth as in the case of *jati*. He explains that the caste system was originally a very flexible system and a person's *varna* was determined by his behaviour rather than by his birth. According to him, the system became rigid under the British rule as they stressed the difference between the various *jatis* and languages prevalent among the Hindus.

This desire to assert oneself as a person detached from his social identity of caste and geographical origin is in keeping with the RSS ideology which seeks to promote to the entire society the ideal of a renouncer.[3] The refusal to accept that there are internal divisions within Hinduism is also a part of the political strategy of Hindu nationalists. The Hindu nationalist politicians, in particular, try to forge alliances between castes with the aim of forming larger blocks which will ultimately lead to the unification of all castes into a single Hindu community opposed to other religious communities.[4] Promoting Hinduism as a militant political movement somehow amounts in this case to the negation of the hierarchical caste structure.[5]

ABSENCE OF A LINK BETWEEN BRAHMIN IDENTITY AND POLITICS AND PERSONALIZED BRAHMIN IDENTITY

This type covers Brahmins who are very conscious of the fact that they are Brahmins but without linking their identity to politics. Their Brahmin identity is built around their way of life and specific values as well as particular professions.

The Issue of the Way of Life

Brahmins who embody this type of attitude refer to a particular way of life that they believe is 'Brahminical'. Many Brahmins of this type consider the sacred-thread ceremony as the beginning of an awareness of their Brahmin identity. From that point onward, they follow a daily routine based on certain rituals performed every morning and evening, which can be summarized as follows: after the morning bath, they observe certain spiritual activities in the form of ritual offerings, recitation of *mantras* or meditation followed by the consumption of food. The regularity of these ritualistic observances varies from person to person, but for some people they represent an essential and indisputable element of their existence related to a 'natural' mechanism.

On the basis of this reasoning founded on the strict observance of rites, a well-known Sanskrit scholar of Agra claims that he is superior because of his religious observances and special knowledge and not because he was born a Brahmin. Fully aware of the issue of ritual pollution, he summarizes a Brahmin's duties as follows: knowledge of the *mantras* and the Vedas, studying, teaching, performing and organizing sacrifices and exchanging ritual gifts. He categorically refuses to talk about politics in this context or, in other words, associate his Brahmin identity with any political issue, although he admits off the record that caste and politics overlap in India today.[6]

It is something sober, slightly not very aggressive.[7]

This is how a young south Indian Brahmin describes his concept of Brahmin identity. He explains that this identity stands for sobriety in the choice of subjects discussed at home and in the manner of dress. It is reflected in the observance of religious practices, regular visits to the temple, listening to classical music and interest in spiritual matters.

Food habits are also an essential element of the Brahmin identity of this group. Its members are vegetarian, many do not eat even onions and garlic, do not drink alcohol and do not smoke. In fact, they avoid any substance that would make them lose control over themselves and arouse their passions. Brahmin ethics are focused on restraint and self-discipline.

Values and Profession

The Brahmins have a great deal of values to give and I still command a great amount of respect from people who may call themselves Brahmins, but also Muslims, Christians, largely because I still commit myself to Brahminical values (...). *Brahminical values consist in a high degree of personal purity, a high degree of self-discipline, a high degree of self-denial, a high degree of truthfulness, a high degree of pursuit of spiritual values* (...). *The Brahmin commitment to spiritual life, to the moral life is what makes him remain a Brahmin* (...). *I am struggling to maintain a high degree of self-discipline, self-denial and pursuit of spiritual and moral values.*[8]

These values are generally mentioned in relation to 'society's expectations' of Brahmins. Society expects a Brahmin to be honest and polite and to observe moral principles. The values generally cited in this context are purity, truth, honesty and sincerity. A Brahmin ought to inspire respect because he has inherited from his ancestors qualities and values that go under the name of *samskar*.

Society also expects Brahmins to be well educated which means that they must practice particular professions.

My father was telling me that I was a disciple of Saraswati, not of Lakshmi.[9]

All Brahmins of this type have a special association with studies and teaching—the major activity in which most of them are engaged. Their ethic makes them engage in intellectual pursuits rather than pursuits with monetary gain—hence the conflict between Saraswati, the goddess of the arts and knowledge and Lakshmi, the goddess of wealth and prosperity. To repeat the words of one of the interviewees, a Brahmin is either a *pandit* (scholar) or a *purohit* (priest).[10]

For many of them, being a teacher is more important than being a Brahmin, or perhaps it is synonymous with being a Brahmin—an essence of their Brahmin identity. A Brahmin lady in Agra told me that she felt that by being a teacher she could be a good Brahmin and perform her routine household tasks more effectively.

There has always been a considerable emphasis on the centuries-old reputation of Brahmins as keepers of knowledge and teachers. In fact, because of this very characteristic, Brahmins have been able to assert themselves as the keepers of society's guiding principles.

I still feel that being born in a Brahmin family, say, the life and the work and the functions should be such for me, should provide a sort of example to the society, an ideal. They provided the rules for the rulers, they were able to get the respect from the society because of that. And this respect is still there.[11]

Finally, the only priest interviewed in Agra did not express any unexpected ideas about identity insofar as he is faithful to the pure tradition of his ancestors. He explained that he got married to carry on the Brahminical tradition, so that his son could take over from him and that he was committed to follow the principles and values expected of a Brahmin in his personal and family life.

All these interviewees in favour of a personalized approach to the Brahmin category, assert the relationship between their specific private duties and principles and teachings found in the sacred texts.

A Politicized but Impersonal Brahmin Category

We will now analyse the interviews that link Brahmin identity with politics, but there is no personal involvement or reference to personal experience. According to these Brahmins, the relationship with politics is expressed in terms of casteism, i.e. the use of caste by politicians as a means to mobilize people and set-up a network of influences or as a strategy for political discourse. This type is characterized by two approaches: a simple acknowledgement of casteism and a criticism of it.

Acknowledgement of Casteism

In 1986–7, I was made aware there is a caste.

Brahmins of this type are characterized by a firm detachment from both the fact that they were born Brahmins and the use of caste for political ends. They are aware that in present-day India caste has become the basis of political discourse and activity. This is particularly true of the 1980s when the issue of job reservations based on caste became the focus of attention while there was a heated debate on the Mandal Commission's report. The Commission had recommended a policy of positive discrimination or affirmative action so that members of Other Backward Classes (OBC), part of the Shudra *varna*, underprivileged groups that did not enjoy official protection, could gain access to government jobs. However, this did not affect on the personal level, the Brahmins of this type. For them, it was simply an acknowledgement of the existing situation. A thirty-two-year-old lawyer declared that he was aware that Brahmins as a community did not carry any weight in the political domain, but apart from that, being a Brahmin did not really affect his way of life.[12]

It would appear that because of their professions (as military officers, doctors or lawyers), the Brahmins of this type were not affected by this kind of political action. In fact, they are not directly affected by job reservations in government service. They are of the opinion that Brahmins do not play a major role in today's social dynamic and that politics is the domain of specialists.

because it is politically exploited, the guy wants vote banks, Brahmins are not a majority of the corporation. Period. His vote bank is sitting elsewhere. (...) I think the people who have a role to play are sitting right there, the politicians and the bureaucrats, whether it is right or wrong.[13]

CRITICISM OF CASTEISM

This type is characterized by criticism of the 'surrounding casteism' but it is still dissociated from the personalization of the Brahmin category.

My caste (...) means that I won't get a fair chance.

This attitude is generally found among students who, due to their lack of experience and their exposure to Westernized urban surroundings do not assimilate Brahminical elements in their basic identity. This impersonal relationship with the Brahmin category is often accompanied by two observations: an awareness of the respect for Brahmins in Indian society and the rigid attitude of their parents' generation towards Brahminical values and practices.

But when they have to face competition to gain access to top quality higher education or government jobs, the issue of caste-based job reservations makes them react and criticize the system.

most of the time it doesn't really matter... what caste I am, but sometimes, when one gives, you know, one is looking for a job like a government job or something, and ... then you have reservations as you know (...), there is no way you get any kind of privilege (...), you have these categories, you have Scheduled Castes and Scheduled Tribes, then you have Other Backward Classes, then you have general . . . so, ok, I'm in general, my chance is gone anyway, it's not a fair test. Otherwise I don't really give it a thought.[14]

Discrimination issues related to the caste hierarchy, which seemed to have disappeared for this section of the youth, seem to have made a comeback through politics, especially through the system of reservations and quotas meant to give the underprivileged classes a greater access to public education.

We started sitting for these competitive exams. At that point, we realized that every Brahmin was falling in U.P. general category and (...) in fact there was this guy who was studying with us, we were so surprised, he was never with his books and he had been to jail twice and we heard that he got through medical, whereas lots of other good students had not (...) and somebody brought this information that he is a S.C. candidate. This will stay in the back of your mind. It may be society which has made us aware of that. We were not so aware of it earlier on. So it doesn't really mean anything as such to be a Brahmin except that we find it disadvantageous in lots of ways for us.[15]

This criticism of discriminative public policies based on caste tends to expose the absurdity of the system. Brahmins of this type, who believe that they are the only ones capable of benefiting from a top quality education because of their experience through the generations, find that they cannot fulfil their aspirations. On the other hand, they feel that the education system, far from being an official priority, offers any way few opportunities to others. A Tamil Brahmin from Chennai explains the situation in the following words:

In order to prevent the domination of any branch by one community or one caste, the governments both at the centre and the states, the governments have a policy of communal regulation by which a Brahmin gets criticized comparing his achievement and his numerical strength in the population of the country as a whole. The Brahmin is about 3 per cent of the population of the country, but he gets more than 10 per cent of the jobs, of the educational opportunities. So educational opportunities and jobs are denied to the Brahmin community merely on the basis of his gifts and marks and merit. The trouble is that the government expenditure on education is a ridiculous fraction of what it costs to conduct education in the country as a whole. Education has a low priority. (...) Today those who could profit by higher education are denied full freedom of opportunity.[16]

They pull out caste for politics.

Other Brahmins of the same type also criticize the exploitation of caste for political purposes, but they have an impersonal relationship with the Brahmin category as they depend on a different system of references, viz., the professional factor. This is so in the case of Brahmins working in the army who are not affected by job reservation policies. But they denounce the exploitation of caste by politicians. Their professional environment actually encourages them to be more open-minded towards other religious communities and castes and seems to reduce communal feelings.

I was in the army, at a very young age I went to the army . . . and there we never talked of any caste and in fact nobody ever asked which caste one belongs to, nobody bothered and . . . therefore the thought never came that as a Brahmin how do I feel or what I should do. It didn't come to my mind at all (...), really it meant nothing to me in terms of awareness . . . till I retired or till I got into politics (...), the politicians have brought in this disease into the Indian society.[17]

Thus Brahmins in the armed forces claim to be fervent champions of Indian secularism, advocating the separation of politics and religion with an equal respect for all faiths. Caste has no importance in their day-to-day existence and its influence has practically disappeared. They criticize politically motivated policies devoid of values and principles and politicians who seek to satisfy their hunger for power by encouraging differences such as caste to create different opinions and groups that they can mobilize in their support. They highlight the fact that this tendency of politicians to exploit controversial issues for strategic purposes is seen all over the world.[18]

Nobody in India, no worker in any industry, in any factory and certainly not in the army and certainly not in the government, is there any thought of caste amongst the common people. Though this caste does work, that certain groups who are interested in promoting their own caste they do it and certain politicians want to exploit the idea of caste because if you create a disturbance or a difference, you make a base for power in a democracy. (...) *In our daily life, there is no caste.*[19]

A POLITICIZED AND PERSONALIZED BRAHMIN CATEGORY: THE ASSERTION OF A NEO-BRAHMANISM

I will now analyse the attitudes of Brahmins who have fully accepted the connection to their *varna*. Being a Brahmin actually makes sense to them in their personal lives (personalized category) as well as in their relationship with socio-political issues in the public sphere. This integration of identity of the Brahmin category is particularly visible in their attitude to positive discrimination policies in favour of underprivileged classes. This attitude corresponds to the phenomenon of neo-Brahminism, as discussed in an article in the *Economic and Political Weekly*, where the assertion of Brahminism is considered in relation to political issues, especially the ideological issues raised by the Mandal Commission Report.[20]

All interviewed Brahmins who have developed such an attitude have a bent towards élitism. The two following types are subdivided according to their modes of reasoning instead of being categorized into groups of individuals, implying thereby that the same person may resort to several modes of reasoning which could connect him to two different types.

THE OPEN ELITIST TYPE

This type includes Brahmins who acknowledge that they have accepted a politicized Brahminical identity related to an elitist attitude, but with an altruistic motive and with the idea of accepting rather than criticizing positive discrimination policies. This type has two variants—one 'responsible' and the other 'natural'.

'RESPONSIBLE' BRAHMINS

There is a responsibility . . . which we have not undertaken well.

The first variant of the open élitist type of Brahmin is the purest and the most extreme. 'Responsible' Brahmins openly declare their support to the idea of looking after the interests of underprivileged classes. They tend to legitimize this process as a social necessity to put an end to inequalities that have persisted throughout the ages.

Actually the S.C., the Brahmins and high castes . . . torture was there. Untouchability was the root cause. We never accepted to embrace them. That's why the untouchables decided to go to politics. And that's because of untouchability that there is so much disintegration in the country . . . casteism has really done harm to Indian culture. I feel that these people must have their due. Things are changing, they have to change.[21]

Viewed from this angle, Brahmins have a role to play. The core of this attitude is in fact linked to one of the main themes of most interviews, viz., what society expects of Brahmins. But unlike the majority, the Brahmins belonging to this 'responsible' variant have decided that they will not allow these expectations to go unheeded. Being a Brahmin means committing oneself to help to create a better world. This attitude seems to stem from a feeling of guilt.

To think as a non-Brahmin, not to be a Brahmin, I find it's very tough because many of the issues were, one has to think on these issues, on things like reservations . . . which have to do with the fact of being a Brahmin or not being a Brahmin. I can't think without acknowledging that I am a Brahmin. And therefore there is, it's like Ambedkar saying, well, how can you speak for us . . . I think there are some points in it in the sense that, till we sensitize ourselves and we're able to acknowledge that there is an ascendancy because for being there for such a long time . . . and . . . there is a responsibility . . . which we have not undertaken well, whether the bureaucrats or the people at large, may be not me, but those who have large plots of land and who have been landlords or . . . I don't think we . . . we have been good human beings . . . not even good, I don't feel we even feel responsible for these days . . . we haven't really had a goal beyond perpetuating all this (. . .). I don't think that equality has come . . . and I really personally feel responsible of bringing that . . . no for . . . which means giving up, which means like, which is like appropriating or stopping to appropriate and to give up, you know . . . I don't know how I will do it but that's what it means to me.[22]

It is a question of being responsible, of acknowledging the evil deeds of the past generations and even of the present generation of Brahmins who benefit by the system and its structural inequalities.

I must confess that there are a number of occasions when I know that we are very virulent, (...) anti certain Brahmins . . . because we are a part of that and we feel an additional responsibility. We would never do it with a person from another community. We would never say he's a Muslim that's why he's bad or he's a Scheduled Caste that's why he's useless, but we would say these Brahmins are like this. Somehow it's because it's a responsibility that you feel within your community, no, and you keep feeling like that. I know I keep feeling like that . . . but you have to make up for all these bloody Brahmins who are . . . I can make up, I don't even know if . . . but this is a feeling that you have to make up for . . . like what is this, all this major, you know, Brahmin-Brahmin break, in these crimes and this corruption thing, every time it's . . . it's Brahmins who are in it, and still, the community is still not willing to accept that it is . . . you know . . . it's a problem.[23]

Admitting that one is a Brahmin can amount today to recognizing the ancestral role of the Brahmin as one who spreads the right knowledge, and for this purpose going against the set ideas of a community proud of its monopoly of knowledge and power.

Being a Brahmin means that you've started with lots of advantages and being a Brahmin from a middle-class educated household means you start with enormous advantages. So that, that thing, you know, that you can be unselfish, so when you don't have at all it's very difficult to be unselfish, when you have so much, then you feel that it's absurd to be selfish.[24]

The relevance like I said, since I am in a position to acquire knowledge, these things, I have been fortunate enough to be given certain things, I think it's necessary to share it. If we don't share what we have, I think we'll be failing completely and we have no one else to blame but ourselves then. If we have failed as a community, if we have been . . . invited the hate of many other communities, it's because of this, that we kept too many things to ourselves, we've privatized very much and we have held that as a position of power, to then control others, I think that's why that has been a major failing. I think we have already lost our relevance because we refused to come down from that position . . . of sharing, we are, I think, we are essentially meant to share what we have . . . and we don't do that.[25]

Being a Brahmin and assuming the moral responsibilities that arise from it makes you first and foremost a good human being.

I believe that the public is private and the private is public . . . so you have to, it has to be free, I mean, it has to be known, there should be nothing that I'm ashamed . . . which would do in private which I would not let the public know then . . . but I wouldn't clip my Brahmin identity . . . in fact, it doesn't, it doesn't affect either the compassion or the empathy which I believe is, has to be integrated to human natures.[26]

'NATURAL' BRAHMINS

I have this feeling that we have never felt insecure.

The 'natural' variant, which is second sub-group of this open type of neo-Brahminism, may be described as 'intermediate'. The attitudes portrayed here reveal a very strong personalization of the Brahmin category displaying a marked élitist conscience, sometimes even more pronounced than in the closed type that we shall take up later, but in a rather implicit approach. Brahmins coming under this variant do not draw attention to their Brahmin origins in their discourse on identity. Their discourse is implicit and impregnated with a tacit Brahminical conscience that could be perceived as 'natural'.

They are more reserved in their attitude towards politics than the 'responsible' variant although they do not want to dissociate Brahmin identity and politics. And their discourses, though marked by a certain detachment, remain clearly an expression of a Brahmin source. Consequently, this variant covers the most paradoxical attitudes: explicit discourses verging on impersonal attitudes while being implicitly deeply personalized and making a distance from politics, though expressing the Brahminical viewpoint.

Unconscious Personalization

The way we speak Tamil is slightly different, it is a dialect, a Brahmin dialect . . . in my case, I speak a very strong Brahmin dialect and because I am at a level where I could not care less, I go on stage with a minister sitting next to me and I speak that Tamil, and if you don't like it, I am sorry for you, I could not care less (...). I would not think of saying that I am a Brahmin and a south Indian and a Tamilian unless you ask me what is your mother tongue and what is your caste, then I would tell you, but I will never imagine saying it, no.[27]

'Natural' Brahmins are characterized by their fierce pride, self-confidence and composure, although they do not associate this type of attitude with the fact that they are Brahmins. The discourse of such Brahmins would not give many open references to personal experiences. The key to their personalization of the Brahmin category is evident more in what is left unsaid or in the fragments of their reasoning which appear to be of secondary importance.

A twenty-six-year-old Brahmin may begin the interview by declaring that being a Brahmin does not mean anything to him and end it on a totally different note presenting arguments with a very meaningful content, but in a casual manner:

I have this feeling that we have never felt insecure. Maybe that's why I don't identify myself as a Brahmin, or people like me who don't care. It's because we always know . . . that, if you live in a context of caste system, there is nothing above a Brahmin, if we start living in that type of society again, there will be nobody above us, they take it for granted (...). You know it, you know that you are the highest and nobody can challenge that, it's there in the Vedas, it's there everywhere (...). I guess that's why, it's just an idea.[28]

Nobody in this variant questions the fact of being a Brahmin. This non-questioning actually implies the absence of responsibility and tends to favour the continuance of existing social structures.

I'm a Brahmin (...) I'm a Brahmin, it's as simple as that.[29]

This tendency can also give rise to ambiguous attitudes that are a mixture of criticism of the élitist character cultivated by Brahmins and a hardly expressed bitterness caused by the end of a 'golden age'.

They competed unfairly all these years, just themselves, into a situation of excellence, naturally in a way, they called it a natural inclination to excellence.[30]

This Brahmin, who criticizes this 'natural inclination to excellence' developed by some Brahmins, harps on this 'natural' approach all through his discourse by projecting the intellectual superiority inherent in his Brahminical origins.

Being a Brahmin of the 'natural' variant is more a matter of journey than of belonging. For example, this thirty-nine-year-old Brahmin speaks of his childhood in an orthodox Tamil Brahmin family that was nevertheless open to Western thinking. His memories are imbued with a sense of guilt, as in the case of the 'responsible' variant, because he is very conscious of having enjoyed enormous privileges. At the same time, he is nostalgic about this period when he had access to the finest intellectual and artistic refinements. He then explains that despite this 'immersion into Brahminism' during his childhood, he is now totally detached from his Brahmin identity. For ideological reasons, he wanted to efface all the conditioning related to his family background. Now, however, he is going through a crisis because he has to decide what aesthetic and moral values he should transmit to his son.

I don't want him to go necessarily through this entire circle of, you know, becoming an agnostic and throwing away certain things and then suddenly realizing O my God, maybe I threw away too much and not really understanding what you threw away and what you kept and so on.[31]

This entire journey seems to illustrate the existence of intermediate attitudes among 'natural' Brahmins that are a result of people breaking away from their initial upbringing where the Brahmin category was very personalized. The association between politics and Brahmin identity is minimal in such cases.

A Reserved Attitude towards Politics

The relationship of this variant with politics would be considered as verging on indifference in some cases.

I don't feel that I need to identify myself with that political party or this political party because I'm part of it. I don't think . . . I would not identify myself with any political party.[32]

But when a criticism of casteism in politics is expressed, even though it may not be particularly aggressive, it remains nevertheless from a Brahmin viewpoint.

If they are trying to bring up the backward classes, then I don't think that all Brahmins should get angry. I don't get angry for this, I get more angry at the BJP type for trying to bring forward upper classes.[33]

The acceptance of reservation policies for the underprivileged classes is, in this case, the result of an attitude of benevolent neutrality. Brahmins of this variant do not feel threatened by such policies like those belonging to the closed type that I shall describe later, nor do they identify themselves with an overtly humanistic attitude like those belonging to the 'responsible' variant.

I understand those people who are trying to say that backward classes should be given more advantages. But I don't feel anything, I mean, I never feel the need to go and join it.[34]

Among such actors, reactions to the new socio-political situation in India can sometimes go beyond the simple observations and express the need to accept it and adapt oneself to the changed circumstances.

Well, you see, contemporary India, they (Brahmins) have, I can say, they are not in the same position which they enjoyed in the past, in the gone by years because, the political power has shifted to, not even to the other higher castes, like the Kshatriyas and the Vaishyas, it has shifted to what are called the intermediate castes or the OBCs. That is the political reality and so, one has to adjust a little and accept it.[35]

Even though they may not openly insist on this point, Brahmins belonging to the 'natural' variant are very conscious of being Brahmins. This means that they are members of an élite class which definitely enjoys certain advantages, but still has to face competition.

A second sub-group of the open type, the 'natural' variant remains moderate when it comes to defending the interests of the backward classes. Although they are aware of the socio-political changes that are taking place and are not opposed to them, 'natural' Brahmins clearly differentiate themselves from the attitude displayed by the responsible variant for whom accepting the other is a priority and a key element of their identity. Their thinking is confined within the bounds of the socio-hierarchical structure based on the caste system, which is central to the closed élitist type that I am now going to describe.

The Closed Elitist Type

The closed elitist type covers Brahmins who are conscious of their ancestral superiority and criticize present-day political trends that are unfavourable to them. Two opposite tendencies will be highlighted in this type, viz., the reaffirmation of the conviction that Brahmins are superior and the discomfort caused by the perception of threat to this superiority.

REAFFIRMATION OF SUPERIORITY

Brahmins belonging to this variant, who are opposed to positive discrimination policies, believe that it is a passing phenomenon, the result of a cyclical political change that will not really affect the élite status they enjoy, because of their exceptional qualities.

You know, in Congress régime, Brahmins were in a dominant position and as long as Brahmin element was dominant in any government, (...) some values were maintained in Indian politics.

This kind of discourse is based on the idea that Brahmins are the true experts in politics. In harmony with a personalized category, it highlights the fact that for generations Brahmins have been the custodians of values that need to be cultivated in society, especially in their role as advisers to rulers. The logical conclusion that follows is that their political role is quite legitimate from the historical point of view.

If you see during the independence movement, most of those who were in the foreground were the Brahmins. One reason they were, Brahmins, if you notice . . . were not a majority part of the government service, they were also not the rulers . . . so, they had really nothing to lose from the British government, and they were the only ones who could come out very openly, and since they had the intellectual background, they knew how to counterargue and how to fight it all. So, by and large, most of those who were into the independence movement were the Brahmins. So, when it took over, when the independence came in, all those who were there, they were obviously to come into power.[36]

This type has developed the view that since Brahmins have been active in public affairs for a long time, they are bound to be interested in supporting common causes. They believe that they belong to the 'enlightened élite' having a civic conscience and interested in working for the common good.

As I said, India is a country of many castes as you make a bouquet. So, in a bouquet there are Brahmins and other castes, but above all, we are Indians. This is how we exhibit unity in diversity, and this thinking of mine is because I am a Brahmin.[37]

Brahmins of this type do not allow themselves to be carried away by selfish aspirations, that is to say, they do not seek to promote the interests of their own community. Unlike other social groups, they are not in a situation where they have to prove anything to society. This attitude is typical of well-to-do Brahmins and is the result of an acute awareness of belonging to an élite group standing at the apex of the economic and socio-religious hierarchy. These Brahmins do not have to stoop to promote the parochial interests of their community like others influenced by casteist parties.

When a scheduled caste, scheduled tribe comes into politics, or bureaucracy, he's overobsessed with the feelings that he and his kinsmen have been deprived, have been kept away from certain things. So, his zeal for putting that right takes precedence over his general doing the right and doing the wrong. And then he tends to do wrong things.[38]

Brahmins expressing this kind of opinion often adopt a didactic attitude and emphasize their exceptional qualities as Brahmins.

The Brahmin brain (...), the excellence and being at the top, that cannot be diminished by laws, or constitutional amendments.

According to this type, Brahmins will shine through because of excellent qualities irrespective of the socio-political context. With generations of eductation and a strong professional background, they have no reason to feel threatened by reservation policies. The backward classes are getting protection because they are underprivileged in socio-economic and educational terms. But the government's efforts to give them a more equitable representation in the field of education and in government jobs do not match up to their needs.

You can never build up a whole society overnight by doing reservations (...) most of the professional work will still be in the hands of the Brahmins (...). By reservation, the U.P. government was able to give admission to the Roorkee University, an Indian university, to a child with 0 per cent mark, just because the Chief Minister that time said no there are seats that all those with the OBC who have applied must sit there. But then, when he went to the university, he would not just understand.[39]

Statements of this kind imply that Brahmins are structurally a part of the élite. They have an intellectual superiority nurtured over generations. They are disciplined and hard-working.

I do believe the discipline, the hard work of the Brahmin is also an explanation of their being at the top, it is not luck, it is not manipulativeness.[40]

They have a wealth of intrinsic qualities that justify and will continue to justify their dominant position. As a matter of fact, it is their intellectual superiority that justifies the absence of any specific policy for their benefit. This is a reversal of the reasoning underlining positive discrimination policies in support of the low castes: stress merit against birth attributes.

I'm still proud of being a Brahmin, because I am there, out of my own merit. I have not been privileged because I was born in a particular caste.[41]

It should be noted that this attitude is diametrically opposed to the humanistic concerns of the responsible variant of the open type because it is situated within the caste hierarchy and characterized by the absence of guilt and the negation of a long history of discrimination.

A SUPERIORITY UNDER THREAT

Other Brahmins from the closed type have a totally different view of reservation policies. They feel that a policy of this kind implies a decline in the social standing of the higher castes, especially Brahmins, who are no longer at the centre of social dynamics.

We were taught when we were young, by our elders that as Brahmins we were the best. However, as the social processes and the political and economic processes have developed in India subsequently, the Brahmin finds that he is encountering a very different kind of reality, which is very different from the self-perception which he has internalized.[42]

The pessimistic and defeatist attitude evident in this viewpoint is based on economic considerations. The Brahmins concerned here would rather be a part of the lower middle classes for whom the terms 'Brahmin' and 'élite' are not quite synonymous.

The poor Brahmin, specially the middle-class Brahmin, specially the . . . intelligent, articulate, educated but lower middle-class Brahmin, specially their girls, their daughters, they find themselves in a great upheaval, and they have great difficulty in deciding whether they are the best, they continue to be the top or that the processes have brought them down together, in the political, social and economic level.[43]

Their precarious economic condition is responsible for the demand that the government should look after them as in the past when Brahmins confined their activities to the religious sphere and their material needs were looked after by society at large.

Brahmins should not have so much money because it was the duty of the society to give them finance, to give them food, to facilitate them, but the duty of Brahmins was to get knowledge and give that knowledge to other people. Now, there is no such work for Brahmins. He is doing business, he is holding money, other things that he should not do.[44]

These demands question the validity of caste-based reservations which do not take into account the economic status of the beneficiary.

Brahmin is generally avoided in the government policies. There is reservation on the basis of caste . . . . There should be reservation on the basis of economic conditions. If a person is weak economically, he should be given reservation to get admission, and starting from the primary school, whatever caste, Harijan, or Brahmin.[45]

Others are conscious of the élitist image of Brahmins all over the world and the unrealistic nature of their demand for separate quotas.

Quite obviously there is not and there cannot be any quota or reservation in jobs, in the employment market for Brahmins . . . who are perceived as the perpetuators of an unequal and unjust social system . . . . Therefore, the reservation system for the Scheduled Castes and later on the reservation system for the OBC, it is widely perceived as an economic, social offense against the Brahmins and a lot of Brahmin families, the daily evening discourse over meal time is a whole range of debates on this issue.[46]

Further, the existing quotas have endangered the traditional professional preferences of the Brahmins, particularly in public administration, and made them turn to the private sector.[47]

I feel good to be a Brahmin, but . . . today, SC and other people like this get more advantages. Brahmins have problems in service jobs. Education was their priority. But today's situation is very bad for Brahmins. Access to service must be by the level of education, not by castes. For Brahmins, it is difficult . . . no promotions for them. So, we went into business.[48]

Finally, such attitudes criticize reservation policies because they encourage a fragmentation process. As we have already mentioned earlier in reference to the nationalistic Hindu ideology, drawing distinctions on the basis of caste is detrimental to Hindu unity.

The political persons and to a good extent, the distortions which later came have divided the society, have fragmented the Hindus. But otherwise, with the original caste system, the Hindus together could make a strong society. Because, the caste system was to bring order according to professions. Widening the gap between castes and use caste for political reasons has put India twenty to twenty-five years back, because of this political thing. For a strong Hindu society, all castes should come together.[49]

This subject of fragmentation has also been addressed in the context of the failure, not of Hindus, but of Brahmins in particular, to unite in order to combat the adverse socio-economic situation from a stronger position.

The Brahmins are basically foolish, they are stupid (...), because they don't understand their self-interest, because it is perceived that there is a great fragmentation among the Brahmins, and two segments of Brahmins cannot get together to safeguard their common Brahmanity cause against the perceived other, whether it is the Dalit or it is the OBC, or the Thakurs or the Jats or whoever . . . the fragmentation among the Brahmins is so deep . . . and their corporate identity is very poor, is very poor.[50]

CONCLUSION

This classification reveals the pluralism underlining the notion of Brahmin identity even as it focuses on a particular aspect of the relationship with politics. A scrutiny of the relationship with politics of the Brahmins who were interviewed reveals a wide range of attitudes. Partial approaches dissociating Brahmin identity from politics include attitudes that tend not to link politics simultaneously to the private and public spheres of Brahmin identity for a variety of reasons related to ideological beliefs, the socio-economic situation and the way of life.

As mentioned in the introduction, I have isolated from these general issues three unifying factors, viz., profession, geographical origin and attitude towards the assertiveness of lower castes, three complementary angles of the political dimension of contemporary Brahmin identity. These three approaches remain in the framework of a politicized Brahmin category whereas the other attitudes included in our typology are too marginal from the perspective of this research.

On the acceptance of a political dimension to Brahmin identity, the discourses presented here stress on the domination of politics by the caste factor. They also show the extent to which politics has become an integral part of the building of caste identity. As in the works of Rajni Kothari, these interviews draw attention to the phenomenon of the 'politicization of caste'.[51]

The three factors that are stressed are complementary for a variety of reasons. As I have already pointed out, the respective analyses are based on different time scales, a long-term analysis for the professional factor, a medium-term analysis for the regional factor and a short-term analysis to gauge the reactions to the rise of the lower castes.

Further, they are based on different geographical areas. The analysis of Brahmins in the armed forces is based on the history of various Brahmin communities belonging to north-west India and even of what is now Pakistan. The regional factor is based on the history and the attitude to identity of Tamil Brahmins. Reactions to the assertiveness of backward classes have been analysed through the attitudes expressed by Brahmins all over India, but with greater emphasis on north Indian Brahmins who are the most recent victims of anti-Brahmin policies.

Lastly, the choice of these three case studies has enabled me to delve deep into the historical and ideological reasons for the impersonal and personalized conceptions of the Brahmin category but always in connection with politics, which is my main interest.

As shown in this chapter, some Brahmins have an impersonal view of the Brahmin category because they practice certain professions. This is true of Brahmins in the armed forces who, though they are aware of the politicization of caste, continue to have an impersonal attitude towards their membership of the Brahmin caste because of the value system prevalent in their professional environment. They therefore constitute the most characteristic example of a Brahmin category that is politicized but impersonal.

Tamil Brahmins, on the contrary, embody the personalized attitude of the Brahmin category in the highest degree having developed a strong identity on the personal level and attitudes that are based on striking historical and political factors. Though the natural and responsible types are found in Brahmins of different geographical origins, they are essentially representative of the attitudes held by Tamil Brahmins.

The third unifying factor refers to the attitudes resulting from the politicization of the Brahmin category, particularly in harmony with the approach developed by the closed élitist type. This type is largely influenced by the political situation that existed in north India since the 1990s. It is a matter of understanding the finer points of the different Brahmin identities formed as a result of facing a strong political 'otherness', in relation to various social, economic and political circumstances.

This chapter thus aimed at a methodical analysis of the whole range of Brahmin attitudes towards politics that I came across in the course of my study. It hinges on the most representative extracts of the sixty odd interviews that I had conducted. I shall refer to some of these extracts again later to appreciate their full significance after having explained in detail the background of such statements.

NOTES

1. 10. These numbers refer to a series of interviews given in detail in the Annexes. Numbers by themselves correspond to interviews conducted in Delhi, while numbers preceded by A refer to interviews in Agra and those preceded by M to interviews in Chennai (Madras).
2. 15.
3. C. Jaffrelot, *Les nationalistes hindous, idéologie, implantation et mobilisation des années 1920 aux années 1990*, Paris: Presses de la FNSP, 1993, p. 68.
4. P. van der Veer, *Religious Nationalism: Muslims and Hindus in India*, Delhi: Oxford University Press, 1996, pp. 52, 134-6.
5. S. Patel, 'On the discourse of communalism', in *Region, Religion, Caste, Gender and Culture in Contemporary India*, ed. T.V. Sathyamurthy, Social Change and Political Discourse in India: Structures of Power, Movements of Resistance, vol. 3, Delhi: Oxford University Press, 1996, pp. 145-79.
6. A12.
7. 14.
8. M3.
9. A16.
10. Also refer to P. van der Veer, *Gods on Earth—The Management of Religious Experience and Identity in a North Indian Pilgrimage Centre*, Delhi: Oxford University Press, 1989, p. 183.
11. A11.
12. 13.
13. A5.
14. 7.
15. A6.
16. M4.
17. 17.
18. See article in the *Sunday Times of India* dated 09/04/95, 'No Politics Please, We're the Elite', on the accusations of the Indian élite against politicians. The author, Kumar Kelkar, says that in the 1960s, following

the glorious years of the freedom struggle and the dawn of independence, these politicians were no longer worthy of our trust as everywhere else in the world.

19. 2.
20. 'Rhetoric of Neo-Brahminism', *Economic and Political Weekly*, Bombay, 01/02/92.
21. A10.
22. 6.
23. 6.
24. 6.
25. 12.
26. 6.
27. M6.
28. 4.
29. 3.
30. 5.
31. 5.
32. 5.
33. 5.
34. 5.
35. 11.
36. 9.
37. A2.
38. 1.
39. 9.
40. A19.
41. 8.
42. A1.
43. A1.
44. A13.
45. A13.
46. A1.
47. See the article, 'The Shifting Sites of Reservation', in *The Hindu* dated 02/12/97 that discusses the movement of the upper castes towards the private sector, both in education and employment, due to the competition triggered by the reservation policy and also in the wider context of globalizaton.
48. A15.
49. A8.
50. A1.
51. R. Kothari, ed., *Caste in Indian Politics*, Delhi: Orient Longman, 1991, pp. 3-5.

PART I

BRAHMIN IDENTITY AND THE PROFESSIONAL VARIABLE

Brahmins in the Army

Profession is a distinct basis of classification in the original *varna* system. This system is in fact a social division based on occupation. Traditionally, Brahmins performed precise functions related to knowledge, especially sacred knowledge. Today, however, Brahmins are present in a wide variety of social and professional spheres. This observation gives rise to a number of questions.

First, we must examine the theory behind the *varna* system. This social organization defining distinct and watertight categories could not have lasted very long. The hierarchical principle of the four *varnas* defined in the *Rigveda* makes way in subsequent texts for various other arrangements, especially in terms of occupation. Thus Brahmins were permitted—or rather permitted themselves, if we assume that they were the authors of these works and the architects of social institutions—to perform functions other than those closely related to sacred knowledge.

Secondly, this observation could lead us to question the place of the profession in the definition of identity and the recognition of being a Brahmin—by recognizing oneself and being recognized by others.

Among the Brahmins, who were interviewed, some were very insistent about their profession being a very significant factor in their lives. Apart from lawyers, teachers and priests, there were also those Brahmins who were professional soldiers who expressed this attitude. This association between Brahmins and the military appeared strange to a Westerner brought up largely on textual references, but it also surprised many Indians I discussed this topic with. A case study of the military profession led me to question the identity of this group made up of individuals who were Brahmins by birth and employed in the army. It also provided material for a better understanding of the impersonal conception of Brahmin identity since Brahmins in the army tend to identify themselves more closely with their professional environment than with their caste. This special relationship between their profession and their Brahmin identity observed among the members of this group gives rise, as we have explained in Chapter 1, to the attitude that recognizes the politicization of caste without, however, personalizing the issue. Thus the relationship of Brahmins in the army to politics focuses on issues they come across in the institution to which they are attached, and not on the status of Brahmins in contemporary Indian society.

Lastly, this case study enables us to evaluate the significance of the profession in the formation of an identity by studying specific historical developments and a deep questioning of values.

CHAPTER 2

History of Brahmins and the Military

A Long-term Analysis: From the Vedas

This first section analysing the professional variable in the definition of Brahmin identity traces the historical development of certain Brahmin communities whose members are professional soldiers. We have stressed the historical conditions explaining the specific nature of this development. Such conditions set these communities apart from other Brahmins until the present time and determined the nature of their socio-political preoccupations. The study of this journey through time throws light on the social and symbolic heritage shared by these Brahmin soldiers. After drawing attention to the traditional references that explain the birth and development of these communities, I will study the recruitment problems faced by their members.

The time scale used in this chapter is the long period going back to the Vedas, as the Brahmins interviewed referred to ancient texts to explain the theoretical foundations of their identity.

We must first isolate the symbolic and textual references specific to Brahmins in the military sphere. Often, in addition to the standard models forming a part of the great Hindu tradition, the figures of martial Brahmins stand out in various ancient texts and in the history of particular groups.

A variety of texts suggest a possible connection between the Brahmin *varna* and activities theoretically reserved for Kshatriyas. They draw attention to the process of social mobility within the *varna* system. The occupational divisions between various social groups led to a critical appraisal and, finally, to arrangements required by their historical evolution.

The Brahmin, who incarnated from *Purusa*'s mouth, performed the social function of transmitting knowledge. Society, as it is described in the *Rigveda*, allowed people to choose their professions but the priest's function was considered to be the noblest of all. In those ancient times, the priest was not only supposed to compose hymns with magical powers but he also had to be a master strategist and an excellent warrior. A Kshatriya could thus preside over his own sacrifices.[1] It was only later that hereditary considerations replaced personal achievements and the system crystallized into castes or closed hereditary groups that became endogamous.

The crystallization of the *varna* system occurred at the time of the later *Samhitas* and the *Brahmanas*, towards the sixth century BC. This process was engineered by the élite, the members of the top three levels, and led to the rise of ritualism—the fundamental role of the initiation ceremony, the importance of sacrifices and wearing the sacred thread. The priest was then no more a strategist or a poet, he was just engaged in a gainful occupation.[2] He became the principal centre of interest, a point of reference for essential values such as violence and the principal target of reform movements.

From this period, the Brahmin as a professional priest stood at the top of the social hierarchy. He embodied the reference values and was considered to be the embodiment of purity. The *varnas* were then a rigid system of activities and functions performed by various social categories differentiated mainly on the basis of their socio-ritual status. The Brahmin, who presided over sacrifices and enjoyed the highest status, was logically the one who was most concerned about his possible impurity.[3]

It was during this time, the time of the *Brahmanas*, in the sixth century BC, that the issue of violence involved in rituals was widely questioned. The Vedic hymns did not condemn sacrificial violence because it was supposed to contribute to the general well-being. It was believed that 'killing during a sacrifice does not amount to killing' and the violence necessitated by the Vedas was equated with *ahimsa*—non desire of hurting—because the Vedas expounded *dharma*, the socio-cosmic order.[4] On the other hand, during the period of the *Brahmanas*, there was a systematic effort to promote non-violence. This change of attitude explains in particular the development of the heterodox Buddhist and Jain doctrines based on the notion of *ahimsa*.[5] This period therefore sees a new approach to sacrificial practices in the very centre of Hinduism, leading to what could be called the ritual theory of *ahimsa*.

This change in attitude towards ritual sacrifices was brought about by the desire to avoid any reference to violence. The first ploy was to substitute sacrificial animals with offerings from the plant world, thus eliminating the presence of blood. But even if the use of plants did not involve any bloodshed, the sacrifice retained its significance and the element of violence was not totally absent. The modalities of the sacrifice thus underwent a change leading to the development of numerous processes for eliminating violence even in the case of animal sacrifice. These processes were acts of appeasement through the use of substances like fire, water or gold that were supposed to eliminate the harmful effects of the use of violence and in a more subtle manner, lead to a linguistic reinterpretation of the murderous act. The *Brahmanas* thus provided the setting for the differentiation between killing and sacrifice, describing the same action with different words. The sacrificial language used euphemisms based on the distinction between human language and the divine language. 'Killing, putting to death' are human terms while 'appeasement, conciliation' are words that belong to the language of the gods. The Brahmin priests had a tendency to dissimulate reality which was too shocking for human sensitivities.[6]

This ritual theory of *ahimsa* had a strong impact on the Brahmin figure following the change in his relationship with violence. Firstly, it was closely linked with reincarnation issues in the sense that it gave rise to several key questions. For example, do specific sacrifices have the power to put an end to the cycle of rebirth (*samsara*)? Or, does the fact that the Brahmin who presides over rituals involving the death of living beings have a negative effect on his *karma*?

The Brahmin, who was the perpetrator of sacrificial violence in Vedic times, became an embodiment of non-violence with the importance given to *ahimsa*. As the logical result of the evolution of the Hindu theory of rituals[7] or the strategy to combat heterodox doctrines,[8] equating *ahimsa* with the Brahmin gave rise to the institution of renunciation.

Social functions thus got organized around the sacrifice as protection of *dharma*. Occupations that were normally associated with a Brahmin at that time were the study and teaching of sacred books, the performance of religious rites for the three higher *varnas* and accepting gifts from them.[9] Only the 'twice-born' Brahmins, Kshatriyas and Vaishyas were qualified to take part in the sacrificial rite. These three groups had a common triple duty, viz., study, sacrifice and giving gifts.[10] These three duties were centred around the sacrificial phenomenon. The duty to study consisted of knowing and practising Vedic knowledge, the study of the Vedas being a corollary of the ability to perform sacrifices. The permission to study also implied the permission to recite religious texts, especially those needed during rituals. Similarly, giving and receiving gifts was an integral part of sacrificial rites. In addition to oblations, the person in whose name the sacrifice was performed had to give gifts to all the Brahmins present and pay a fee to the priests performing the sacrifice.[11]

Through his priestly functions, the Brahmin became a divine being. The Sanskrit word *brahman* in its multiple meanings points to this overlap between the Brahmin's social and religious functions and his divine character. The word *brahman* is first and foremost an appellation of the Absolute: the Pure Being, the Pure Consciousness and Beatitude. When it is in the neuter gender, it could be the name of a ritual formula and represent the totality of Vedic learning. When it is in the masculine gender, it designates a specific priest who silently supervises the solemn ritual of the Vedic sacrifice. And lastly, it even becomes a synonym of the Vedas.[12]

As a reaction to this Brahmin supremacy, the *Upanishads*, which appeared between the fourth and third century BC, contributed to the spread of the anti-ritualistic viewpoint implicitly opposed to the *varna* system. The *Upanishads* adopted a more dynamic attitude towards life than the Vedic tradition, implying that man needed to progress from generation to generation. This dynamism was introduced into the idea of reincarnation which only later became an instrument justifying the inequality of birth.[13]

Buddhism also criticized the *varna* system and preached more liberal and egalitarian ideas. By breaking away from Brahmin orthodoxy, the Buddhist tradition protested against the institution of caste and its hierarchical implications in terms of purity and unequal access to education. Buddhism says that social distinctions are unavoidable in a way, but it does not mean that one should question the basic principle of equality of all human beings.[14]

With the passage of time and increase in population, it was inevitable that there should be some deviation from the original *varna* system. The theoretical system of social division based on occupation, as it was originally defined, could not embrace moving social realities. Social groups got diversified and the functions attributed to different *varnas* overlapped and were intermixed. The main categories made way for mixed varieties. This process becomes evident through the study of changes in successive reference works as well as in precise circumstances.

Various reference books report this change. Firstly, the Manava Dharmashastra (Laws of Manu), even though it is evidently a manifestation of the Brahmin renaissance as a reaction to opposing movements such as the teachings of the *Upanishads* and Buddhism, shows a great deal of changes in comparison to the Vedic teachings. The élite priestly class, which was keen on restoring the hierarchy of the *varna* system, could not disregard at the same time the change in mentality and practices.[15] The Brahmin continued, nevertheless, to be considered as the master of all creation and a figure to be admired. But in terms of occupation, there is mention of situations where unorthodox activities were probably accepted. The chapter on duties related to subsistence and morals indicates the means of subsistence allowed to a Brahmin. Living on gifts and donations was the most meritorious and prestigious means of existence for a Brahmin, especially if these gifts were given freely without being asked for. However, a Brahmin was allowed to till land even though agriculture is described as *pramrta*—linked to death—certainly because this activity involves the death of living creatures. It was even possible, as a last resort, to engage in trade for a livelihood.[16]

The *Puranas* too are a valuable source of information about the development of activities that Brahmins were allowed to engage in. The *Bhagavata Purana* mentions four ways in which Brahmins can sustain themselves in the following order of preference: gleaning grain from a reaped field, begging for grain from door to door, accepting various articles as gifts and finally various other occupations like agriculture and cattle farming.[17] The *Brahma Purana* goes even further. It says that in conditions of adversity, the vocation of a Kshatriya or a Vaishya is recommended for a Brahmin, but this option should be exercised only in case of extreme difficulty, in order to avoid a chaotic mixture of occupations.[18] This text then refers to the category of mixed castes or races, resulting from the mobility of status within the *varna* system. It is explained that a Brahmin who commits evil deeds loses his status. Further, a Brahmin who engages in activities reserved for Kshatriyas or Vaishyas has to join their ranks and finally, if he deviates from his duties, is reduced to the status of a Shudra.

This lowering of social status was explained in such texts as a result of misalliances. If a Brahmin begins to practice a profession peculiar to Kshatriyas, it is because he is born of a Kshatriya mother.[19] It was actually ritual status that gave birth to this theory of mixed castes who were despised for being ritually impure. This phenomenon has been understood as a result of the difficulties that arose in assimilating the tribal peoples in the Aryan social structure. Brahminical literature is very concerned about ritualistic status, which is quite logical because it is this status that gave the Brahmins their unique position in society.

But social status in ancient India needs to be analysed from two points of view, the ritualistic and the economic and political. The ritualistic status was difficult to change. It had to change for the entire group and over a period of several generations. Social mobility consisted in denying its importance or in a change in the actual status in economic and political terms. The last process can be seen in the contradiction that exists between various textual sources. As a matter of fact, the list of *varnas* or occupations appears to be rather theoretical and does not reflect the true social conditions if we take into consideration sources other than the Dharmashastras. The Kayastha community is a typical example of this possible change of status. The Kayasthas are supposed to be the descendants of Brahmins married to Shudras and are consequently of a lower ritualistic status. However, they have succeeded in elevating themselves to a status that is higher than their original theoretical status because of their importance in society as an educated community.[20]

It should be noted that the intermingling of different peoples was also responsible for this process of change. As a matter of fact, the history of north India is replete with invasions and large-scale migrations. Persian invasions from the sixth century BC and Greek invasions from the third century BC followed by the coming of the Scythians, the Parthians and the Huns made a deep impact on Indian society.[21] India's communications with the outside world, mainly through the overland routes in the north-west and Central Asia, permitted not only trade but also the exchange of ideas in the artistic, religious and political realms.[22]

The Gupta period (fourth to fifth century AD) was the most important phase in this transition. It was a period of great upheaval resulting from the interaction between external invasions and internal changes.

First, it must be noted that the various texts analysed earlier relate to this period. The Puranas are compilations that cannot be precisely dated because they often consist of passages written at different periods. It would appear, however, that the oldest parts of the *Bhagavata Purana* go back to the fifth and sixth century AD.[23] The Laws of Manu too, although they are supposed to go back to the hoary past, are believed to have been written at about the same time and the oldest portions between the second and the third century AD.[24]

We must especially take into account the coming of the Huns who are supposed to have invaded north India towards the end of the fifth century AD and caused a major displacement of population. As a result of these migrations, most Brahmins had to adapt themselves to the new conditions of life. There are indications that many migrant Brahmins sought the protection of one king or another. They received in return, among numerous other gifts, villages and lands that provided them a means of subsistence. Being close to the king, they could continue to practice their priestly duties, preside over royal sacrifices and find employment as astrologers. Some of them were also employed as ministers in the royal court. Finally, among these disparate occupations, it is mentioned that they also performed the functions of composers of music, writers, doorkeepers and soldiers. This last occupation was permitted only in times of distress according to the textual references quoted above, or in exceptional circumstances as a fight against the mixing of castes, for safeguarding *dharma* or protecting the twice-born.[25] In the following pages, we will focus our attention on this very professional sector.

Apart from the specific traditional references mentioned above, Brahmin soldiers are characterized by distinctive activities involving a cross between the two original *varnas* and defined according to the development of specific communities.

Brahmin and Kshatriya *varnas*, though they are quite distinct from each other in theory, have always had close relations leading first to the intermingling of the two categories until the appearance of an emblematic figure belonging simultaneously to both.

Indeed, although the *varna* system has been presented as an unadulterated example of the hierarchical principle, it admits relations based on complementarity. It is obvious that the two social units represented by the Brahmin and the Kshatriya had to cooperate in the performance of sacrifices, the Brahmin as the person presiding over the sacrifice and the Kshatriya as the supreme ruler, on whose behalf the sacrifice was performed. But their relationship could also be of a more antagonistic nature. The Brahmins could resort to fasting, either individual or collective, as a form of protest to prevent the king from reducing their privileges.[26]

This confrontation often turned into a real competition between the two categories. The tensions between them were expressed in terms of functions and status, i.e. in the division of temporal and spiritual powers as well as in the competition for the highest ritualistic status. It was clear that aspirations to temporal power could not be confined to the Kshatriyas alone and non-Kshatriyas managed to obtain the status of Kshatriyas by becoming kings. This illustrates the distinction between the ritualistic status and the real status. To validate his new status the non-Kshatriya king had to get a proper genealogy prepared. For this, interaction with Brahmins was indispensable. Being in charge of royal genealogies, they were the only ones who could provide the validation. This particular function gave them a higher ritualistic status besides allowing them to play an active role in establishing temporal power.

It took several centuries for the development of this type of arrangement and it became a widespread practice only during the Gupta period, when the various Puranas were composed. These texts go even further in pointing out the intermingling of the two categories and mention cases of Brahmins performing the functions of Kshatriyas and vice-versa.[27] Other texts too deal with the overlapping of the two highest *varnas* leading to the creation of an emblematic figure belonging to both categories at the same time.

Examples of this extreme overlapping of the two categories are found in many texts. For instance, Madeleine Biardeau has done a joint analysis of a temple in the Pondicherry area and a legend connected with it. The empty space between the two sanctuaries of the temple is occupied by a row of seven *munis*, wearing either royal crowns or the topknot of Brahmin ascetics. These seven *munis* are opposed to seven enemy warriors or *viras*, evil princes who did not respect the tenets of *dharma*. These two clans are the protagonists of a legend that narrates how the *munis* combined in their persons the virtues of the Brahmin and the skills of the warrior. The *munis* were thus Brahmins who led an ascetic life but, when confronted with the wicked *viras*, they were forced to take up arms to protect the gods.[28]

Ascetic warriors are a manifestation of such an overlapping of functions. The ascetic, who aspires to a life of detachment and the practice of *ahimsa*, seemingly wants to distance himself from the use of violence. However, apart from his tendency to withdraw himself from the world, the ascetic is often shown as possessing immense powers as a result of his asceticism. These powers approximate the world of magic and in many legends they are not always portrayed as benevolent. The ascetic thus affirms his power by performing exploits, often magical and often violent. Historically speaking, it is the Naga ascetics who engaged in activities involving defence and trade in Hindu pilgrimage centres and faced the hostility of the Muslims.[29]

Furthermore, the epics remain the major source of characters combining in their persons the ethics of the Brahmin and the warrior. The *Mahabharata* begins with the episode of Rama, a Brahmin, who rid the earth of Kshatriyas twenty-one times. The Kshatriya women then sought Brahmins ascetics to bear them sons. It was still the golden age of *Kritayuga*, when the four *varnas* were satisfied, through the practice of *dharma*, with performing their own functions. But when *dharma* underwent a crisis, an overlapping of activities between Brahmins and Kshatriyas really started.

Several Kshatriyas like Bhishma gave up their hereditary ethic to adopt that of the Brahmin ascetics. On the other hand, some Brahmins adopted the martial ethic. A major shift happened in the life of the Brahmin ascetic Drona when he got married. His wife, Kripi, was the daughter of a heroic Brahmin named Saradvat Gautama better known for his warlike propensities than for his attachment to Vedic studies. Kripi was hungry for royal power, while her twin sister Kripa had inherited a liking for arms. After producing a son, Ashvatthama, who neighed like a horse, the finest royal animal, Drona declared his desire to acquire wealth and arms. He obtained arms from another Brahmin warrior, Rama. The creation of Brahmin warriors was a sign of degeneration, a period of crisis when *dharma* was not observed, because the Brahmin warrior defended the weakened Kshatriyas.[30]

Such cultural references constitute the basis of a symbolic heritage of Brahmin warriors. It is one way of understanding the specific traits of these Brahmins. We must now determine the social attitudes of these specific communities. The majority of Brahmin communities who resorted to martial activities are linked to the agro-military sphere. This term refers to the trajectory of these Brahmins, who in the course of history first turned to occupations linked with agriculture and then towards the army.

Although they are little known, warrior Brahmins were the subject of an ethnographic study commissioned by the Government of India in the late nineteenth and early twentieth century in its desire to get to know the different communities of India. An entire collection of studies was prepared for the army under the title *Caste Handbooks for the Indian Army*. The volume on Brahmins deals with their history and origin, their classification and geographical distribution, their religious habits, dress and their peculiar characteristics as well as problems related to recruitment.

The historical introduction traces the development of Hinduism through the confrontation between Brahmin supremacy and strong heterodox doctrines like Buddhism and the impact of historic events outside. It also emphasizes the fact that many *rishis* had strong links with the martial ethic. They play as proof of the ancient Brahminical lineage of Brahmin warriors like Rama, the destroyer of Kshatriyas and the protector of Brahmins, who rid the earth of all Kshatriyas to avenge the killing of his father by a domineering king.[31] There is also a reference to the historical circumstances that led some Brahmins to practice farming, as pointed out earlier. Some of these Brahmins, who were obliged to abandon their lands, had to take employment in the army as it was 'the only type of job that they could accept without losing their caste'.[32] Brahmin communities from an agricultural background, especially those from what is today eastern Uttar Pradesh, were given preference for recruitment in the Bengal Army during the first half of the nineteenth century. Their Brahmin status was an important factor both for the recruits and for the colonial power. The Bhumihars of Bihar are a typical example of this process. This group, whose Brahmin status was a subject of controversy, used its entry into the military profession as a means for moving up the social ladder. At the same time, from the viewpoint of the military authorities, their Brahmin status, even though dubious, was a guarantee of their high social status which helped them in their strategy of involving the local élite.[33]

There follows a description of the religious practices and dress common to all Hindus or peculiar to different sects. The Brahmin is shown as being proud of his traditions and dress.[34] He was supposed to live frugally, but in his day-to-day life would be very particular about his food and clothes, especially in terms of purity and cleanliness.[35]

It is pointed out that during recruitment it was necessary to gather information about their geographical origin and *gotra* to verify their affiliation to a particular Brahmin *jati*. Brahmins were mainly selected for two regiments of the Bengal Army and, in a less systematic manner, for the Hyderabad contingent.[36]

But all Brahmin communities were not equally suitable for recruitment in the army. It appears that their geographical origin was very important to determine their military qualities. This problem of geographical distribution refers to the traditional classification of Brahmins according to their place of origin. One of the most widely accepted classifications of Brahmin communities subdivides the *varna* into two groups—the Gauds in the north and the Dravidas in the south. The Gauds are further subdivided into Sarasvats, Kanyakubjas or Kanaujiyas, Gaudras,

Utkala and Mithila and the Dravidas into Maharashtra, Andhra, Dravida, Carnata and Gujrat.[37]

It is pointed out that only the Gauds are considered suitable for military recruitment and among them only the Kanaujiyas, Gaudras and Sarasvats. The Kanaujiyas provided three-fourths of the Brahmin recruits. Their name is derived from the ancient city of Kanauj on the banks of the Ganges. This community consists of five sub-groups among whom the Kanaujiyas proper are reputed to be the best soldiers.[38] There are also a large number of Bhumihars, the community with a dubious lineage often linked with Thakurs and Rajputs. The Gaudras, originally from Haryana, are depicted as being ignorant and bigoted and not suited to make good soldiers. Finally the Sarasvats coming from an agricultural environment in Punjab enjoy a reputation of being good soldiers even though very few are recruited, except those who are taken as Dogras, like the Mohyals, a community I would like to highlight.[39]

This manual about the recruitment of Brahmins in the army is extremely interesting even though it does not contain an exhaustive list of all the communities involved. Among the Sarasvat Brahmins, who according to this document are little inclined towards a military career, one group indeed that seems to have a long history and a deep awareness of its martial character is the Mohyal community.

The Mohyal community consists of seven original clans, now known as *jatis*: Datt, Vaid, Chibbar, Bali, Mohan, Lau and Bhimwal. Each of these castes traces its lineage to the dawn of time through the *gotra* named after the *rishi* who was the founding father of the line. In the case of the Mohyals, these founding fathers are better known for their involvement in worldly matters than for their attachment to rituals.[40] These *rishis* belong to the epic tradition that we have already mentioned earlier. The Datts are descendants of Bharadvaj, father of Dronacharya who was the mentor of the Kauravas, while the Balis are descendants of Parashara, grandson of Vasistha and father of Vyasa who is said to be the author of the *Mahabharata*.[41]

The historical trail connects them with Islamic lands as they are mentioned in the battle of Karbala. They are supposed to have governed Kabul between AD 830 to 950. They were also known to be landowners in Arabia. The term Mohyal is said to indicate their agricultural background. One of the most widespread theories connects this name, which is certainly not more than six or seven hundred years old, to the term Mahipal or Mahiwal meaning landowner. The historical phenomenon of the passage of Brahmin communities from the religious to the agricultural sphere, that we have explained earlier, is wholly applicable in their case. The process of giving land as a reward or payment for services rendered to a king linked the community to agricultural functions.[42]

But the Mohyal community is not the only one to be linked with the agro-military sphere. Several other communities have followed a similar path. They are grouped together under the term Shastra-Upjivi Brahmins and are described as Ayachaks, those who do not accept charity to survive and as Apratigrahik or non-mendicants. They mostly share the same *gotras*. The Chitpavans of Maharashtra, Tyagis of Uttar Pradesh and the Bhumihars of Bihar can be counted amongst these communities.[43]

Very striking example, the Chitpavan Brahmins have a long history of heroic conquests. They were involved in plunder during their battles with Muslim invaders. Later, in the early twentieth century they reinterpreted their history to portray themselves as the traditional, noble defenders of Hinduism. An analysis of the personality of Godse, Gandhi's assassin and a member of this community, reveal several characteristics peculiar to the Chitpavans. Godse was violently opposed to Gandhi's doctrine of non-violence, passive resistance and praise of womanhood. He believed that the rejection of the martial ethic would imperil India's vital strength. As a matter of fact, the Chitpavans traditionally combine the status of Brahmins and the attributes of Kshatriyas. And because of the absence of warrior castes in Maharashtra, they were able to occupy this empty slot. Further, in his socio-political plans for India's future, Gandhi wanted to marginalize the traditional élites and push them to the periphery of Indian society. As a Brahmin, Godse was a part of these traditional élites. He felt that his socio-economic status was threatened, especially because the Chitpavan community had started losing its importance in the late nineteenth century. Various factors were responsible for this decline: the neglect of traditional values due to the rise of commercial activity in Bombay, an improvement in the fortunes of rival groups and the tremendous upheaval brought about by the colonial rule.[44]

With a clearer idea of the specific traits of these military Brahmin communities, both in symbolic terms and regarding their social origins, we can now take up the question of their historical development, especially the role they played during the colonial period, by studying the recruitment strategies of the British.

Indeed, this study of Brahmin communities, such as the Mohyals and other related communities, closely associated with the army can be fully appreciated only by analysing the recruitment policies followed by the colonial rulers. The martial traits of particular Brahmin communities may have been encouraged or curbed during different periods of colonial domination leading to the systematization of the theory of martial races which served for a long time as a reference.

The recruitment of Brahmins in the army has to be addressed in the larger framework of recruitment strategies introduced by the British to keep the 'pearl of the British Empire' under their control. The Sepoy Mutiny of 1857 upset their strategy and put the Brahmins in a completely new position. Let us look at this evolution, in detail.

In India, the eighteenth century was a period of transition between two eras—the decline of the Mughal Empire and the struggle between various European powers to gain control over the country. The formation of Indian regiments became a necessity for the latter to establish their territorial presence and defend their economic interests. The French were the first to form Indian units, under the command of Europeans, in the 1740s. The British followed in their footsteps in the late 1750s by setting up their own companies of sepoys and forming them into battalions. The colonial rulers decided to import the European system of grouping soldiers into companies, based on the rationalization of human organization introduced from the sixteenth century onward, a period of military revolution.[45]

Thus the British undertook the professionalization of their three armies in Bengal, Bombay and Madras through the East India Company. But these three armies had very different internal structures due to the marked difference in their situation and the practices they followed. As a result, each of the three armies developed specific traits that the British had to take into account when defining their recruitment strategies.

The recruits in the Bombay Presidency came from vastly different social status. Among the lower castes and tribes, the largest number of recruits were from the Mahar community and, until 1857, they accounted for almost one-sixth of the Bombay army. Gradually, however, the higher castes with martial traditions realized the advantages of being associated with the British and started encouraging the recruitment of parents and friends to bring about a greater homogeneity in the units. Further, the British themselves gradually got familiar with the social hierarchy operating under the caste system and started identifying themselves more with the higher strata of Indian society. As a result, they only resorted to recruitment from the lower castes in times of war.[46]

But it is the study of the Bengal Army that enables assessment of this trend more clearly. The recruitment policy in Bengal rested on a narrow social base. After the 1760s, groups of soldiers who had served in Muslim armies since the fifteenth century, mainly Rajputs and Brahmins from Bihar and Awadh (the area to the north of Benares in what is now eastern Uttar Pradesh), were enrolled in the Bengal Army. Communities belonging to the Gaud Kanaujiya category of Brahmins, discussed earlier, were the main source of Brahmin recruits before 1857.

British officers in Bengal seemed to have been closer to the local centres of power than their compatriots in Bombay and Madras and were therefore more sensitive to matters relating to social status. All issues related to caste received the highest consideration. This attitude encouraged soldiers to refuse to accept orders from men of a lower status and also to stress the strict observance of religious taboos. The upper caste men in the Bengal Army enjoyed certain privileges as compared to the armies in Bombay and Madras. They were allowed to cook their food separately and were even exempted from overseas service, which apart from being considered uncomfortable, was also held to be a religious taboo.[47]

Low-caste men were finally excluded from the ranks of this army, first as a matter of practice and later, after 1855, through appropriate regulations.[48] Owing to the domination of high caste

Hindus, the Bengal Army consisted of homogeneous battalions based on caste. It was in fact an army where there was a 'total victory of caste'.[49] This gave rise to a new solidarity in the settlements under the control of the military authorities, but it did not lead to the destruction of the ancient solidarity links which were operating in villages from where the soldiers were recruited. It is quite clear that allowing and encouraging such practices was bound to have certain consequences in this context of management of foreign troops, and these practices may be considered as one of the main factors that led to the 1857 Mutiny which started within the Bengal Army.[50]

1857 is not only a symbolic date arbitrarily selected by historical convention but it marks an important turning point in the history of the British Raj, especially in terms of military recruitment strategies. An analysis of the famous Sepoy Mutiny can be divided into three points, based on the three ingredients that Philip Mason defines as the causes for any mutiny, viz., the absence of healthy relations between officers and men, discontent among the public which has the army's sympathy and a fortuitous crisis that acts as a catalyst.[51]

The absence of friendly relations between officers and ordinary soldiers raises the question of discipline connected with the facts mentioned earlier regarding the encouragement by the British authorities of 'caste feelings' among the Bengal sepoys. This strategy based on the unconditional acceptance of current practices may have helped in the maintenance of good relations within the military hierarchy for a short while but it also contained the seeds of a conflict that could be triggered by the slightest error.

The second cause of this revolt, viz., the opposition to British colonial domination, was of a more general nature. For the sepoys, the annexation in 1856 of the princely state of Awadh, to which many of them belonged, was a great shock. The rural population in north India was generally very receptive to the discontent among the soldiers. The colonial administration was swept away for a while in large parts of north India by the wave of uprisings during this period leaving power in the hands of local chiefs, as in Allahabad and Meerut.[52]

Finally, the crisis itself was triggered by two decisions taken by the British authorities regarding two matters that affected the sensitivities of the upper castes, especially the Brahmins. The first decision concerned the exemption from overseas service enjoyed by the sepoys of Bengal. The decision in 1856 to put an end to this privilege provoked a violent reaction among the sepoys, some of whom believed that it was a ruse to convert them to Christianity.[53] The second decision too concerned a religious taboo. The army planned to introduce a new rapid action rifle for which the soldiers had to bite the cartridges to remove them from their casing. This exposed them to the risk of coming into contact with impure substances such as beef fat.[54] Further, the atmosphere of insecurity was aggravated by the threat of erosion of the near monopoly of recruitment enjoyed by the upper castes with the absorption of new recruits from Punjab. The annexation of Punjab by the British had taken place quite recently, in 1849, and the latter now had access to a new source of soldiers among the Hindus, Muslims and Sikhs trained by the Sikh rulers. These forces, which were initially dismantled, were subsequently absorbed in order to avoid any change in the organization of companies. Consequently, each regiment of the Bengal army posted in the new provinces was permitted to enrol in its ranks up to two hundred Punjabi soldiers.[55]

The combined results of these factors led to the outbreak of the mutiny in Meerut on 1 May 1857. As far as the British were concerned, these events led them to reflect deeply on the sociological and geographical dimensions of their recruitment strategies. An analysis of the socio-cultural origins of the troops responsible for these uprisings clearly pointed to the concentration of high castes and the dangers of recruiting soldiers from a restricted area which had solidarity networks extraneous to the military organization. The mutinous upper castes were thus ostracized after 1857.[56] They were kept out of the army officially although some of them like the Brahmins, as we shall see later, managed to get into the categories favoured by the new recruitment policy based on geographical rather than sociological factors.

In terms of pure military organization, this revolt confirmed the fears of the British about the unification for the Bengal, Madras and Bombay armies into a single homogeneous body. During the mutiny, the latter two armies had served as a reserve force and a counterbalance to the mutinous sepoys of the Bengal army. Further, as far as the internal organization of troops was concerned, it was deemed necessary to secure the watertight compartments formed on the basis of social and religious differences in Indian society in order to avoid the risk of contagion in case there was another revolt in the future. The result was the diversification of the internal organization of regiments with the intention of avoiding standardization that could prove dangerous later.[57]

On the basis of these observations, the British started categorizing the Indian population for purposes of military recruitment thus giving rise to a lasting trend: the theory of martial races, which assumed the proportions of a dogma and an ideology for some but was considered as a pure myth by others.

The involvement of Brahmin communities in the army should be viewed from the wider perspective of recruitment policies and theories based on this controversial concept of 'martial races'. This category, invented by the British after the Sepoy Mutiny, included communities who got recruited systematically since they fulfilled two main criteria that were more or less official, viz., loyalty to the Raj during the 1857 conflict and conformity with specific martial characteristics in geographical, ethno-cultural or psychological terms. The Brahmins figured prominently in this debate because, though they—together with the Rajputs—were favoured by the recruitment policy prevalent before 1857, were responsible for the revolt launched in Awadh. The ideological discourses in support of this theory are based on geographical and racial arguments and references to caste.

It appears that the geographical origin of various communities is of primary importance. Giving preference to people from the north-west in the matter of military recruitment is obviously a trend that is best summarized by the term 'Punjabization' of the Indian army.

The early 1860s witnessed the formulation of a territorial strategy based on the exploitation of the animosity between communities belonging to different regions. Thus in the north, the troops from Hindustan counterbalanced troops from Punjab while, at another level, the armies of Bombay and Madras served as a counterweight to the Bengal army. This equilibrium between the four major components of the Indian army was one of the main principles behind the recruitment strategy pursued in the

1860s and 1870s. But from the 1880s onwards, the geographical orientation of these policies tilted in favour of Punjab and Nepal.[58]

From then on, many groups came to occupy a privileged place in colonial attitudes and policies. A series of government publications entitled *Handbooks for the Indian Army*, mentioned earlier, provides information about the history, religious affiliation and behavioural traits constituting the distinctive character of each of these groups. Kumaonis, Garhwalis, Jats, Gujars and Ahirs, Muslims of Punjab and Hindustan—Pathans and Sheikhs—Sikhs, Gurkhas of Nepal and Dogras were the officially recognized martial races who provided a new source of recruitment.[59]

The last category, viz., the Dogras, formed on a geographical base, made it possible to continue the recruitment of certain Brahmins who, though they were the members of a socially despised and ostracized group, belonged to the north-west of the country which was now the preferred area of recruitment.[60]

The term Dogra is derived from *Durgara*, the ancient name of the state of Jammu. But with the change in policy for the selection of military personnel, several other groups belonging to neighbouring areas or to sections that were not normally recruited were also included in this category. The Dogra Brahmins were mostly Gaud Sarasvat Brahmins who originally belonged to Punjab and the surrounding areas.[61] Mohyal Brahmins were recruited under this category, as indicated earlier, but also recruited in some Sikh regiments.[62]

The 'Punjabization' of the army was also prompted by geostrategic reasons, viz., the Russian threat which became quite serious in the late 1870s and forced the British to prepare for an attack from the west.[63] F.S. Roberts played a crucial role in the new military strategy. An analysis of his writings brings to light one of the main factors not yet mentioned in the theory of martial races, viz., its racist character.

A comparative study of books written before and after 1857 enables us to assess this trend. For example, the fascination of Albert Hervey, an officer in the Madras army, for his south Indian soldiers led him to claim that there was no other army as disciplined as the Madras army in the whole of Europe. In his book published in 1850, he extols the moral strength, courage, endurance and loyalty of his soldiers. However, F.S. Roberts, commander-in-chief of the Madras army from 1880 to 1885, had a different opinion. According to him, there was no comparison between the Gurkhas of Nepal or the martial races of north India and the 'effeminate people' of the south.[64] Obviously, the poor performance of the Madras army was a reality in the 1880s, but instead of advancing more concrete justifications like the loss of combativeness or the higher average age of the soldiers, the British authorities used racial factors to explain the failure.[65]

This trend is also a result of the theories of human evolution formulated in Europe in the second half of the eighteenth century. Many of the ideological publications mentioned earlier insist on the Aryan ancestry of these martial races. For example, Mac Munn's book is a typical example of the spread of these racial concepts in matters of recruitment during the 1930s. He traces this notion of martial races to the advent of Aryans in India and insists that they were the descendants of the 'original white races'.[66] It is interesting to note that this ideological debate on the legitimization of some strategic groups, which gathered force during the 1880s, leaves the Brahmins out of this Aryan lineage although there are indisputable references to this issue in other contexts and at other times.[67]

These ethnographic studies conducted during the colonial period resulted in the categorization of the Indian population and the legitimization of martial races/classes not only on the basis of psychological and physical traits or those related to climate and geography, but also of socio-historic notions that were more or less reshuffled to suit their own purposes. However, in addition to the colonial view, we must also take into account the way various communities portrayed themselves as having a strong image and a martial character, the most prominent among them being the Sikhs, Muslims, Marathas and Gurkhas.[68] These studies, undertaken in the interests of research and for purposes of codification and classification, were nevertheless a part of the colonial plan to inspire obedience and loyalty through the portraits of perfect soldiers, perfect men and perfect subjects with the aim of controlling a population so truly difficult to define.[69] They managed to establish a strategy that was initially adapted to the prevailing circumstances but developed into a long-lasting recruitment trend based on largely stereotyped judgements. The Brahmin was thus depicted in fairly standard colours in the various publications of this type and was strongly characterized as a person 'given to intrigue'. Thus a person belonging to the Brahmin *varna* was viewed with suspicion in matters of military recruitment.

As far as caste is concerned, references to it in military recruitment strategies initially consisted of eliminating the upper castes, i.e. Brahmins and Rajputs, who had participated in the 1857 uprising, but changed later to include members of these same upper castes for training as officers of the Indian army.

After the revolt, a Commission was set up under Maj. Gen. Peel, Secretary-General of War, to examine the organization of the Indian army and recommend judicious changes. The members of the Commission, all non-Indians, and others who were consulted could not arrive at a consensus except on the need to avoid too many references to caste during recruitment. The Commission's recommendations were otherwise quite vague: e.g. 'The indigenous army should include different nationalities and castes, mixed randomly in each regiment.' In 1860, it was decided to keep those regiments of the Bengal army that had remained faithful to the Crown and to add to them Punjabi and low-caste units formed in 1857-8. The armies of Madras and Bombay remained largely unchanged. These decisions clearly indicated that the upper castes of Awadh had fallen into disfavour with the British authorities.[70]

Thus the Brahmin's status changed completely in the eyes of the colonial government: from being placed at the top of the social hierarchy as a member of the élite favoured in recruitment policies, he became the embodiment of the recruit to be avoided and, by definition, a member of a group having non-martial traits.

A stereotyped portrait of the Brahmin was indeed painted in many books. Mac Munn points out that it was surprising that Brahmins were recognized as soldiers for many generations, referring to the Brahmins of Awadh in the Bengal army, as their numerous religious taboos and peculiar food habits often constituted a major obstacle for the proper performance of military activities. He explains that this group received many distinctions but that it was also prone to indiscipline with a well-recognized tendency towards intrigue.[71]

The special manual on Brahmins in the *Handbooks for the Indian Army* also refers to these flaws in the Brahmin psychology. It points out that the Brahmin is the most conservative of all Indians. He is supposed to have a higher intelligence than all other groups. In the past, the tendency of officers to allow Brahmins to follow their own customs affected the efficiency of the army. But the policy followed after 1857 insisted on the *esprit de corps* and sense of military honour.[72] It was this type of publication that spread the myth of martial races through an ideology mixing theories of race with geographical and caste considerations.

The second historical dynamics when Brahmins were in the forefront of the military strategies deals with the Indianization of the Indian army, through the search of suitable élites. This refers to the desire of Indian leaders to participate in the decision-making process in the army which was always partially under colonial domination. The Brahmins, who were officially black-listed as a rebellious caste after the 1857 uprising, were wooed once again when the proposal to train Indian officers for the army was under serious consideration. The first debates took place even before a reference body was set up.

At the time of the 1857 uprising, there were Indian officers who were influential at the company level but they had no real authority at the level of the battalion where British officers were fully in control. The British assessment of the role of Indian officers during the 1857 uprising was a story of failure considering that they had not played their role as intermediaries between British officers and Indian soldiers by communicating to their superiors the early signs of discontent among the latter. After considering various reform schemes, it was decided to entrust Indian officers with greater responsibility with the aim of increasing their efficiency and widely applying the principle of promotion by seniority. This process received a fresh impetus in the late 1880s, when the Indian National Congress became influential enough to voice its demands, particularly regarding the appointment of Indians to higher military posts. But the negotiations on this issue did not produce any concrete results.[73]

It was only after World War I that this question was taken up seriously and some thought was given to the introduction of special training courses to give the Indians access to positions of responsibility.[74] In 1918, even though the record of Indian officers was not particularly brilliant, the Indian nationalist movement pressurized the British authorities to take up the subject in all earnest. After World War I, the British were ready to give concessions to their colonies, which in the case of India were formalized in the Montagu-Chelmsford Report. The former, the Secretary of State for India, and Lord Chelmsford, the Viceroy of India, presented a report in 1918 as a follow-up to the Montagu Declaration of 20 August 1917 on the aims of the new British policy on self-government within the framework of the Raj. Apart from leading to the promulgation of the Government of India Act of 1919, which modified the working of commercial governments, these reforms allowed the assertion of the notion of responsibility of self-defence from the right to self-government as defined in this report.[75]

Despite difficulties, the decision to Indianize the army was finally implemented, particularly because of the loss a large number of British officers between 1914 and 1918. Various schemes were introduced during the 1920s. The first one proposed to train ten cadets per year by sending them to England to the Royal Military College in Sandhurst. These young officers, known as King's Commissioned Indian Officers, were posted in an English battalion for a year before joining their Indian regiment. Another training programme was started in India, at Indore, but without any success. The nationalization of the Indian army advanced slowly and even if the training programme in Sandhurst had progressed as planned, it would have been far from sufficient. The Indian Sandhurst Committee set up in 1925 was asked to examine the problems responsible for the slow progress of this scheme. Factors such as the high rate of failure of Indian cadets at Sandhurst (30 per cent as compared to 3 per cent for English cadets) and the high cost borne by the family to send a son to England gave rise to the idea of setting up a military academy in India.[76]

The establishment of the Military Academy in Dehra Dun played a crucial role in the Indianization of the army. As early as 1922, Dehra Dun was chosen as the site for the Prince of Wales Royal Indian Military College, but it was only after the Indian Sandhurst Committee presented its report that it was decided to set-up an institution in India similar to the one in Sandhurst. In addition to admitting more Indian cadets to Sandhurst, the idea was to train sixty Indian King's Commissioned Officers in an Indian military academy which was finally set-up in Dehra Dun at the end of 1932 under the name Indian Military Academy (IMA).[77]

The academy was supposed to be a model institution and it is so even today. The Indian Sandhurst Committee had clearly defined its hopes of creating in the IMA an institution capable of conducting large-scale recruitment covering the entire sub-continent without any bias regarding social and geographical origin of the candidates. However, things turned out quite differently. To begin with, candidates were selected in equal measure from among soldiers serving in the ranks belonging to the martial classes as well as from the élite classes such as big landowners, Brahmins and princely families.[78] Thus the Brahmins figured officially once again in the recruitment strategy of the British, this time as members of an élite class characterized by its high level of education.

But continuing our study of the recruitment of Brahmins, especially by means of a quantitative analysis, is a difficult task because it must be noted that it is very difficult to obtain information about the caste of military personnel.

Yet, the work done by Apurba Kundu gives a clear view of the situation, through the specific study of the Indian Military Academy (IMA). He has studied the geographical distribution of officers trained in Dehra Dun and has been able to show that the recruitment trends introduced after 1857 continue to this day.[79] His work covers two periods, the period between 1932 and 1936 when the IMA was set-up and the more recent period between 1978 and 1982. He brings to light the fact that even more than hundred years after the Sepoy Mutiny, the over-representation of north-west India in the army persists.

As we have already seen, Brahmins from these regions, who have been considered suitable for recruitment in the army for a long time even through social categories other than caste as in the case of the Dogras, could indeed remain faithful to their martial traditions. This trend is visible in the names of Brahmins who were interviewed or in the names of authors whose books we consulted, viz., Sharma, Khanduri, Datt (Mohyal) and whose origins can be linked to Delhi, Garhwal or Punjab.

Having defined the historical context of the association of certain Brahmin communities with the military sphere, we have now to understand the contemporary manifestations of such an association after Independence. Highlighting the strong martial culture among military Brahmins will help us to fully understand the impersonal conception of the Brahmin category that has developed among these communities, as I have shown in my typology.

NOTES

1. R. Thapar, *Ancient Indian Social History—Some Interpretations*, Delhi: Sangam Books, 1984, pp. 126-8.
2. This modification of the religious function was a response to the change in the nature of the Gods who showed less vigour and heroism and became involved in more worldly and day-to-day matters (Shrirama and I. Deva, 'Crystallization of the Traditional Pattern of Stratification in India', in *Social Stratification in India*, ed. K.L. Sharma, Delhi: Manohar, 1992, pp. 11-12.
3. P.G. Hiebert, 'India: the politicization of a sacred society', in *Religions and Societies: Asia and the Middle East*, ed. C. Caldarola: Mouton Publishers, 1982, pp. 291-2.
4. M. Biardeau, 'Le Brahmanisme ancien, ou la non-violence impossible', in *Violences et non-violences en Inde*, ed. D. Vidal et al., Paris: Editions de l'EHESS, Purusartha, 1994, pp. 126-7.
5. U. Tahtinen, *Ahimsa—Non-Violence in Indian Tradition*, London: Rider and Company, 1976.
6. B. Oguibénine, 'De la rhétorique de la violence', in *Violences et non-violences en Inde*, ed. D. Vidal et al., Paris: Editions de l'EHESS, Purusartha, 1994, pp. 81-95.
7. H.P. Schmidt, 'The origin of Ahimsa', in *Mélanges d'indianisme à la mémoire de Louis Renou*, Paris: E. de Boccard, 1968, pp. 647-52.
8. L. Dumont, *Homo Hierarchicus*, Paris: Gallimard, 1992, p. 335. L. Dumont, *La civilisation indienne et nous*, Paris: Armand Colin, 1975, p. 54.
9. J.N. Bhattacharya, *Hindu castes and sects: an exposition of the origin of the Hindu caste system and the bearing of the sects towards each other and towards other religious systems*, New Delhi: Munshiram Manoharlal, 1995, p.18.
10. S. Lévi, *La doctrine du sacrifice dans les Brahmanas*, Paris: PUF, 1966, p. 82.
11. M. Biardeau and C. Malamoud, *Le sacrifice dans l'Inde ancienne*, Paris: PUF, 1976, p. 27.

12. M. Biardeau, *L'hindouisme—anthropologie d'une civilisation*, Paris: Flammarion, 1981, pp. 24-6.
13. Shrirama and I. Deva, 'Crystallization of the Traditional Pattern of Stratification in India', in *Social stratification in India*, ed. K.L. Sharma, Delhi: Manohar, 1992, pp. 14-16.
14. R. Thapar, *Ancient Indian Social History—Some Interpretations*, Delhi: Sangam Books, 1984, pp. 28-32.
15. Shrirama and I. Deva, 'Crystallization of the Traditional Pattern of Stratification in India', in *Social Stratification in India*, ed. K.L. Sharma, Delhi: Manohar, 1992, pp. 22-5.
16. *The Ordinances of Manu*, tr. A.C. Burnell, Delhi: Oriental Reprint, 1971, p. 79.
17. *Bhagavata Purana*, tr. G.V. Tagare, vol. 9, Delhi: Motilal Banarsidass, 1976, pp. 964-5.
18. *Brahma Purana*, vol. 35, Delhi: Motilal Banarsidass, 1985, p. 613.
19. Ibid., pp. 618-19.
20. R. Thapar, *Ancient Indian Social History—Some Interpretations*, Delhi: Sangam Books, 1984, pp. 128-36.
21. L.P. Sharma, *Ancient History of India*, Delhi: Vikas Publishing House, 1981, pp. 108-98.
22. Institut Français d'Etudes sur l'Asie centrale (IFEAC), *Inde—Asie centrale, routes du commerce et des idées*, Aix-en-Provence: Editions Edisud, 1996.
23. *Brahma Purana*, vol. 33, Delhi: Motilal Banarsidass, 1985, p. xvii. *Bhagavata Purana*, tr. G.V. Tagare, vol. 7, Delhi: Motilal Banarsidass, 1976, p. xxxiv.
24. B. Walker, *Hindu world : an encyclopedic survey of Hinduism*, Delhi: Munshiram Manoharlal, 1983, vol. 2, p. 28.
25. S. Datta, *Migrant Brahmanas in northern India*, Delhi: Motilal Banarsidass, 1989, pp. 147-51.
26. C. Malamoud, 'Remarques sur la dissuasion dans l'Inde ancienne', in *Violences et non-violences en Inde*, ed. D. Vidal et al., Paris: Editions de l'EHESS, Purusartha, 1994, p. 59.
27. R. Thapar, *Ancient Indian Social History—Some Interpretations*, Delhi: Sangam Books, 1984, pp. 131-4.
28. M. Biardeau, 'Brahmanes combattants dans un mythe du Sud de l'Inde', *The Adyar Library Bulletin*, Madras, 1967-8, pp. 521-7.
29. V. Bouillier, 'La violence des non-violents, ou les ascètes au combat', in *Violences et non-violences en Inde*, ed. D. Vidal et al., Paris: Editions de l'EHESS, Purusartha, 1994, pp. 215, 218-25.
30. M. Biardeau, 'Le Brahmanisme ancien, ou la non-violence impossible', in *Violences et non-violences en Inde*, ed. D. Vidal et al., Paris: Editions de l'EHESS, Purusartha, 1994, pp. 134-5. *Le Mahabharata*, com-

mented by M. Biardeau, Paris: Flammarion, 1985, pp. 52-3, 61, 66, 109-17.
31. *Le Mahabharata*, commented by M. Biardeau, Paris: Flammarion, 1985, p. 53.
32. Capt. A.H. Bingley, *Caste Handbooks for the Indian army – Brahmins*, Calcutta, Government of India, repr. 1918, p. 7. The problems related to the confrontation between traditionally accepted Brahminical values and a military career will be discussed in Chapter 3.
33. S. Alavi, *The Sepoys and the Company—tradition and transition in northern India 1770-1830*, Delhi: Oxford University Press, 1995, pp. 49-52.
34. This factor would play an important role in triggering the Sepoy Mutiny of 1857, as explained later.
35. Capt. A.H. Bingley, *Caste Handbooks for the Indian army – Brahmins*, Calcutta, Government of India, repr. 1918, pp. 41-6.
36. Ibid., pp. 47-53.
37. J.N. Bhattacharya, *Hindu castes and sects: an exposition of the origin of the Hindu caste system and the bearing of the sects towards each other and towards other religious systems*, Delhi: Munshiram Manoharlal, 1995, p. 24.
38. The problem of vegetarianism in the confrontation between the Brahmin ethic and the warrior ethic is discussed later in the book.
39. Dogra is a martial category, in accordance with the theory of martial races that is defined later.
40. H.A. Rose, *Glossary of the tribes and castes of the north-west frontier and the protected territories of the north-west frontier provinces*, Delhi: Amar Prakashan, 1919 (reed. 1979), vol. 3, p. 132.
41. P.N. Bali, *The History of the Mohyals—A Legendary People*, Bombay, Popular Press, 1986, pp. 4-10.
42. Ibid., pp. 24-5.
43. Ibid., pp. 13, 41-2.
44. A. Nandy, 'Rencontre ultime : la dimension politique de l'assassinat de Gandhi', in *Miroir de l'Inde : études indiennes en sciences sociales* , ed. L. Lardinois, Paris: Maison des Sciences de l'Homme, 1988, pp. 273-91.
45. S.P. Rosen, *Societies and military power: India and its armies*, Delhi: Oxford University Press, 1996, pp. 172-3.
46. Despised after 1857, the Mahars were once again in demand during World War I. A Mahar Regiment was created in 1917 but disbanded in 1921. During World War II, Dr. Ambedkar pressurized the government to start recruiting them again, which led to the creation of another Mahar Regiment in September 1941. S.P. Cohen, 'The Untouchable Soldier: Caste, Politics and the Indian Army', *Journal of Asian Studies*,

Association for Asian Studies: Ann Arbor (Michigan), 1969, 28(3), pp. 454-8.

47. K.L.M. Saxena, *The military system of India (1850-1900)*, New Delhi: Sterling Publishers, 1974, pp. 13-16. Lt. Gen. S.L. Menezes, *Fidelity and Honour—The Indian army from the seventeenth to the twenty-first century*, Delhi: Viking, 1993, pp. 147-50.
48. D. Omissi, *The Sepoy and the Raj—the Indian Army, 1860-1940*, London: Macmillan Press, 1994, p. 4.
49. P. Mason, *A Matter of Honour—an account of the Indian army, its officers and men*, London: Jonathan Cape, 1974, p. 125.
50. S.P. Rosen, *Societies and military power: India and its armies*, Delhi: Oxford University Press, 1996, p. 178.
51. P. Mason, *A Matter of Honour—an account of the Indian army, its officers and men*, London: Jonathan Cape, 1974, p. 313.
52. C. Markovits, ed., *Histoire de l'Inde moderne: 1480-1950*, Paris: Fayard, 1994, p. 341.
53. The order issued on 1 September 1856 stated that 'no native recruit shall be accepted who does not at the time of his enlistment undertake to serve beyond the sea, whether within the territories of the Company or beyond them'. K.L.M. Saxena, *The military system of India (1850-1900)*, Delhi: Sterling Publishers, 1974, p. 14.
54. P. Mason, *A Matter of Honour—an account of the Indian army, its officers and men*, London: Jonathan Cape, 1974, pp. 269-73. Lt. Gen. S.L. Menezes, *Fidelity and Honour—The Indian army from the seventeenth to the twenty-first century*, Delhi: Viking, 1993, pp. 157-8.
55. D. Omissi, *The Sepoy and the Raj—the Indian Army, 1860-1940*, London: Macmillan Press, 1994, pp. 4-5.
56. P. Mason, *A Matter of Honour—an account of the Indian army, its officers and men*, London: Jonathan Cape, 1974, p. 314.
57. K.L.M. Saxena, *The military system of India (1850-1900)*, New Delhi: Sterling Publishers, 1974, pp. 232-6. Before 1857, some regiments were organized on the principle of a 'general mixture' where men from different castes and classes intermingled in each company. It was noticed, with reference to the events in 1857, that social and religious differences in these regiments encouraged the development of an *esprit de corps* which enabled an individual soldier, irrespective of his caste and religion, to identify with the spirit of his regiment. But other systems were also continued and various homogeneous companies based on geographical or socio-economic factors were included in the same regiment. S.P. Cohen, 'The Untouchable Soldier: Caste, Politics and the Indian Army', *Journal of Asian Studies,* Association for Asian Studies: Ann Arbor (Michigan), 1969, 28(3), p. 237.

58. D. Omissi, *The Sepoy and the Raj—the Indian Army, 1860-1940*, London: Macmillan Press, 1994, p. 11.
59. See map in G. Mac Munn, *The Martial Races of India*, London: Sampson Low, Marston & Co., 1932, before index.
60. See Tables that enable us to assess the changes in the social bases of recruitment between 1858 and 1914, especially the marked decline in the number of Brahmin recruits: D. Omissi, *The Sepoy and the Raj—the Indian Army, 1860-1940*, London: Macmillan Press, 1994, pp. 7, 20.
61. Lt. Col. W.B. Cunnningham, *Handbooks for the Indian army—Dogras*, Calcutta, Government of India, repr. 1918 and 1932, pp. 56-8.
62. Interview with Lt. Gen. Z.C. Bakshi (a Mohyal Brahmin), 11/08/1995.
63. D. Omissi, *The Sepoy and the Raj—the Indian Army, 1860-1940*, London: Macmillan Press, 1994, p. 12.
64. Lt. Gen. S.L. Menezes, *Fidelity and Honour—The Indian army from the seventeenth to the twenty-first century*, Delhi: Viking, 1993, pp. 286-9.
65. D. Omissi, *The Sepoy and the Raj—the Indian Army, 1860-1940*, London: Macmillan Press, 1994, pp. 13-16.
66. G. Mac Munn, *The Martial Races of India*, London: Sampson Low, Marston & Co., 1932, pp. 9-12.
67. For example, refer in chapter 4 to the overlapping of the terms Brahmin and Aryan in the Dravidian movement opposed to these two categories.
68. D. Omissi, *The Sepoy and the Raj—the Indian Army, 1860-1940*, London: Macmillan Press, 1994, p. 24.
69. Ibid., pp. 23-32.
70. Ibid., pp. 8-9.
71. G. Mac Munn, *The Martial Races of India*, London: Sampson Low, Marston & Co., 1932, pp. 271-2.
72. Capt. A.H. Bingley, *Caste Handbooks for the Indian army – Brahmins*, Calcutta, Government of India, repr. 1918, p. 41.
73. D. Omissi, *The Sepoy and the Raj—the Indian Army, 1860-1940*, London: Macmillan Press, 1994, pp. 155-60.
74. Discussion with Brig. C.B. Khanduri, a historian. See in this connection his book, *Field Marshal K.M. Cariappa—his life and times*, Delhi: Lancer Publishers, 1995, pp. 102–3.
75. C. Markovits, ed., *Histoire de l'Inde moderne: 1480-1950*, Paris: Fayard, 1994, pp. 440-1.
76. J. Gaylor, *Sons of John Company—The Indian and Pakistan Armies 1903–1991*, New Delhi: Lancer Inernational, 1993, pp. 22-4. P. Mason, *A Matter of Honour—an account of the Indian army, its officers and men*, London: Jonathan Cape, 1974, pp. 455-6. Lt. Col. G. Sharma, *Indian army through the ages*, Delhi: Allied Publishers Limited, 1979, pp. 263-6.

77. Maj. Gen. C.N. Das, *Traditions and Customs of the Indian Armed Forces*, Delhi: Vision Books, 1984, pp. 364-7.
78. Lt. Col. G. Sharma, *Nationalisation of the Indian army—1885-1947*, Delhi: Allied Publishers Limited, 1996, p. 129.
79. A. Kundu, 'The Indian Army's Continued Overdependence of Martial Races' Officers', *Indian Defence Review*, Delhi, July 1991.

CHAPTER 3

Brahmin Identity in the Armed Forces

In the previous chapter I traced the trajectory of Brahmin communities which were associated with the army throughout their history but had to adapt themselves in more recent times to the constraints imposed by the theory of martial races. Although this theory has been widely criticized and denounced after Independence as a myth propagated by the British colonial regime, so as to implement its famous 'divide and rule' policy, it has had a profound influence on military recruitment policies in India. The tendency towards the overrepresentation of some groups in the army holds true even today.[1] The study of these Brahmins reveals the adjustments made by some groups and the subterfuges employed by them to counter the strategies used by the authorities as well as communities competing for recruitment. For example, the Mohyal Brahmins, as mentioned in the previous chapter, sought recruitment under the category of the Dogras, classified as a martial race, to ensure their place in the army.

Brahmins steeped in the military tradition adhered to it even after Independence, especially since officers' posts were considered suitable for middle-class Brahmins commensurate with their level of education and social status. However, with the advent of Independence and democracy, the social base of the military élite widened considerably and family connections had to make way for merit and aptitude in the recruitment process.[2]

As far as military traditions are concerned, they continued after Independence, but after the 1960s a career in the armed forces no longer enjoyed the same prestige and respect. I intend to examine the reasons behind this change by studying the attitudes of Brahmins now serving in the armed forces. To understand the peculiar nature of these Brahmins, this chapter delves into the foundations of their contemporary identity as linked to an 'impersonal' approach. Having found out how and why military traditions gained ascendance over Brahminical traditions, it is possible to understand the prestige attached to martial values. This respect, nevertheless, has ceased to attract the younger generation which is more concerned about the growing disadvantages of a career in the armed forces as compared to a career in the civilian sector.

Let us begin with the notion of traditions and values. It is generally associated with a military career in countries where the army is more involved in maintaining order than in seeking political power. In India, the importance attached to these values and traditions is linked to the legacy of the British colonial rule. Brahmins in the armed forces, whom I interviewed, were very articulate about their profession brushing aside references to their caste identity. They spoke of the Indian army as an institution having strong ethical principles and democratic convictions that encouraged apolitical and secular attitude and discouraged parochialism with reference to religion or caste.

We had this feeling of prestige of belonging to the army... this feeling has disappeared.[3]

The values propagated by the military as an institution are central to the discourse of Brahmins who have retired from the armed forces; those who are still in service refused to be formally interviewed. Further, this tendency is linked to the belief that only the older generation attaches prestige to traditions and values while the younger generation opts for criteria like social status or financial gains, as we shall see in the second part of this chapter. It is nevertheless true that insistence on this prestige is usually the most noticeable feature of articles and publications related to the army. In other words, it is the highlight of the image that is sought to be projected. This prestige is connected with the notion of duty, a specific way of life and values associated with a military career.

The notion of duty is central to the attitude of a professional soldier. Performing one's duty is an essential part of the code of ethics followed by all military men and it is akin to one of the fundamental principles of Indian civilization, viz., the socio-cosmic order of *dharma*.[4]

The *Bhagavad Gita* is the perfect illustration of the invocation to duty as the nucleus of the military ethic. When it extols devotion and disinterested action, the *Gita* actually refers to the ethic of the Kshatriya, the *varna* of kings and warriors. A man must not cease to perform his duty till the moment of his death. Krishna constantly encourages Arjuna, the model warrior of the Pandava clan, by showering praises on the warriors who laid down their lives for a just cause. It is a question of duty for duty's sake and it means that the soldier must perform the task assigned to him without expecting anything in return. He must not strive to win appreciation nor should he fear condemnation. He should do what is expected of him in a spirit of renunciation. This does not mean acting without purpose but giving up the fruits of action while performing one's duty.[5]

This ethic of renouncing the fruits of one's actions could be compared to the notion of renunciation implicit in the concept of *ahimsa*. It was the result of the evolution of the Brahmin figure who, as we have seen in the beginning of the previous chapter, from being the master of sacrificial violence gradually came to embody non-violence.[6] But as one of the Brahmin military officers we interviewed pointed out, religious renunciation is egoistic in nature while renunciation in the army is related to the 'duty of protecting the Nation'.[7]

In the army there is no question of individual salvation, it is always individual duty in relation to a collective national cause. 'Service Before Self' is the motto of every military man and particularly of officers. The ethos of an officer can be briefly described as follows: safety, honour and the country's welfare always come first, the honour, welfare and comfort of the men under his command come next, while his own comfort and safety always come last. This is the motto inscribed on the pediment of the Indian Military Academy in Dehra Dun.[8] Officers have a major role in motivating their men and ensuring the smooth progress of operations they are entrusted with. Performing their duty in perfect coordination with their men is an essential element of the relationship between officers and soldiers.[9] In addition to this devotion to duty, military men are attached to a particular way of life and specific values that enable them to function independently, free from all ties and references associated with civilian life.

Being in that environment, you are brought up in a certain manner, which subconsciously . . . you are imbibing a certain value system. You see the point is that, suppose I am . . . say in the house of my children, they may know nothing about the Brahminical ethos but they will know a lot about the army. They will know how the army people function, what do they do, how do they go about things . . . .[10]

Military activities are essentially group activities. Different solidarity networks are created in this manner, but always within the military sphere. Working in a closed environment totally isolated from civilian public space gives rise to a particular style of working. Sharing a day-to-day existence, that is sometimes rough and tiring, strengthens the bonds within each unit giving rise to a strong 'esprit de corps'.[11]

This separation between military and civilian space explains why the general public looks at military men as a 'breed apart' having an élitist nature. The reason is that in the Indian context the British had a tendency to give too much importance to a career in the military to satisfy their needs of colonial domination and this tendency persisted after Independence for reasons of 'tradition' and 'security'. Politicians use the pretext of security to shroud in secrecy anything that has to do with the military, especially the military budget. The attachment to traditions is a result of the desire of military men to present themselves as a unique group, proud of its customs and its values.[12]

There are many such values mentioned in the publications that I consulted or in the statements made by the Brahmins interviewed. Honour seems to top the list.[13] Respect and self-esteem serve as the foundation of a conscious effort to build a collective feeling of pride at every level of the military hierarchy and in the army as a whole. Honour is followed by patriotism, honesty, loyalty, professionalism, feeling of unity and courage.[14]

Leena Parmar, a sociologist, talks of the 'professional socialization' in the army through which soldiers share the same subculture in terms of phraseology, dress habits, physical training and the values of discipline, punctuality and loyalty.[15] These values must be personified first and foremost by the officers who as distinguished members of the military hierarchy are expected to carry forward the fine military tradition and behave like perfect gentlemen.[16] Personal attitudes marked by morals and a sense of manners must be combined with irreproachable professional standards.[17]

It is interesting to note that military officers occupy the highest place in public esteem. A survey entitled '*Public Reverence—50 Years After Independence*' conducted by the Mode Institute on 13 August 1997 in five cities, viz., Bangalore, Calcutta, Chennai, Delhi and Mumbai, during which about a thousand persons were questioned, gives us an idea of the extent of this esteem. The poll concerned bureaucrats, advocates, doctors, businessmen, military officers and top-ranking sportsmen. The four parameters for judging them were honesty, courage, efficiency and contribution to the nation's well-being ; for each of these parameters, military officers came out on top.[18]

There is a certain similarity between some of these military values and values considered as Brahminical by the non-military Brahmins who were interviewed. Honesty, in particular, is a value common to both, but what seems to be a characteristic of the psychological approach peculiar to the military is actually that a personal quality should be valued only when it is used for the proper functioning of the group. Values mentioned by non-military Brahmins like integrity, morality and sincerity are essentially qualities that enhance the worth of an individual.

Respect is also one of the principles stressed by both military and civilian Brahmins. But here again, the military approach differs from any self-centered concerns. The respect of military values and traditions by the general public and by the rulers is absolutely necessary for maintaining the morale of the troops and indispensable for the proper functioning of the military apparatus as a whole. The military career, built around such values, constitutes a very elaborate reference system able to marginalize aspects of the civilian domain. Brahmins, who are professional soldiers, claim indeed that they are estranged from the theoretical Brahminical model, i.e. the teachings of the ancient books on religious matters.

The army, which stands apart because of this distinctive ethos, is also considered to be a unique model for its ability to fit into Indian society's scheme of things. The secular and apolitical character of this institution makes it a key element of the ideology pursued by the Indian state since Independence.

Being a homogeneous body built on sound values, the Indian army is usually referred to as a 'holy cow' as it is considered to be an institution above criticism embodying the basic principles of

Indian democracy.[19] The Brahmins we interviewed proudly defended these characteristics. The perception of the Indian army is of an institution totally free from bias as far as caste and community are concerned and standing above political intrigue and manoeuvring.

The army has always been a great leveller of castes.[20]

The Indian Army is an institution that symbolizes the diversity of the country and brings together all castes, religions and geographical regions in a spirit of harmony. I will now take up the relationship between its functioning and reference to caste and community through the opposing tendencies of asserting one's caste identity and practising a functional secularism, in the post-Independence context.

In the army nobody cares, they are all mixed. And this is what people don't know. While the British were here, more than 150 years, these so-called low caste people made some excellent soldiers. And so did the higher caste people, the Brahmins made excellent soldiers (...). And there were Brahmin regiments of the East India Company. And there were Brahmins in the army, amongst the common soldiers, even during the British days. Chamars, the bootmakers, there were Chamar regiments, they did excellently well. Among the Ramdasia Sikhs, they did excellently well.[21]

Although mixing castes and communities in the army is a historical fact, the long history of various regiments consisting of specific groups contributed to the crystallization of caste identities. After Independence, the Government of India decided that it would no longer create new caste-based regiments in accordance with the traditional theory of martial races. The new regiments that were created were mixed regiments, the Parachute Regiment being a typical example.[22] However, in addition to maintaining the old regiments, which now admitted members of different castes but maintained old names and traditions, the army had to give in to demands from caste-based organizations even as late as in 1962-3. At that time, the *All India Yadav Mahasabha* representing the Yadav caste brought indeed pressure on the government for creating a separate Yadav Regiment.[23]

Also, the identities of some groups, formed precisely due to their assimilation in the army, could not disappear overnight following a government order. The building of the identity of the Jat community, officially recognized as a martial race, is quite characteristic of this process. Jat identity was fragile and almost non-existent in the pre-colonial era, but the beginning of the twentieth century witnessed the rise of a well-structured group with a strong identity following its conversion to the Arya Samaj ideology and its assertion in the army. The Arya Samaj, a socio-religious reform movement, attempted to modify Hindu religious practices in response to Western criticism. Its founder, Swami Dayananda, rejected the system of *jatis* considered to be retrograde and too particularistic and reintroduced the system of *varnas* which was closer to Western individualistic values.[24] Under the influence of Swami Dayananda, the Jats claimed the Kshatriya status and the right to wear the sacred thread, especially in the army to counteract their humiliation and revilement by the Brahmins. On the basis of illusory notions about their past, for example the belief that the 1857 uprising was the rallying point for their community, the Jats created a 'natural' military identity going back to the pre-British period in opposition with the colonial interpretation, inclined to place their community at a rather low level in the caste hierarchy.[25]

The Mohyals have a similar history in the sense that their group identity was mainly built around their military activities, but the difference is that, being Brahmins they did not have to claim a higher status. Their attitude is nonetheless ambivalent. They try to minimize the importance of their Brahmin *varna* by laying stress on their military background and claiming that they have a 'natural' aptitude on the basis of historical links between Brahmins and the military.

Mohyals do not like to be called Brahmins . . . . We are Brahmins . . . but not priests (...). *We are Brahmins but with a difference.*[26]

In his book on the Mohyals, P.N. Bali emphasizes from the very first page the paradox according to which the members of this community 'gained recognition over the years as a martial race because of their heroic deeds although their ancestors were Brahmins'.[27] Their refusal to accept a Brahmin identity in the religious sense is accompanied by assertions about the Kshatriya functions performed by some Mohyals throughout history or the existence of illustrious Brahmins like Dronacharya, the accomplished strategist who taught the art of war, in the *Mahabharata*. This Brahmin sect, which decided to combat Muslim invaders, made a vow to fight by giving up all their links with the priesthood. Though they constitute only a small proportion of the total Brahmin population, the Mohyals as a martial race have a strong presence in the army having been recruited in the Dogra, Sikh and British regiments.[28]

This ambivalent attitude can be partly explained by the strong system of military values and the typical spirit of the Indian Army, which encourages its members to avoid all reference to their belonging to a particular caste or community. This does not however stop individuals from being conscious of specific historical links between their groups and the army.[29]

The Indian Army, described by Maj. Gen. D'Souza as the 'best example of secularism' during a seminar on minorities and cohesion in 1996, is indeed a privileged space where men of different castes and religions live and work together and share their religious festivals.[30]

I went to the army . . . and there we never talked of any caste and in fact nobody ever asked which caste one belongs to, nobody bothered and . . . therefore the thought never came that as a Brahmin, how do I feel or what I should do. It didn't come to my mind at all . . . and therefore I functioned in an environment where not only Hindus of various castes were there, there were Muslims, there were Christians and over all in the army we have a very different atmosphere where religion really doesn't matter . . . to the extent that it's not that people are non religious, everybody is very religious . . . but everybody respects every other religion.[31]

All references to the army's internal functioning emphasize its role as a melting pot where men from different socio-cultural backgrounds mix together to form a homogeneous body and practise religious tolerance which is the 'living ideal' of a united India.[32]

As for the theory of martial races, even though its repercussions are still being felt as pointed out earlier, the official ideology aims at full-scale national integration and the rejection of old communal policies, except in the case of Gurkhas from Nepal who are treated as a special case. The policy laid down in the early 1990s is to have within the next twenty-five years an army consisting of regiments made up of men from various ethnic groups and geographical regions—an 'all-class, all-India mix'.[33] As far back as the 1950s, Field Marshal K.M. Cariappa, tried to mix Sikh soldiers of different ranks in the religious hierarchy, but without much success.[34] Later, during the 1960s, this trend crystallized in a 'secularized theory of martial races' highlighting the martial characteristics peculiar to each group. The idea was to preserve the strong martial traditions within a largely egalitarian structure. Y.B. Chavan, who was then Defence Minister, remarked that when it is a question of defending the Indian nation, all soldiers are equally martial, no matter what their caste or class is, encapsulating his point of view in the interesting phrase: 'We are all Kshatriyas now'.[35]

This same view was expressed by two Brahmin military officers we interviewed.

Caste is a profession. You said profession, you said you feel because of profession. As a Brahmin, I should be a religious teacher or I should be a school teacher, or I should be some very highly educated person doing research or doing something . . . damned hell, I'm a damned good engineer and I am a damned good soldier, that's the end of it.[36]

I subscribe to the view that these four classifications, Brahmins, Kshatriyas, Vaishyas, Shudras, which have been made are not by birth. Today, as a military officer, I am a Kshatriya. I am not a Brahmin for my 38 years of service in the army, I am a Kshatriya. I am not a Brahmin, I do nothing as a Brahmin, why should I be called a Brahmin? Just because I was born a Brahmin, it's not correct.[37]

By insisting that they are Kshatriyas rather than Brahmins, these Brahmin soldiers support the theory that defines caste on the basis of occupation, which was in fact the original *varna* theory.

Another trait of the Indian army I would like to highlight here, apart from its melting pot dimension is its role as an instrument of state policy. S.P. Cohen, an expert on the Indian Army, describes this trend in the following terms, 'The Indian Army remains an outstanding example of an apolitical, professional force, almost the model of a bureaucratic instrument of state policy'.[38]

Of all the armies in developing countries, the Indian Army is a truly remarkable institution that interacts smoothly with the country's political leadership even as it maintains its distance, especially as compared to the situation in neighbouring Pakistan. Some people are of the opinion that this balance has always existed in India as a result of the system of checks and balances built into the *varna* system. For example, the Kshatriyas as warriors were dependent on the Brahmins from whom they learnt the art of war.[39] But it was mainly during the British colonial period that this apolitical tendency took root as also the Indian Army's willingness to cooperate with the civilian government.[40]

Under the British rule, the possible links between the military and political spheres could be expressed through two major issues—either by allowing caste and communal feelings to gain an upper hand in the army and encouraging factions that would side with one party or another during conflicts or taking an ideological stand on matters related to the country's Independence. But in both cases, the majority of military men in India have displayed a neutral attitude as an expression of the distance maintained by the army from party politics.[41]

After Second World War and with the advent of Independence, this essentially British tradition of separating civilian and military authority was considered to be good for the country. The army thus became a favoured instrument that would strive to maintain the country's stability, integrity and security.[42]

It was with the same idea in mind that one of the Brahmin officers we interviewed categorically rejected any affinity for his *varna* and declared that, on the contrary, he was very proud of being in the army:

We had our own share in developing our own country. I don't talk about patriotism and all that, that's all nonsense, forget it. . . . We have a lot of work to do, we have to bring stability. Our country is stable today in India, a good part of that is the credit of the army. It takes no part in politics, but it kept our country stable for fifty years. And I am very proud to be a part of that army.[43]

In the same spirit, another officer said that serving in the army was for him synonymous with working for the nation's well-being.[44]

The object of a soldier's duty and loyalty is the country and not the political party in power or the head of the government. Various political changes have occurred in India without any fear of a military coup d'état. On the contrary, the army has always provided protection and has silently watched over the proper functioning of parliamentary democracy. Since it is widely accepted as a melting pot of diverse castes and communities, the Indian Army is the preferred symbol and institution for ensuring the country's unity and integrity.[45]

Despite its apolitical nature, in recent years the army has been in the public eye on several occasions, e.g. the political stir caused by the dismissal in December 1998 of Admiral Vishnu Bhagwat and the attempts by the ruling party to exploit the Indian Army's victory against Pakistan in 1999 in Kargil for electoral gains. It remains nevertheless a model institution.[46]

Brahmins serving in the army continue to be proud of the secular and apolitical character of this professional body. Their values, their style of working and their pride are derived, without apparent conflict, from their belonging to this professional organization rather than to their belonging to a particular caste. There could however be a conflict between the values associated with the traditional Brahmin ethic and those associated with the military ethic.

Ahimsa is behind us.

A Brahmin officer from the Mohyal community summed up his thoughts in this brief and incisive statement explaining later that, as far as his sense of values and morality are concerned, he is inspired by the way the army functions and not by any caste ethic.[47]

As we saw at the beginning of Chapter 1, at the time the *Brahmanas* were composed, the Brahminical function was intrinsically linked with the notion of *ahimsa*, following the development of Buddhist and Jain heterodoxies based on this principle and the adoption of a new approach to sacrificial practices within the Hindu fold itself. This was the origin of the practice of renunciation which finally superimposed itself on the existing Brahminical values and, consequently, the Brahminical function changed focus to self-denial, the search for purity and vegetarianism.[48]

It is interesting to observe that these last values were at the very core of the crisis leading to the uprising of 1857. Two decisions taken by the British authorities at that time were perceived by the upper castes, particularly the Brahmins, as a negation of these values.[49] It would therefore appear that military values and way of life come in conflict with traditional Brahminical values. This was in fact the main argument of the colonial anti-Brahmin propaganda after 1857, especially with regard to violence. This apparent contradiction of values may be the reason for Brahmins serving in the army to stress the legitimacy of their situation : members of the Brahmin *varna* and still fully involved in the military career. Brahmins, who were targeted by the colonial rulers after the mutiny, defended their professional abilities. They objected that although they were born Brahmins, they had the right to claim that they could be good soldiers.

So, being a Brahmin, when I say has no difference to me, I mean, my ancestors were . . . medical . . . doctors and army. Some of my ancestors were in Ranjit Singh's army, nearly 200 years ago. So that is perfectly normal routine for a Brahmin to be a general in Ranjit Singh's army. Nothing unusual.[50]

They explain moreover that they are hardly aware of committing violence when they function as soldiers.

They had no so called moral compulsions as people have now that if you are a soldier you are a killer.[51]

Even if the public thinks differently today, they insist that they are totally detached from the practice of violence as such and only serve as tools in the exercise of violence for legitimate purposes. If there is violence, it is used for safeguarding the nation's integrity and defending its interests. For some of these Brahmins in the army, the police force embodies the 'other' that has to be despised because it is the true agent of violence.

This notion is widely shared by public opinion, as demonstrated by the diametrically opposite images of the army and the police presented by the press.[52] The heroism displayed by soldiers in a particular conflict is contrasted with the violent behaviour of the police in various incidents all over the country.[53] Newspaper articles with suggestive titles like 'Police Unprofessional' and 'Police Need to Develop a Human Face' contrast the army's humaneness and professionalism with police violence.[54] Unlike the army, which is held to be secular and apolitical, the police force has a tendency to be biased during communal conflicts to the detriment of the minorities, especially Muslims, and is implicated in various scandals involving criminals and politicians.[55] The aggravation of the situation during the last few years has led to a multitude of articles on the urgent need to reform this unpopular force and has recently prompted the Delhi Police to appoint a special officer to supervise relations with the media.[56]

Guided by the unambiguous benchmarks laid down by the institutional framework of the army regarding the principle of secularism and the absence of involvement in politics, Brahmins in the armed forces are soldiers first. And like other military men, their demands are based not on the caste factor but on a comparison with the benefits enjoyed by their civilian counterparts. Profession is the criterion for their identity. What matters first is the prestige attached to a job in the armed forces as compared to the civil services, and not caste considerations.

Indeed, when Brahmins in the armed forces claim that they are being unfairly treated, it is never on account of caste unlike Brahmins in Tamil Nadu or Brahmins elsewhere after the application of the recommendations of the Mandal Commission, as we shall see in Part II and III.

A Brahmin army officer of the Mohyal community emphatically states that the Mandal Commission Report is of no importance for his community.[57] Reservation policies are not valid in the armed forces where officers and soldiers are judged on merit without any reference to the caste hierarchy.[58] This same principle of merit was cited in a case before the Supreme Court in response to a recommendation by the then President K.R. Narayanan that members of Scheduled Castes and Scheduled Tribes should be given greater access to the post of judges. Reporting on the matter, the magazine *India Today* said that adopting this approach in the case of the armed forces would amount to opening Pandora's box.[59] However, as things stand today, it would have no meaning in the armed forces where the integration of men belonging to the lower castes is nothing new, even though the system of assessment and recognition of services is not based on caste. Assessment is an internal matter in the armed forces and is not linked to social origins. If any comparison has to be made, it would be with the members of the civilian services in connection with the issues of working conditions and élite status.

The observation by military personnel of striking disparities in the working conditions of military and civilian personnel refers in general to the hostile material environment leading to a difficult psychological environment.

Military duty is traditionally linked all over the world with postings in distant places. As we have seen earlier, it was this factor of transfer to distant places, especially overseas, that provoked Brahmins in 1857 because they believed that such travel was polluting. Apart from the troubled domestic situation following independence and the emergence of various secessionist movements and Hindu-Muslim conflicts which needed the presence of the armed forces, the Indian Army is in great demand for international operations.

The number of emergency operations increased in Punjab and in Jammu & Kashmir as well as in the tribal areas of the north-east. Interventions in Sri Lanka (India's 'Vietnam' according to S.P. Cohen) and the Maldives in the late 1980s widened the Indian Army's field of action which had already become international with the three wars with Pakistan and clashes with China, in harsh climatic conditions and on extremely difficult terrain.[60] To these operations may be added the peacekeeping operations in Somalia involving difficulties totally unknown to civilians.[61]

We may add to the above the decline of other services provided by the government, especially looking after the families of men serving in non-family stations in terms of health care and problems related to land ownership. Letters addressed to magistrates remaining unanswered, the need to bribe railway officials to obtain a train reservation when going home on leave are but some of the signs of the growing disinterest of public authorities and civilians in general towards the hardships faced by military personnel.[62] The necessity of living outside the civilian social circuit even in normal times and taking part in operations in risk-prone areas, can give rise to a strong feeling of isolation and physical isolation may eventually lead to psychological isolation.

The different types of duties assigned to the army entail

different disadvantages for its personnel. In the first place, the growing number of operations on the domestic front creates totally different problems for army men such as the danger of politicization and dealing not with an outside enemy but with their own countrymen.[63] This type of law and order operation brings army men in close contact with the police who they do not hold in high esteem.

Further, the army's normal duties take its members away from their family and friends. Apart from missions in foreign lands, the normal pattern of posting of an officer in the army is four years in a high altitude station followed by two years in a 'peace station'. This means that most of them are away from their homes and families at least half the time and about half to two-thirds of their total period of service in spent in field operations.[64] This practice of isolating military personnel is also a result of the continuance, even after 1947, of the British institution of the 'army cantonment' which separates the military from the rest of the population.

To this must be added the disadvantages of adhering to values and a way of life based on order and discipline that can sometimes create a feeling of being stifled. All these factors together that express the differences perceived by military men between themselves and their civilian counterparts are incorporated in the debate on the concepts of 'relative deprivation' and 'relative gratification'.[65]

The feeling of deprivation is a result of the combination of several factors such as frequent transfers and being cut-off from social civilian circles. This affects the daily rhythm of family life and children's education in the case of married men and amounts to plain and simple loneliness in the case of bachelors. But this same lifestyle may be seen as a source of gratification from other points of view.[66] In the first place, there is gratification in terms of the honours won by a soldier at different stages of his career in the form of medals and recognition. There is also group gratification which is the backbone and the driving force of military culture. Finally, there is so-called gratification in the form of special allowances and perquisites that were effective in the past but are now on the decline, as mentioned earlier. This last point is today the main reason for the 'relative deprivation' experienced by military men in relation to civilians. The feeling of being cut-off from the core of society is now most accurately perceived by military men in terms of salaries, promotion avenues and other factors related to social status.

When I retired from the army, I didn't have enough money, they pay the army very little, so I worked in industry.[67]

Right from 1947, the Indian Army maintained that it promoted values like courage and honour and, even more, the principle of loyal service to the state and freedom from all political and communal tensions. For a long time these characteristics gave an aura of prestige to a military career, even more so because there was not much financial disparity between the different sectors of the economy immediately after Independence. But this golden age is long past. A young cadet in the prestigious Indian Military Academy in Dehra Dun interviewed by a reporter from *The Hindu* in 1997 said, 'This profession gives you a lot of satisfaction. But, if you are only after money, then it is a different matter.'[68]

The 1960s were a turning point and disturbed the existing equilibrium between the military and the civilian sector. In his analysis of the Indian middle-class, Pawan K. Varma refers to this period as the 'end of innocence'. Following the decline of ideological references, such as the legacy of Gandhi and Nehru, the founding fathers of the Indian National Congress, which were a source of ethics and idealism, more pragmatic issues related to consumption and purchasing power became a major cause of concern for the Indian middle class. It was about this time that the private sector started growing in India. New social strata like the entrepreneurial class and business and trading communities began climbing the social ladder thanks to the favourable institutional framework set up by Indira Gandhi to facilitate the systematic development of a capitalist economy. The 1970s witnessed a rapid economic growth which encouraged the rise of consumerism in India.[69]

As a result of these economic upheavals, the armed forces ceased to be attractive for the younger generation which could choose between a career in the army and the possibility of a rapid rise in the private sector. In addition, there was a decline in the situation of military personnel as compared to the civil services. Until 1953, military men earned salaries that were comparable to those earned by their counterparts in the civil services. But gradually the gap between the two started widening, especially after 1962, due to the high rate of inflation.[70]

These socio-economic changes led to a shift in the references used by the élite where values and prestige, which were of prime importance in a military career, could no longer compete with financial gains. To be a part of the élite, one had to earn a large salary. A survey conducted for the defence services in 1994 by MARG revealed that 50 per cent of the young men who were polled expressed a preference for a career in the private sector, the most obvious choice for young university graduates today. When choosing a profession, money is the main criterion for people of all ages. In the case of the civil services, the advantages mentioned were access to power and prestige and also opportunities for corruption. As for a career in the armed forces, the remuneration is not at all attractive in view of the difficult working conditions and frequent transfers.[71] To add to this, the comparative advantages enjoyed by military personnel in the form of special allowances, membership of clubs and official cars no longer appear attractive considering the much better perquisites offered by the private sector.[72] Finally, there are the problems regarding promotions. A military career is not considered exciting, as it does not offer the attraction of more and more interesting posts demanding greater responsibility. All these factors taken together are responsible for a significant fall in the status of military personnel, which can be symbolically perceived in terms of the order of precedence on ceremonial occasions in relation to their civilian counterparts.[73] These disparities are particularly flagrant in the case of the superiority enjoyed by the much-envied Indian Administrative Service.[74]

This lack of interest in a military career has inevitably led to a dramatic shortage of recruits to the officers' cadre.[75] It has also progressively given rise to sociological changes in the officers' cadre with the recruitment of young men from lower social strata who in the normal course would have joined the ranks.

But in India, as in the old Europe, not now, now there is a great levelling in Europe. Whether you are an officer, or whether you are a ranker, it's much the same. In India, it's changing also . . . very fast. But sixty-seventy years ago, an officer was of an upper social strata, a common soldier was from a lower social strata.[76]

After the 1960s, it became quite clear that the armed forces had lost their ability to attract the Indian élite and had become a popular career with the rapidly growing middle-class. This trend became more apparent after 1970 when the officers' corps became more attractive to the middle-class Indian as a career option. In the late 1970s, the senior officers did not hesitate to describe the intellectual calibre of officer cadets as 'mediocre'.[77] Thus there was a marked change in the social origin of officers trained in the IMA in Dehra Dun. Earlier, they belonged to the Westernized upper middle class or princely families and were sons of officers, but now they come from a much more modest background. About 50 per cent of the cadets come from a military background of whom 10 to 15 per cent are the sons of junior officers (JCOs) or non-commissioned officers (NCOs) while the remaining 50 per cent come from a civilian background, many of whom are from rural areas and underprivileged classes. The financial conditions offered by the army are the most obvious explanation for these changes in an age when the private sector offers numerous openings.[78] This state of affairs led a high-ranking army officer to make this embittered comment:

In the old days, officers contested and resigned. Because they came from a certain background, had sufficient private income, and believed in honour and integrity. Now they come from the middle class. Which means they have got little to fall back on.[79]

The attitude of the Mohyal community is equally defeatist. The military career no longer attracts young Mohyal Brahmins for obvious financial reasons and also because of a decline in the prestige traditionally attached to a career in the armed forces. This community is thus losing its traditional military character. The Mohyal Mahasabha has been organizing in this changing context professional training programmes to fulfil the need for professional reorientation within the community.[80]

To conclude, it clearly appears that the socio-political demands of Brahmins working in the army are dissociated from the notion of caste. The definition of the 'other' is the result of their professional dynamics. It means that they have been building an identity which is dissociated from the *varna* system, i.e. from the relationship between caste and occupation and from caste hierarchy. Brahmins serving in the army, like their peers belonging to other castes, define their social position in comparison with the one of civilians of a similar status and not with other competing castes as in the case of Brahmins in other professions. The absence of a reservation policy in the armed forces in favour of underprivileged classes has prevented these warrior Brahmins from joining the ranks of Brahmins embittered by the political exploitation of caste to their detriment.[81]

The attitude of these Brahmins towards society finds its roots in an all-encompassing professional value system, far detached from any caste matter, which is utterly specific. Most of these communities, who come from north-west India, hold positions that are diametrically opposed to those of the Brahmins belonging to the extreme south. The Brahmins of Tamil Nadu indeed stand out because of the personalization of their relationship with the Brahmin category. Firmly anchored in the history of south India during the last century, especially in relation to anti-Brahmin politics, the identity of Tamil Brahmins appears as particularly strong and structured. It forms the basis of our next case study for understanding the relationship between Brahmin identity and geographical origin.

NOTES

1. See the analysis of the Indian Military Academy in the previous chapter.
2. T.K. Barua, 'The role of the military in South Asia with special reference to India and Pakistan', *VIth European Conference on Modern South Asian Studies*, Paris: CNRS, 1978, p.3.
3. Interview with Maj. Gen. K.K. Mehta, 30/07/98.
4. Brig. B.K. Khanna, 'Ancient military heritage in India and current relevance', *Strategic Analysis*, New Delhi, August 1995, p. 679.
5. Brig. K.K. Singh, *Overcoming crisis in leadership, Indian army*, Delhi: Manas Publications, 1998, p. 82.
6. The Brahmin, who had renounced all worldly goods, succeeded in recreating within himself the fire of the sacrificial rite by digesting the offerings given to him. H.P. Schmidt, 'The origin of Ahimsa', in *Mélanges d'indianisme à la mémoire de Louis Renou*, Paris: E. de Boccard, 1968, pp. 637-83.
7. Interview with Lt. Gen. M.S. Gosain, New Delhi, 27/05/95.
8. R. Kadian, *India and its army*, Delhi: Vision Books, 1990, p. 110.
9. Brig. B.K. Khanna, 'Ancient military heritage in India and current relevance', *Strategic Analysis*, Delhi, August 1995, p. 689.

10. 17.
11. Brig. B.K. Khanna, 'Ancient military heritage in India and current relevance', *Strategic Analysis*, Delhi, August 1995, p. 687.
12. 'A closer look at the holy cow', *The Pioneer*, 08/01/99.
13. See one of the reference works on the Indian army: P. Mason, *A Matter of Honour—an account of the Indian army, its officers and men*, London: Jonathan Cape, 1974.
14. Lt. J. Jaggi, 'Military Values', *Sainik Samachar*, vol. 42, no. 1223, 15/10/95, pp. 72-3.
15. L. Parmar, *Society, Culture and Military System*, Jaipur: Rawat Publications, 1994, pp. 187-8.
16. This image is used to attract young recruits to the officers' cadre. See, for example, the advertisement for a 5-year short service commission appearing in daily newspapers all over the country. It says, 'You'll be a gentleman for the rest of your life. Do you have it in you?'.
17. Brig. B.K. Khanna, 'Ancient military heritage in India and current relevance', *Strategic Analysis*, New Delhi, August 1995, pp. 690-1.
18. Bureaucrats polled the least votes. 'Army officers high in public esteem', *The Hindu*, 22/08/97.
19. See Lt. Gen. S.C. Sardeshpande, 'The Army: Perspective of a "Holy Cow"', *USI Journal*, Delhi, 1992, pp. 341-5.
20. 2.
21. 2.
22. S.P. Cohen, *The Indian Army—Its contribution to the development of a Nation*, Berkeley: University California Press, 1971, pp. 187-8.
23. T.K. Barua, 'The role of the military in South Asia with special reference to India and Pakistan', *VIth European Conference on Modern South Asian Studies*, Paris: CNRS, 1978, p. 4.
24. C. Jaffrelot, *Hindu nationalist movement and Indian politics, 1925 to the 1990s: strategies of identity building implantation and mobilisation*, Delhi: Penguin Books, 1996, pp. 11-15.
25. N. Datta, 'Arya Samaj and the making of Jat identity', *Studies in History*, Delhi: Sage Publications, 13,1, n.s., 1997, pp. 97-119.
26. Interview with Vice Admiral N.P. Datta, 30/07/1998.
27. P.N. Bali, *The History of the Mohyals—A Legendary People*, Bombay, Popular Press, 1986, p. III.
28. Interview with Lt. Col. Z.C. Bakshi, 11/08/95.
29. This ambivalent attitude can also be explained by the contradiction between Brahminical and military values regarding violence, as we shall see later.
30. *The Times of India*, 27/10/98.
31. 17.
32. *Sainik Samachar*, vol. 42, no. 1223, 15-01-1995, pp. 24, 27, 31, 41.
33. 'Changing the mix', *India Today*, 15/12/92, p. 45.

34. Interview with Lt. Col. Gautam Sharma, Delhi, 16/03/95. See Brig. C.B. Khanduri, *Field Marshal K.M. Cariappa—His Life and Times*, Delhi: Lancer Publishers, 1995.
35. S.P. Cohen, *The Indian Army—Its contribution to the development of a Nation*, Berkeley: University California Press, 1971, pp. 190-1.
36. 2.
37. 17.
38. S.P. Cohen, 'The Military and Indian Democracy', in *India's democracy: an analysis of changing State-society relations*, ed. A. Kohli, Jersey: Orient Longman, 1991, p. 99.
39. R. Kadian, *India and its army*, Delhi: Vision Books, 1990, p. 128.
40. S.P. Cohen, 'The Military and Indian Democracy', in *India's democracy: an analysis of changing State-society relations*, ed. A. Kohli, New Jersey: Orient Longman, 1991, p. 103.
41. S.P. Cohen, *The Indian Army—Its contribution to the development of a Nation*, Berkeley: University California Press, 1971, pp. 133-5.
42. Maj. P.S. Bhatia, 'Army, politics and national integration', *Sainik Samachar*, Mumbai, vol. 42, no. 1223, 15/01/95, p. 74.
43. 2.
44. Interview with Lt. Gen. M.S. Gosain, Delhi, 27/05/95.
45. L. Parmar, *Society, Culture and Military System*, Jaipur: Rawat Publications, 1994, pp. 186-7.
46. See articles in *The Times of India*, Delhi, 21/12/98, *The Hindu*, Delhi, 27/04/99 and *Courrier International*, Paris, no. 461, 02/08/99, p. 18.
47. Interview with Lt. Col. Z.C. Bakshi, Delhi, 11/08/95.
48. Renunciation thus became the fourth and last stage in the life of a Brahmin after the first three stages, viz., life as a Vedic student, a householder and a hermit living in the forest. M. Biardeau, *L'hindouisme—anthropologie d'une civilisation*, Paris: Flammarion, 1981, pp. 37-8, 67-8, 75-6.
49. The decision to put an end to exemption from overseas service, considered to be polluting, and the introduction of a new rapid-action rifle whose cartridges had to be removed from their casing by biting on them which would have brought the soldiers into contact with impure substances like grease made from beef fat (see Chapter 2).
50. 2.
51. 2.
52. The Indian Army is nevertheless accused occasionally of violating human rights, notably in the course of its operations in Jammu & Kashmir. See *The Times of India*, 10/04/95.
53. We may take the case of Delhi, Punjab, Kerala, West Bengal and Bihar (*The Hindu*, 26/05/97; *The Pioneer*, 27/11/94; *The Indian Express*, 25/10/98; *The Hindustan Times*, 13/01/99; *The Pioneer*, 12/01/99).

The article in *The Hindustan Times* about police excesses in Calcutta is entitled, 'Making fun of a policeman costs an innocent young man his life'.

54. *The Hindu*, 20/01/98 and *The Times of India*, 06/04/95. Also see 'Police and professional lapses' in *The Hindu*, 20/01/95 and 'Humanising the police' in *The Hindu*, 02/12/97.
55. See articles by Asghar Ali Engineer, 'Will our policemen change?' in *The Hindu*, 07/06/97, 'The police and the minorities', in *The Hindu*, 06/02/98 and V.N. Rai's book, *Combating Communal Conflicts (Perception of Police Neutrality during Hindu-Muslim Riots in India)*, Delhi: Renaissance Publishing House, 1999. On the subject of the politicization and criminalization of the police, see two articles written by army officers comparing the police and the army: Lt. Gen. S.K. Sinha, 'The Police in India', *Indian Defence Review*, Delhi, vol. 8 (4), October 1993, pp. 69-71. Rear Admiral S. Singh, 'The Indian Police Force: Politicised and Enfeebled', *Indian Defence Review*, Delhi, vol. 8 (4), October 1993, pp. 72-6.
56. *The Times of India*, 01/04/99. As regards the need for reforms, see *The Hindu*, 18/04/97, 12/08/97, 17/11/98, 10/01/99.
57. Interview with Maj. Gen. K.K. Mehta, Delhi, 30/07/98.
58. In a self-portrait published in *The Hindu*, a Brahmin from Tamil Nadu explains why he is keen on a military career although he wanted to become a doctor. This was due to the existence of reservation policies since the 1940s that are unfair to Brahmins in South India—('1948 My Watershed Year', *The Hindu*, 30/03/97).
59. *India Today*, 25/01/99, pp. 20-4.
60. S.P. Cohen, *The Indian Army—Its contribution to the development of a Nation*, Delhi: Oxford University Press, rev. ed., 1990, pp. 204-6.
61. 'Don't they deserve better?', *Sunday Review, Times of India*, 15/01/95: Army Day.
62. 'Army fighting alienation', *The Pioneer*, 18/01/99.
63. The army was called only 476 times to perform such operations between 1956 and 1970 but it was called 369 times between 1980 and 1984 ('Army for the road', *The Times of India*, 24/01/95).
64. S.P. Rosen, *Societies and military power: India and its armies*, Delhi: Oxford University Press, 1996, pp. 208-9.
65. L. Parmar, *Society, Culture and Military System*, Jaipur: Rawat Publications, 1994, pp. 138-47.
66. Ibid., p. 191.
67. 2.
68. *The Hindu*, 09/12/97.
69. P.K. Varma, *The great Indian middle class*, Delhi: Viking, 1998, pp. 66-70, 89-90, 108-9.
70. S.P. Cohen, 'The Military and Indian Democracy', in *India's*

democracy: an analysis of changing State-society relations, ed. A. Kohli, New Jersey: Orient Longman, 1991, p. 105.

71. 'Army last on career choice', *The Times of India*, 07/02/95, 'A better deal for our army', *The Times of India*, 15/02/95.
72. 'Military hires pvt. firm to study pay difference', *The Times of India*, 16/10/94.
73. 'Why an Army career has ceased to be attractive', *The Hindu*, 25/04/95.
74. 'Messy military appointments', *The Hindu*, 16/03/97; 'Short-changing the armed forces', *The Hindu*, 20/07/97.
75. It was officially announced in 1997 that there was a shortage of 13,000 officers ('Officers' posts being filled up: Army chief', *The Hindu*, 09/12/97).
76. 2.
77. S.P. Cohen, *The Indian Army—Its contribution to the development of a Nation*, Delhi: Oxford University Press, rev. ed., 1990, pp. 215-16.
78. 'Change of guard', *The Telegraph*, 29/06/97.
79. 'Restoring parity', *India Today*, 30/11/91, p. 142.
80. Interview with Maj. Gen. K.K. Mehta, New Delhi, 30/07/98; interview with Vice Admiral N.P. Datta, Delhi, 30/07/98.
81. A Mohyal Brahmin was thus able to assert that the Mandal Commission Report, the most recent and the most striking version of such anti-Brahmin policies, does not affect his community. (Interview with Maj. Gen. K.K. Mehta, Delhi, 30/07/98.)

PART II

BRAHMIN IDENTITY AND THE REGIONAL VARIABLE

Tamil Brahmins

The idea of studying Tamil Brahmins in order to assess the importance of the regional factor in the definition of Brahmin identity was a result of the interaction of several elements. In the first place, what struck me after an overall assessment of the sixty odd interviews conducted in the course of this study was the cleavage between the north and the south. This regional difference between the persons interviewed is visible in the rather vague views expressed by north Indian Brahmins regarding their belonging to the Brahmin *varna* and the generally more structured and well thought-out views of south Indian Brahmins.

There are many explanations for this tendency. First, we must note that the caste structure is quite different in these two regions, especially where the upper castes are concerned. In the north, there are many castes that are placed quite close to the Brahmins in the social hierarchy like the Khatris, the Kshatriyas and the Kayasthas. On the other hand, the south is characterized by a significant absence of these castes as a result of which the Brahmins finds themselves quite isolated. From the sociological point of view, there is a polarization of the caste system in south India with the Brahmins on one side and the Shudras and Adi-Dravidas on the other.[1] Then come the merchant castes who, as we shall see later, have reaped the benefits of the Dravidian movement.

Consequently, the Brahmin identity of Tamil Brahmins evolved in a very distinctive manner unlike the north where it allowed itself to merge into a higher caste or upper class identity as seen in many of the interviews. To this we may add other geographical and historical factors. The south, for example, was quite sheltered from outside invasions and the consequent cultural influences, unlike the north where the Brahmins especially belonging to the north-western part of the country were forced to leave their native villages, as we saw in Part I. Finally, it must be noted that numerically, the position of Brahmins in the north is different from their position in the south. In Tamil Nadu they represent only 3 per cent of the total population of the state as against 9 per cent in Uttar Pradesh.[2] This is one of the main keys to understand why they could not have followed the same socio-political trajectory. All these elements together have contributed to the preservation of the 'purity' of south Indian culture, especially the Brahminical traditions.[3]

The political history of the south provided an ideal setting for the creation of a 'Brahmin category', as a central reference in political discourse and action, that gave rise to ideological debates based upon the opposition of Brahmin and non-Brahmin. We will first study the birth and growth of this category in the history of Tamil Nadu before presenting the views of contemporary Tamil Brahmins regarding their identity.

CHAPTER 4

Brahminism in the History of South India

Medium Period: From the Late Nineteenth Century

Tamil Brahmins, who enjoyed a privileged position in society in terms of status and function, were the focus of colonial attention in the second half of the nineteenth century. They stood at the top of the religious hierarchy and also held all the top posts in the British administration as a result of their access to education for many generations. Consequently, they became the object of discriminatory policies leading to their segregation and making their community the most meaningful political category in the early twentieth century. The conflict between Brahmins and non-Brahmins has been indeed for the major part of the twentieth century the pivot of politics in Tamil Nadu.

The privileged social position of the Brahmin minority supported by the British led to a reaction from the majority—non-Brahmins—demanding socio-political measures to end Brahmin supremacy. The Brahmins expressed their supremacy through overall social dominance and by demonstrating their political awareness.

This domination, though conspicuous in many spheres, has to be looked at in details. Let us first consider their spiritual role. Apparently, as a result of the strong *bhakti* tradition in Tamil Nadu implying a direct relationship between the devotee and the deity, they were reduced to playing an instrumental role since they were engaged as priests mainly by kings and dominant non-Brahmin agrarian groups.[4]

Their socio-economic influence was not negligible but, at the same time, it was not excessively disproportionate. The electoral list drawn up by the Madras Presidency in 1918 gives us a fairly good idea of the links between caste and economic class. According to the census figures, Brahmins in urban areas constituted only 20.38 per cent of the population deemed to be affluent while those in rural areas constituted 15.27 per cent.[5]

But their presence was overwhelming in the fields of education and government jobs, even though some non-Brahmins groups from educated backgrounds were also well represented in the colonial administrative services.[6] It was the British themselves who took official cognizance of this predominance and its disadvantages.

After the introduction of Lord Macaulay's education policy in 1835 aimed at creating persons who were 'Indian in blood and colour, but English in taste, in opinions, in morals, and in intellect', the British authorities changed their attitude.[7] They realized that the élite groups who had access to this type of education were concentrated among a limited number of castes and families, most of them Brahmin. If we look between 1864 and 1880, in the entire Madras Presidency, 59 per cent of the children who had completed their secondary education and 63 per cent of university graduates were Brahmins even though they constituted only 3 per cent of the total population.[8] As a result of their predominance in the educational field, it was found that from the 1850s certain Brahmin families were monopolizing key posts in the government. During this period, the revenue office in Nellore district had on its rolls almost fifty employees belonging to the same Brahmin family. The situation was equally grave in other parts of south India. In 1918, in the princely state of Mysore, Brahmins held 70 per cent of the administrative posts even though they constituted only 3.6 per cent of the state's population.[9]

When the various concerned authorities were asked for their opinion in the second half of the nineteenth century, they expressed the fear that Brahmins would oppose measures of general interest because of their monopoly. This problem was further aggravated by the fact that Brahmins acquired landed properties in the districts where they were posted. They were also known for their nepotism and opposition to the betterment of the socio-economically underprivileged classes. The British, who were guided in their actions by moral and strategic principles, could not afford to neglect the overwhelming majority of the population and frame policies that served only the interests of the local élites who were out to make the most of the prevailing system. The British, who were initially more concerned about the Muslim population, subsequently turned their attention to the non-Brahmins among the Hindus and, after various surveys, they took the decision in 1913 of reserving at least 50 per cent of government jobs for the latter.[10]

But concomitantly, with the expansion of the education system after the 1890s, there emerged an educated non-Brahmin middle-class which migrated towards Madras, the centre of political and administrative activities, to fulfil its aspiration of sharing power and influence with the Brahmins on a more equitable basis.[11] This urbanization process seems to have been at the core of the identity problem that led to the birth of the non-Brahmin movement. Groups of non-Brahmin landlords were able to maintain their dominant position in rural areas. But in the cities, the overrepresentation of Brahmins in government posts, especially from the nineteenth century onwards, accentuated the difference between Brahmins and non-Brahmins and added to the latter's frustration. Brahmins in urban areas benefited by their higher status in both the socio-ritual and economic hierarchies, while the other upper castes of orthodox non-Brahmins, in the same context, were simply labelled as 'non-Brahmins'.[12]

The emergence of the Brahmin community as a modern educated middle-class determined to dominate the urban milieu is one of the main reasons for the development of a political awareness among the non-Brahmins, initially those belonging to the forward castes like the Vellalas. The Brahmins started segregating themselves in the cities. They had separate canteens in the universities, separate waiting-rooms in railway stations and special restaurants in cities where non-Brahmins were not allowed.[13] The Vellalas and other communities of the same status, most of whom were rich and respected land-owning families in rural areas, were treated as ordinary Shudras in the cities. One would have thought that the *varnashrama dharma*—the ancestral principle of hierarchy—had been imposed once again in a modern urban context.[14] The struggle against these discriminatory practices gathered strength as it brought together all strata of society and radically changed the social dynamic. It was time to start a full-fledged political agitation. But even in the political field the Brahmins wielded considerable influence.

Nineteenth-century urban Brahmins constituted indeed the core of the country's intellectual élite that laid the foundations of politics in modern India. The only ones capable of defining politics by reinterpreting India's past and its sacred books were Brahmin scholars. They were the best interpreters of this dominant religious nucleus and had inherited the right to do so. They were indeed the only ones capable of performing this function due to their socialization and education.[15]

Just as Lord Macaulay had expected, Hindus belonging to the higher and middle classes, who had received a Western education and the majority of whom were Brahmins, were behind the revivalist movements. These movements were inspired by the principles of science and rationalism, much revered in the West, and sought to apply them to Hinduism. However, this intellectual élite maintained an ambivalent attitude towards the colonizers and their views. Wanting to take advantage of the colonial system which was already in place, it was torn between two opposing approaches—it could either develop ancestral models as identity reminders or reject them as they were likely to hinder progress. This élite was thus torn between hostility towards the colonizers and a desire to imitate them.[16]

In Tamil Nadu, the political awareness of the Brahmin community found a wide expression. Pre-Independence political history is characterized by the prominent role played by Brahmins in Madras Presidency. Until the mid-1930s, the majority of leaders and members of the Tamil Nadu Congress party belonged to the Brahmin caste and the English-speaking educated élite. The type of politics and the use of English as a means of communication restricted the choice of leaders and political participation. Consequently, the Brahmins became the first group to be entirely politicized. Information collected in 1942, when Congress activists were arrested during the 'Quit India' movement, illustrates this trend as 20 per cent of the listed prisoners were Brahmins. As a result of the high proportion of Brahmins in the Congress party in Madras Presidency, the opposition to Brahmins became synonymous with opposition to the policies of the Congress, especially those related to the country's independence. As a matter of fact, the founders of the non-Brahmin movement insisted that the end of Brahmin predominance should be a pre-condition for the country's Independence.[17]

As a protest against the social supremacy of the Brahmins in south India, the non-Brahmin élite got together to start the 'non-Brahmin movement' which sowed the seeds of the Dravidian movement that would sweep Tamil Nadu later.

Opposition to the Brahmins crystallized in the south Indian Liberal Federation, later transformed into a political party, the Justice Party, and the publication of the non-Brahmin Manifesto in 1917. The leaders of this movement were members of non-Brahmin upper castes such as the Vellalas, Reddys, Kammas, Velamas and Nairs and the higher merchant castes. It was an expression of the frustration of these castes to the ever-growing influence of Brahmins, especially in the urban areas.[18]

The activists of the Justice Party were opposed to the Congress's ideological views and basic policies. This party had in its fold members representing diverse tendencies. There were atheists, socialists and even conservatives. Their political priorities were the recruitment of more non-Brahmins in the colonial administration and opposition to 'Brahminism', not so much in terms of caste as of attitude, in order to define a general programme for the social betterment of non-Brahmins.[19]

They succeeded in obtaining the twenty-eight reserved seats for non-Brahmins out of a total of ninety-eight elected seats in the Madras Legislative Council under the Government of India Act of 1919. The Justice Party won the elections in 1920 and dominated the discussions in the newly constituted Legislative Council. In response to its demands, the government took several measures for selective admission on a communal basis to institutions of higher education funded by the government as well as government services in an attempt to curb Brahmin dominance. This process led to the passing of the Communal Government Act in November 1927 which introduced a system of communal quotas for government jobs. The Act decreed that out of every twelve posts, five would go to non-Brahmin Hindus, two each to Brahmins, Anglo-Indians/Christians and Muslims and one to other categories.[20]

Even as it opposed the political ideology of the Congress, the Justice Party adopted a pro-British ideology and skirted the issue of freedom struggle. It laid emphasis on Tamil pride, thus triggering the politicization of cultural symbols and preparing the ground for the more far-reaching Dravidian movement.

The political leanings of this movement, when judged in perspective, appear as a series of reactions to the modernization of Tamil society and a protest against the twentieth century. In cultural terms, the non-Brahmin movement of the first decade of the twentieth century can be interpreted as a result of the changing social equations between the Brahmins and non-Brahmin groups, especially the Vellala landlords.[21] But apart from a conflict of interests, it could also be read as a result of the desire of these particular non-Brahmin groups to re-establish the special relationship they had with the Brahmins, before the latter decided to break away following changes in property laws and in the patronage enjoyed by the former.[22]

It must be noted that this confrontation between Brahmins and non-Brahmins, which formed the ideological bond that held the Dravidian movement together in its early stages, would soon lose its power and make way for other socio-cultural issues. The different tendencies within the movement laid stress on the glory of Dravidian culture which became a new rallying point. During the 1940s, Dravidian leaders gave priority to internal reforms in the Madras Presidency, insisting on religious reforms and the redistribution of power. They relegated the issues related to independence to the background unlike the Congress, which was then the second largest party in the Madras Presidency and looked at social and economic problems from the national viewpoint. After Independence, these differences in attitude proved to be advantageous to the Dravidian movement which could claim forty years of experience in dealing with social issues, specific to the Madras Presidency.[23]

As far as its internal organization was concerned, the Dravidian movement expressed itself through several mouthpieces. In the same anti-Brahmin spirit as the Justice Party, E.V. Ramaswamy Naicker founded the Self-Respect League in 1925. But he declared that his aim was to go beyond the upper class non-Brahmins, who had given birth to the Justice Party, and work for the unification of all non-Brahmin Hindus, without any internal discrimination, thus giving non-Untouchable Hindus of a low social status their first opportunity in Indian history to assert themselves politically.[24] Later, in 1944, he set-up the Dravida Kazhagam. Two parties emerged from this movement, the Dravida Munnetra Kazhagam in 1949 under the leadership of C.N. Annadurai and the All India Dravida Munnetra Kazhagam formed by M.G. Ramachandran in 1972.[25]

These numerous changes led to the juxtaposition of new priorities and, later, their superimposition on the ideological foundations of the Dravidian movement. But apart from the change in priorities introduced by rival parties in Tamil Nadu and their ideological swings, one social factor remained firmly anchored in the Tamil soil as a result of the anti-Brahmin spirit of the movement and that was the application of reservation policies.

The concept of caste-based quotas, born in India as a result of the predominance of Brahmins in the social and political fields, led to serious thinking about the problems of people situated at the opposite end of the hierarchy. This process was a result of the dichotomy between the two socio-political categories active in south India, viz., Brahmin and non-Brahmin and led to the categorization of underprivileged population.

The term 'backward classes' may have several connotations, but it is most commonly used in two senses.[26] In the first place it is a generic term that includes the legally recognized categories of Scheduled Castes (SCs) corresponding to the untouchable castes, Scheduled Tribes (STs) or the tribal peoples belonging mainly to central, east and north-east India and the Other Backward Classes (OBCs), communities belonging to the Shudra category. In a more restricted sense, it could be equivalent to the term OBC.

The classes that are now grouped together under the category of Scheduled Castes stand at the bottom of the traditional Hindu caste hierarchy. In the early twentieth century, this issue entered the political scene in the guise of 'depressed classes', although the first numerical estimates became available only in the 1920s, in south India.

At that time the Scheduled Tribes were sometimes included in this category of 'depressed classes'. It was only in 1930 that they were recognized as a separate category on the basis of specific criteria such as distinctive tribal, social, religious, linguistic and cultural characteristics, associated with their spatial and cultural isolation from the general population and their state of backwardness.

The main problem linked to these categories (SCs and STs) is about their exact number and their official stigmatization, which in effect is a double-edged weapon giving them certain advantages but at the same time officially classifying them as having a very low status. The criteria for identifying these people vary from survey to survey. According to J.H. Hutton, Census Officer in 1931, access to water and public places, literacy and poverty level as well as the possibility of maintaining normal 'non-polluting' relations with the higher castes, especially in terms of exchange of services with the Brahmins, can be considered some of the important criteria. Dr Ambedkar maintained that the common point for all 'untouchables' was the contempt and humiliation heaped on them by the upper castes. The distinction between rich and poor, forward and backward, educated and uneducated had no relevance for him. But the committee in charge of the census rejected this approach in view of the fact that 'untouchability' linked with the contempt of upper castes and the resultant taboos is not as easy to identify in the northern and eastern parts of the country as in the southern (Madras) and western (Bombay) parts. A list of these groups was prepared in 1936 and new additions were made as the years went by.[27]

The Constitution of Independent India is a significant document in respect of the efforts made to improve the lot of SCs and STs. Article 46 states that it is the state's duty to carefully promote the educational and economic interests of underprivileged groups, especially SCs and STs by protecting them from social injustice and other forms of exploitation. Apart from its determination to monitor their condition (Art. 164(1), 338, 339), the Constitution contains several measures in their favour such as reservation of seats in the national Parliament (Art. 330) and in the state legislative bodies (Art. 332) for a period of 40 years (Art. 334) and preference for appointment to government posts (Art. 335).[28] Although commissions appointed later have laid stress on economic considerations and the level of education, caste remains the basic element for identification of SCs and STs to this day.

What about the OBCs? As pointed out earlier, the term

Backward Classes in the acronym OBC has many meanings. Its connotations change according to the perceptions of the committees and commissions set up to improve the conditions of these underprivileged classes. For example, the term acquired a technical significance in the first decade of the twentieth century in the princely state of Mysore in the context of the non-Brahmin movement then in full swing in south India. So in 1921, 'backward' communities were defined as 'all communities other than Brahmins who are not adequately represented in public service'. But gradually the term 'Backward Classes' was accepted to designate the underprivileged classes placed above the 'untouchables'.[29]

The highly combustible situation in south India influenced the constitutional provisions in this regard. In the Constituent Assembly, delegates from Madras, Mysore and Bombay reported their regional experiences of the use of this term and its precise technical definition and this prompted the central government to take special note of this category. Two Supreme Court judgements in April 1951 reopened the debate on this category.[30] They opposed the legal foundations of caste-based reservations in south India giving access to some institutions of higher education and government jobs. They tended in fact to restrict reservation policies to the groups that could be considered a part of the Backward Classes category mentioned in Article 16(4) of the Constitution. These judgements touched off widespread political protests in south India and led to the addition of paragraph 4 to Article 15, which became the first amendment of the Indian Constitution. Article 15(4) clarifies the expression 'any backward class of citizen' as stated in paragraph 4 of article 16 by defining social and educational backwardness as a condition for the application of preferential policies, to prevent socially advanced groups from benefitting vague communal policies.[31] But these constitutional measures did not lead to the formulation of a central policy regarding OBCs.

The states of the Indian Union are not obliged by the Constitution to scrupulously follow the opinions expressed by various national commissions on Backward Classes, especially regarding the specific groups to be favoured. Hence the situation varies from one state to another. However, three major zones can be set apart. Firstly, the east-central one stretching from Assam in the north-east, across West Bengal, Orissa and Madhya Pradesh right up to Rajasthan where the Backward Classes category is not made great use of. An intermediate model is found in Jammu & Kashmir, Punjab, Uttar Pradesh and Bihar. However, it is the peninsular zone covering Andhra Pradesh, Karnataka, Kerala and Tamil Nadu in addition to Maharashtra that is the bastion of policies favouring these backward classes.[32]

At the Union level, the Kalelkar Commission was appointed in 1953 as a sequel to the new trends established by the first constitutional amendment. It was entrusted with the task of identifying communities, apart from SCs and STs, who could be considered as backward classes in social and educational terms and asked to draw up a list of these communities. The report published in 1955 was widely criticized for recommending the use of caste as a criterion for selecting communities needing protection as this would lead to the continuation and even the reinforcement of existing caste differences.[33] The Commission was fully aware of this major problem, especially since general caste data were not available as the 1951 census had given up the practice of noting a person's caste in view of the reservations expressed above. The Commission argued that despite its desire to dissociate caste from economic and social backwardness, it had recommended the caste criterion because Indian society is not based on a purely economic structure but on notions of birth, caste and social hierarchy.[34]

The Mandal Commission appointed in 1979 was faced with the same dilemma. But though it used different sources of information and also different social, economic and educational criteria for selection, the caste factor continued to be an essential element of identification. The Mandal Commission Report thus recommended that in addition to the 22.5 per cent seats reserved for SCs and STs, a further 27 per cent should be reserved for OBCs in government jobs and professional and technical education institutions funded by the central and state governments.[35] But the reservation of seats in the field of education has not yet been enforced at the central level. The states, on the other hand, follow different policies in this respect, as we shall see in the case of Tamil Nadu.

The use of the caste criterion to measure the backwardness of communities needing protection in the social and educational realm is quite paradoxical. Prompted by the desire to put an end to the supremacy enjoyed by the upper castes, especially Brahmins, for thousands of years, these commissions used caste as a criterion to identify the communities needing protection thus reinforcing the practice of caste-based discrimination which they were supposed to curb. The Mandal Commission had to face the same type of criticism as the Kalelkar Commission, even more so because this whole exercise ran counter to the Congress's social ideal of an egalitarian classless and casteless society formed at the time of Independence.[36]

In the specific case of Tamil Nadu, the process of positive discrimination was the most evident because of the peculiar historical circumstances in south India, leading to an early awareness of Brahmin dominance. The reservation policies introduced after Independence and the negotiations that led to the first amendment to the Constitution in 1951 made Tamil Nadu a pioneer in this field. The percentage of seats reserved for various categories of underprivileged communities have increased over the years. From 16 per cent for SCs and STs and 25 per cent for OBCs in 1964, these figures went up to 18 per cent and 31 per cent in 1971 in accordance with the recommendations of Tamil Nadu's first Backward Classes Commission.[37]

But the most controversial debates started in the 1980s. The AIADMK ministry decided in 1980 after a series of reverses, just before it went out of power, to raise the OBC quota from 31 per cent to 50 per cent. The Supreme Court declared the order unconstitutional and asked the Tamil Nadu government in 1982 to appoint a new Backward Classes Commission. The contradictory findings of this Commission published three years later only increased the political turmoil and the OBC quota of 50 per cent remained in force. The enforcement by the V.P. Singh government of the Mandal Commission Report at the centre in 1990 reopened the debate. The AIADMK leader, Jayalalitha, openly criticized the ceiling of 27 per cent fixed by this report and launched a relentless struggle to obtain a quota of 69 per cent. Out of this total, 50 per cent seats were meant for Backward Classes, 18 per cent for SCs and 1 per cent for STs thus maintaining the *status quo* in the political realm in Tamil Nadu. In 1984, Jayalalitha managed to get the President's assent and this measure became constitutional thanks to a new amendment

(85th) to the Constitution.[38] These 69 per cent reserved seats are available in government jobs as well as in educational institutions funded by the Tamil Nadu government.[39]

The entire twentieth-century south Indian history starting from the late 1910s and ending in the late 1990s is marked by the struggle against Brahminism as a form of socio-political domination. But in north India, it was only after the publication of the Mandal Commission Report that the importance of the Backward Classes was really recognized. This new political issue together with numerous historical factors throws light on the disparity of the socio-political situation of Brahmins in north and south India. An important aspect of this disparity is related to language. Brahmins have a well-defined stand on linguistic issues, which are central to the Dravidian movement. As a living embodiment of the Aryan influence, Brahmins indeed remain to this day at the centre of debates in which language and politics are intertwined.

The dominance of Brahmins in the colonial educational and administrative systems in south India led, as we have seen, to the adoption of a general programme for the social betterment of non-Brahmins. But after the introduction of concrete measures in the form of reservation policies in their favour, the debate shifted to the historical and ideological plane and turned into a confrontation between Aryans and Dravidians.

In this context, the term 'Dravidian' has a double meaning—racial and linguistic. A Dravidian is one who speaks one of the Dravidian languages, mainly Tamil, Malayalam, Telugu and Kannada, and is a part of the racial heritage shared by south India that is different from that of the Aryan invaders from the north from whom the Brahmins descend. But Dravidianism as a political weapon developed mainly in Tamil Nadu. This geographical limit is due to the status of the Tamil language considered to be the oldest of all the Dravidian languages spoken in modern India, and the socio-political situation peculiar to this area polarized around the opposition between Brahmins and non-Brahmins.[40]

This blatant opposition is due in a large measure, as we have mentioned earlier, to the isolation of Brahmins from the other upper castes of south India, a situation which does not exist in the north. Tamil Brahmins in particular always enjoyed a very high position in the social hierarchy. Even at the beginning of the eighteenth century, they dominated the bureaucracy and were practically the only ones to have access to Sanskrit religious books.[41] Unlike the north where the opposition between Hindus and Muslims was the main issue, in the south it was the opposition between Brahmins and non-Brahmins. But we are following Nicholas B. Dirks when he rejects a primordial tradition as the reason for the gulf between these two strata of the population and looks instead at the historical processes that gave rise to this antagonism between caste identities.[42]

First of all, I would like to highlight the fact that the non-Brahmin perception was greatly influenced by the research conducted by Orientalists on Dravidian culture. A great deal of ethnographical research was conducted in south India on the division between Aryans and Dravidians. There was a widespread belief that Dravidian culture was inferior to the great Sanskrit tradition. The ancient Dravidian culture and religion were criticized because of the absence of a written tradition and the observance of barbaric rites. But the works of some scholars, notably those of the Revd Robert Caldwell, ran counter to this tendency. As a matter of fact, Caldwell took up the defence of the rich and ancient Dravidian culture and praised the Tamil language which, he claimed, was as expressive and methodical as Sanskrit. He rejected the assumption that the Dravidian languages were derived from Sanskrit. Caldwell's theory was that Sanskrit was first brought to south India together with a particular type of Hinduism based on idol-worship by the Aryan Brahmins who settled down in this region. Tamil was spoken by the Dravidian chieftains, soldiers and farmers who, even though they were never conquered by the Brahmins, were described by the latter as Shudras.[43]

The works of some Orientalists largely criticized Brahmin domination in the social and literary fields and in the practice of Hindu law. Some of them even criticized Brahmin debauchery evident in the observance of certain rituals and the institution of temple-dancers (*devadasis*). However, the British colonial authorities adopted an ambivalent attitude towards the Brahmins. At first, the Brahmins were viewed with favour and they soon became the preferred informers and administrative assistants of British officers. This was a result of their ability to make the most of the new opportunities available to them in the form of education and jobs, which later became a major point of criticism against them and gave birth to the non-Brahmin movement. Secondly, as keepers of the great Sanskrit Hindu tradition, they protested against the spread of missionary activities. They were nevertheless forced to make some adjustments of a strategic nature. When consulted by the government on matters relating to Dravidian rites, they tended to fabricate a rigid and highly Sanskritized version of Hinduism that satisfied the moral requirements of the colonial rulers. So by forging a Hinduism that was exclusively Sanskritized and ossified, the Brahmins themselves paved the way for the anti-Aryan and anti-Brahmin Dravidian movement.[44]

A real Dravidian renaissance then took place. Inspired by the writings of such Orientalists, numerous associations were set up to study the origins of Dravidian culture and stimulate interest in the promotion and the study of Tamil literature and poetry. This led to the reinterpretation of Sanskrit reference texts like the *Ramayana* with the aim of tarnishing the image of the Aryan hero Rama and glorifying the Dravidian Ravana as a powerful heroic character.[45] Every effort was made to develop a pure Tamil language completely free from the influence of Sanskrit in terms of vocabulary and literary themes.[46] Tamil poetry, particularly that of Subramanya Bharati, as well as music, theatre and dance distinctly linked with Tamil culture were highlighted.[47] Different organizations were established for this purpose. In 1942 the Tamil Isai Sangam, an academy for the promotion of traditional Tamil music was set up as a rival to the Madras Academy founded by Brahmins in 1926. Another institution, the Tani Tamizh Iyakham was set up to promote the Tamil language. Hostility to Hindi and Sanskrit was accompanied by a hostility to their cultural representatives, the descendants of the Aryan invaders from the north, i.e. the Brahmins. This organization was associated with the political wing of the Dravidian movement, as far as 1916, through the south Indian Liberation Front and later the Justice Party.[48]

Theories about the glory and the antiquity of Tamil culture were exploited for political purposes. The Dravidian movement tried to promote the idea that it was the Aryans who were inspired by the Dravidians and not vice-versa. But the Brahmins, who were responsible for the hierarchy based on birth, had imposed their views and founded their power on the *varna* system. The non-Brahmins, who were proud of their Dravidian heritage, evidently opposed this theory. The Vellala community in particular found it profitable to follow this ideology. Placed second in the social hierarchy after the Brahmins, the Vellalas claimed that they were the original Dravidians, as orthodox as Brahmins, in their practice of the original Tamil religion, *Saiva Siddhanta*.[49]

E.V. Ramaswamy Naicker who spearheaded the Dravidian political movement clearly treated the Brahmins as being synonymous with the Aryans. In this context, the caste (*varna*) was considered in racial terms and this enabled the non-Brahmins to assert that the Brahmins and Dravidians did not belong to the same race.[50]

The south Indian Brahmins reacted by highlighting their numerous contributions to the ancient Tamil civilization and the validity of the hierarchy imposed by the *varna* system as well as the principles laid down in the Shastras, especially those of the *varnashrama dharma*.[51] Later, the Brahmins were admitted into the Dravidian movement, following a change in the political strategy then based on language.

Linguistic issues indeed, which were central to the formation of the Dravidian movement, continued to play a significant role in the ideological viewpoints on the relations between south and north India. The Tamil language brought together the Brahmins and non-Brahmins of south India against the north even as conflicts about the use of Sanskrit and Tamil continued to create a rift between the two communities.

The idea that the quarrel between Brahmins and non-Brahmins could be patched up by sharing a common language, viz., Tamil, was put forward by the poet C. Subramania Bharati who was very conscious of this common cultural heritage and opposed to the sectarian views promoted by the Brahmins in support of a social organization based on the *varnas*.[52] A Brahmin interviewed in Chennai shared his views on the subject:

There is no movement called Dravidian Movement at all. Our art is there, our culture is there, our music is there . . . it has been there for several centuries. The language is there also (...). Dravidian is a Sanskrit word. But they want to use this distinction for political purposes. There is no pure Aryan, there is no pure Dravidian.[53]

After Independence, this approach was used for political gains. For many years, propaganda was carried out through artistic mediums like theatre, cinema, poetry and literature to project the renaissance of Dravidian culture. Brahmins were equally involved in this effort. One of the Brahmins interviewed in Chennai relates his experiences in the artistic and political domains:

I entered into theatre, I wrote 23 plays, all in Tamil. They were performed about 5,000 times throughout the country in various places (...). *While I was doing all this, I also entered films, I have acted in about 180 films. I have scripted about 14 films and directed 4 films. And I ventured into journalism. Now, I am in charge of this journal, this journal is about 30 years old, it is . . . political analysis is the force of this journal. It is a magazine of comment, political analysis and comment.* (...) *many of my plays were political satires. That is how I got interested in politics.*[54]

After this first phase, the DMK strategy concentrated on specific political issues like language.[55] Language is indeed an essential element of identity. It is possible to identify a particular ethnic group settled in a particular area by its language. This process is completely in accordance with the views of the Dravidian movement intent on highlighting the distinctive views of south Indians in the political arena at the national level.[56]

The Dravidian movement which had become a witch-hunt targeting individual Brahmins eventually lost its anti-Brahmin character. It must be noted, however, that from the very beginning of the movement its relationship with Brahmins was somewhat paradoxical. Non-Brahmin objectives oscillated between the fierce condemnation of Brahmins and desperate attempts at reconciliation. As far back as 1920, the Justice Party, which was then in power, was quite favourable to Brahmins in some respects and this led to the birth of a rival non-Brahmin faction within the party. In 1930, the Justice Party approved the admission of Brahmin members.[57] The 1930s still remained a decade of conflicting relationships with agitations led by non-Brahmins against the introduction of Hindi as a compulsory language in schools by Rajaji (C. Rajagopalachari), the Brahmin Chief Minister of the Congress government in Madras. This measure was a symbol of the superiority of Aryan Brahmins in Tamil society.[58] It also corresponded to the Congress plan to bring about national integration. But this only roused Tamil parochial feelings, especially after the crushing defeat of the Dravidian Movement in the 1936 elections. The first anti-Hindi agitation launched in 1937-8 formed a part of the demand for the creation of a separate Dravida Nadu. The situation was further aggravated because the Tamil Brahmins were quick to learn Hindi just as they had learnt English and also because the Sanskrit roots of the Tamil dialect used by Brahmins made it easier for them to learn the language. All these factors together made it easy for the Dravidian leadership to incite anti-Brahminism and oppose the introduction of Hindi.[59]

But it was mainly in the decade between the late 1950s and the late 1960s that the DMK asserted the acceptance of Brahmins in the Dravidian movement. The enemy was no longer the Brahmin community as such but Brahminism as a whole with less emphasis on ostracism. The strong anti-Hindi feelings in Tamil Nadu were exploited by the DMK in its fight against the Congress, a party whose interests were more national and 'northern' and not specifically limited to the Tamil region. This made it easy to overlook all differences of class and caste and rally the entire Tamil population to put up a fight against the domineering north.[60]

This shift of 'key adversary' has been the trigger for a new perception of Tamil Brahmins. The enemy to be targeted was the northern Hindi culture against which all Tamil-speaking people, including Brahmins, united in a spirit of fiery Tamil nationalism.[61] During the 1960s, the Brahmin versus non-Brahmin conflict receded further into the background to make way for the north-south opposition as the major political rift.[62] Before the 1962 elections, the DMK chief, C.N. Annadurai, made it clear that the Dravidian movement was not hostile to Brahmins but to Brahminism, as a matter of attitude.[63]

Rajaji's radical change of approach during the anti-Hindi debate is quite symbolic of this development. On India's first Republic Day on 26 January 1950, Hindi became the country's official language according to Article 343 of the Constitution. Taking a stand that was diametrically opposed to his earlier stand in 1938, the Brahmin Rajaji, who had become one of the leaders of the conservative Swatantra Party, declared that this decision was a 'tyranny, insane, unjust and discriminatory'. There was severe tension not only among students, who were worried about gaining access to administrative posts following the imposition of Hindi as the official language, but also among the rest of the population which nursed more than one grievance against the Congress government, especially regarding the food shortage in October 1964.[64]

The debate continued. Hindi was declared the official language of the Indian Union, but the position of English as the *lingua franca* of the élite all over India became stronger.[65] In the debate in 1965, the use of English in government communications was at the centre of the demands advanced by Tamil leaders, both non-Brahmins and Brahmins, like Rajaji.[66]

Thus the DMK finally acquired legitimacy in the eyes of the Brahmins, during the 1960s, after it discarded its anti-Brahmin image.[67] The specifically anti-Brahmin ideology of the Dravidian movement faded away gradually and the immense popularity enjoyed by Jayalalitha, a Brahmin, is the most recent example. But as we have seen earlier, there has been no change in the reservation policy in Tamil Nadu and it continues to be chiefly responsible for the crystallization of the identity of the Brahmins, as will be shown in the next chapter. Finally, though anti-Hindi agitations are a thing of the past, some conflicts related to language are still alive, driven by old animosities.

Upholding the supremacy of the Tamil language and strongly opposing Hindi as the national language remain indeed a major preoccupation among the population and political parties in Tamil Nadu. Other linguistic demands favour the use of Tamil in place of English. Nevertheless, most parents want their children to learn English which continues to occupy a prominent place in the educational system, especially at the university level.[68]

However, it is the conflict between Tamil and Sanskrit that is extremely disquieting as it revives old enmities between Brahmins and non-Brahmins. Recent debates focus on the Tamil Nadu government's decision to use only Tamil for religious ceremonies (*puja* and *archana*) in Hindu temples. The Hindu Temples' Protection Committee (HTPC) appealed to the Madras High Court against the Tamil Nadu government's tendency to interfere in temple rituals. The HTPC, which is in favour of Sanskrit, points out that the use of Tamil would go against Articles 25 and

26 of the Constitution which state that rituals and *mantras* cannot be changed. The debates on Sanskrit are a sensitive matter as they are seen to be related to Brahmin hegemony, the old demon that continues to torment Tamil Nadu.[69]

Several cultural and linguistic groups inspired by the Dravidian movement reacted forcefully to this opposition to the efforts to give Tamil its due place and even criticized the Tamil Nadu government of not being firm enough on this issue. In response to this criticism, the latter announced a new education policy for 1999, declaring Tamil as the medium of instruction from the beginning of the school year. This meant that the government would recognize and give aid only to those schools that taught Tamil and used it as a medium of instruction.[70] Various Tamil scholars also brought pressure on the Tamil Nadu government, especially the Minister for Tamil language and culture, M. Tamizhkudimagan, to introduce drastic policies to enforce the use of Tamil in higher education.[71]

In May 1999, the government appointed a committee to examine the question of making the use of Tamil as a medium of instruction compulsory in all government schools. On the basis of the recommendations of this committee, which supported this policy, the government issued an order declaring Tamil as the only medium of instruction up to Class V, in schools under its jurisdiction. In response to an appeal filed by the representatives of several schools, the Madras High Court delivered a judgement in April 2000 against the government's order. Declaring such practices anti-constitutional in view of the principal of equality before the law (Article 14), the High Court endorsed the absolute and exclusive nature of the right of parents to choose the medium in which their children should study.[72]

The Tamil Nadu government had been strongly criticized for such positions displaying the parochial mindset of the Dravidian movement as in the decision to change the name of Madras to Chennai or the introduction of *pujas* in Tamil. It therefore appears that although the Dravidian movement claims to be atheist and is firmly opposed to the caste system on an ideological plane, after having reached a position of power it finds itself embroiled in conflicts related to caste and religion. By exploiting the same Brahmin-non-Brahmin conflict while formulating its political programmes, it has reinforced casteism. Having got rid of the Brahmin threat, the emergence of internal factions claiming a share of the power have only accentuated the importance of caste in administrative and political circles in Tamil Nadu.[73] The DMK's record is quite remarkable in this respect. The unequal development of communities grouped under the head 'non-Brahmin' seems to be the reason behind the crisis that has afflicted the party for some time. These different groups have not had equal access to political and economic resources because of their own peculiarities and also because of their strategic position in the social dynamic. The communities whose social fortunes have improved are now turning away from ideological issues limited to regional Dravidian interests and aspiring to take part in national debates. Others, who have remained in the same place, blame the DMK's incompetence for their stagnation.[74]

All along the twentieth century, this binary opposition between Brahmins and non-Brahmins in Tamil Nadu led to internal restructuring. The non-Brahmins were themselves divided into several communities, each having a different socio-economic status and decided to go beyond these differences in the dynamic of socio-political strategies. Brahmins too had to evolve within a certain predetermined set-up. Being the targets of reservation policies hostile to their interests and referred to in negative terms in the ideological and social programmes of the Dravidian movement, Tamil Brahmins had to devise tactics to counter these moves. Even though the Dravidian anti-Brahmin ideology is no longer one of the key elements of the political debate in Tamil Nadu, Tamil Brahmins still find themselves facing psychological, social and economic problems and have developed an identity and attitudes that mirror this long history of discrimination. In the next chapter we will draw a portrait of these contemporary Tamil Brahmins.

NOTES

1. N.B. Dirks, 'The Politics of Caste and Race in Contemporary Southern India', in *Caste Today*, ed. C.J. Fuller, Delhi: Oxford University Press, 1996, pp. 268-9.
2. Figures of the 1931 Census, in view of the fact that later census data do not provide information regarding caste: *Census of India*, Government of India, 1931.
3. See Chapter 4.

4. D.A. Washbrook, 'Caste, class and dominance in modern Tamil Nadu—non-Brahmanism, Dravidianism and Tamil nationalism', in *Dominance and state power in modern India, Decline of a social order*, ed. F.R. Frankel and M.S.A. Rao, Delhi: Oxford University Press, 1989, vol. 1, p. 211.
5. C.J. Baker, *The Politics of South India, 1920-1937*, Cambridge: Cambridge University Press, 1976, pp. 90-5.
6. D.A. Washbrook, 'Caste, class and dominance in modern Tamil Nadu—non-Brahmanism, Dravidianism and Tamil nationalism', in *Dominance and state power in modern India, Decline of a social order*, ed. F.R. Frankel and M.S.A. Rao, Delhi: Oxford University Press, 1989, vol. 1, p. 212.
7. P.K. Varma, *The great Indian middle class*, Delhi: Viking, 1998, p. 2.
8. P. Radhakrishnan, 'Backward Classes in Tamil Nadu: 1872-1988', *Economic and Political Weekly*, Mumbai, 10/03/90, p. 509.
9. M.S.A. Rao, *Social movements and social transformation*, Delhi: Manohar, 1987, p. 209.
10. P. Radhakrishnan, 'Communal Representation in Tamil Nadu, 1850-1916', *Economic and Political Weekly*, Mumbai, 23 (31), 21/07/93, pp. 1586-9, 1596.
11. P. Radhakrishnan, 'Backward class movements in Tamil Nadu', in *Caste—its twentieth century avatar*, ed. M.N. Srinivas, Delhi: Viking, 1996, pp. 112-13.
12. M.R. Barnett, 'Cultural nationalist electoral Politics in Tamil Nadu', in *Electoral Politics in the Indian States—Party systems and cleavages*, ed. M.R. Barnett et al., Studies in Electoral Politics in the Indian States, vol. 4, Delhi: Manohar, 1975, pp. 75-6.
13. F.R. Frankel, 'Middle Classes and Castes in India's Politics prospects for political accomodation', in *India's democracy: an analysis of changing State-society relations*, ed. A. Kohli, New Jersey: Orient Longman, 1991, pp. 232-3.
14. M.R. Barnett, 'Cultural nationalist electoral Politics in Tamil Nadu', in *Electoral Politics in the Indian States—Party systems and cleavages*, ed. M.R. Barnett et al., Studies in Electoral Politics in the Indian States, vol. 4, Delhi: Manohar, 1975, pp. 25-6.
15. A. Nandy, *At the Edge of Psychology, Essays in Politics and Culture*, Delhi: Oxford University Press, 1990, pp. 52-3.
16. P.K. Varma, *The great Indian middle class*, Delhi: Viking, 1998, pp. 3, 6.
17. M.R. Barnett, 'Cultural nationalist electoral Politics in Tamil Nadu', in *Electoral Politics in the Indian States—Party systems and cleavages*, ed. M.R. Barnett et al., Studies in Electoral Politics in the Indian States, vol. 4, Delhi: Manohar, 1975, pp. 1972-4.
18. P. Radhakrishnan, 'Backward class movements in Tamil Nadu', in

Caste—its twentieth century avatar, ed. M.N. Srinivas, Delhi: Viking, 1996, p. 113.

19. M.R. Barnett, 'Cultural nationalist electoral Politics in Tamil Nadu', in *Electoral Politics in the Indian States—Party systems and cleavages*; ed. M.R. Barnett et al., *Studies in Electoral Politics in the Indian States*, vol. 4, Delhi: Manohar, 1975, p. 74.
20. P. Radhakrishnan, 'Backward class movements in Tamil Nadu', in *Caste—its twentieth century avatar*, ed. M.N. Srinivas, Delhi: Viking, 1996, pp. 113-14.
21. V.N. Viswanathan, 'Dravidian movement: an epiphenomenal study', in *Caste, politics and society in Tamil Nadu*, ed. G. Palanithurai, Delhi: Kanishka, 1994, p. 8.
22. D.A. Washbrook, 'Caste, class and dominance in modern Tamil Nadu—non-Brahmanism, Dravidianism and Tamil nationalism', in *Dominance and state power in modern India, Decline of a social order*, ed. F.R. Frankel and M.S.A. Rao, Delhi: Oxford University Press, 1989, vol. 1, p. 243.
23. M.R. Barnett, 'Cultural nationalist electoral Politics in Tamil Nadu', in *Electoral Politics in the Indian States—Party systems and cleavages*, ed. M.R. Barnett et al., *Studies in Electoral Politics in the Indian States*, vol. 4, Delhi: Manohar, 1975, pp. 76-7.
24. F.R. Frankel, 'Middle Classes and Castes in India's Politics prospects for political accomodation', in *India's democracy: an analysis of changing State-society relations*, ed. A. Kohli, New Jersey: Orient Longman, 1991, p. 234.
25. G. Palanithurai, ed., *Caste, politics and society in Tamil Nadu*, Delhi: Kanishka, 1994, pp. 77-82. *Reservation for Backward Classes, Mandal Commission report of the Backward Classes Commission*, Delhi: Akalank Publications, 1980, pp. 279-80.
26. M. Galanter, *Competing equalities, Law and the Backward classes in India*, Delhi: Oxford University Press, 1984, p. 155.
27. M. Galanter, *Competing equalities, Law and the Backward classes in India*, Delhi: Oxford University Press, 1984, pp. 121-39, 147-53.
28. *The Constitution of India*, Government of India, 1991, pp. 14, 41, 92-4.
29. M. Galanter, *Competing equalities, Law and the Backward classes in India*, Delhi: Oxford University Press, 1984, pp. 154-8.
30. A.C. Kapur, *Constitutional history of India*, 1765-1984, Delhi: S. Chand & Company, 1985, pp. 468-9.
31. M. Galanter, *Competing equalities, Law and the Backward classes in India*, Delhi: Oxford University Press, 1984, pp. 159-67.
32. Ibid., pp. 180-4.
33. P. Radhakrishnan, 'Caste, Politics and the Reservation Issue', in *Illfare in India, Essays on India's Social Sector in Honour of S. Guhan*, eds. B.

Harriss-White and S. Subramaniam, Delhi: Sage Publications, 1999, pp. 170-1.

34. J. Mishra, *Equality versus justice—the problem of reservations for backward classes*, Delhi: Deep & Deep Publications, 1996, pp. 49-50.
35. This figure of 27 per cent, although much lower than the proportion of OBCs in Indian population which is 52 per cent, was decided upon because a Supreme Court judgement has fixed a ceiling of 50 per cent for reservation of seats under Articles 15(4) and 16 (4) of the Constitution (*Reservation for Backward Classes, Mandal Commission report of the Backward Classes Commission*, Delhi: Akalank Publications, 1980, pp. 63–4).
36. P. Radhakrishnan, 'Caste, Politics and the Reservation Issue', in *Illfare in India, Essays on India's Social Sector in Honour of S. Guhan*, eds. B. Harriss-White and S. Subramaniam, Delhi: Sage Publications, 1999, p.171. The ideological debates on this subject are taken up in Chapter 7.
37. *Reservation for Backward Classes, Mandal Commission report of the Backward Classes Commission*, Delhi: Akalank Publications, 1980, pp. 15–16.
38. P. Radhakrishnan, 'Caste, Politics and the Reservation Issue', in *Illfare in India, Essays on India's Social Sector in Honour of S. Guhan*, eds. B. Harriss-White and S. Subramaniam, New Delhi: Sage Publications, 1999, pp. 173-9.
39. See article by P. Radhakrishnan in *The Hindu* on the details of the political manoeuvres leading to this measure: 'The quota conundrum', *The Hindu*, 09/02/95.
40. E.F. Irschick, *Politics and Social Conflict in South India—The Non-Brahmin Movement and Tamil Separatism, 1916-1929*, Berkeley and Los Angeles: University of California Press, 1969, pp. 275-6.
41. Ibid., p. 5.
42. N.B. Dirks, 'The Politics of Caste and Race in Contemporary Southern India', in *Caste Today*, ed. C.J. Fuller, Delhi: Oxford University Press, 1996, pp. 269-71.
43. E.F. Irschick, *Politics and Social Conflict in South India—The Non-Brahmin Movement and Tamil Separatism, 1916-1929*, Berkeley and Los Angeles: University of California Press, 1969, pp. 277-9.
44. N.B. Dirks, 'The Politics of Caste and Race in Contemporary Southern India', in *Caste Today*, ed. C.J. Fuller, Delhi: Oxford University Press, 1996, pp. 275-6, 287-9.
45. E.F. Irschick, *Politics and Social Conflict in South India—The Non-Brahmin Movement and Tamil Separatism, 1916-1929*, Berkeley and Los Angeles: University of California Press, 1969, pp. 283-4, 294.
46. The sociologist, M.N. Srinivas, presents the Dravidian movement in its cultural dimension—the rejection of the *Ramayana* and the

purification of Tamil from Sanskrit influences—as the most elaborate form of opposition to the Sanskritization movement: M.N. Srinivas, *Village, Caste, Gender and Method—Essays in Indian Social Anthropology*, Delhi: Oxford University Press, 1998, pp. 92, 99.

47. G.J. Samuel, *Tamil identity and resistance to Sanskrit*, Chennai: Institute of Asian Studies, 1998, pp. 49-50, 54-5.
48. V. Ramaswamy, 'Tamil Separatism and Cultural Negotiations: Gender politics and Literature in Tamil Nadu', *Social Scientist*, vol. 26 (5-6), Delhi, May-June 1998, pp. 61-3.
49. E.F. Irschick, *Politics and Social Conflict in South India—The Non-Brahmin Movement and Tamil Separatism, 1916-1929*, Berkeley and Los Angeles: University of California Press, 1969, pp. 289-92, 295-7.
50. N.B. Dirks, 'The Politics of Caste and Race in Contemporary Southern India', in *Caste Today*, ed. C.J. Fuller, Delhi: Oxford University Press, 1996, pp. 275-6, 281-3.
51. E.F. Irschick, *Politics and Social Conflict in South India—The Non-Brahmin Movement and Tamil Separatism, 1916-1929*, Berkeley and Los Angeles: University of California Press, 1969, pp. 298-9.
52. Ibid., pp. 285-8, 300.
53. M12.
54. M4.
55. M.R. Barnett, 'Cultural nationalist electoral Politics in Tamil Nadu', in *Electoral Politics in the Indian States—Party systems and cleavages*, ed. M.R. Barnett et al., Studies in Electoral Politics in the Indian States, vol. 4, Delhi: Manohar, 1975, pp. 77-8.
56. V.N. Viswanathan, 'Dravidian movement: an epiphenomenal study', in *Caste, politics and society in Tamil Nadu*, ed. G. Palanithurai, Delhi: Kanishka, 1994, p. 89.
57. D.A. Washbrook, 'Caste, class and dominance in modern Tamil Nadu—non-Brahmanism, Dravidianism and Tamil nationalism', in *Dominance and state power in modern India, Decline of a social order*, ed. F.R. Frankel and M.S.A. Rao, Delhi: Oxford University Press, 1989, vol. 1, p. 213.
58. F.R. Frankel, 'Middle Classes and Castes in India's Politics prospects for political accomodation', in *India's democracy: an analysis of changing state-society relations*, ed. A. Kohli, New Jersey: Orient Longman, 1991, p. 235.
59. N. Subramaniam, *Etnicity and populist mobilization—political parties, citizens and democracy in south India*, Delhi: Oxford University Press, 1999, pp. 126-9.
60. M.R. Barnett, 'Cultural nationalist electoral Politics in Tamil Nadu', in *Electoral Politics in the Indian States—Party systems and cleavages*, ed. M.R. Barnett et al., *Studies in Electoral Politics in the Indian States*, vol. 4, Delhi: Manohar, 1975, pp. 83-4.

61. D.A. Washbrook, 'Caste, class and dominance in modern Tamil Nadu—non-Brahmanism, Dravidianism and Tamil nationalism', in *Dominance and state power in modern India, Decline of a social order*, ed. F.R. Frankel and M.S.A. Rao, Delhi: Oxford University Press, 1989, vol. 1, p. 238.
62. This difference between north and south India goes beyond the bounds of political manoeuvring. The theme of a 'common background' uniting the four south Indian states of Kerala, Karnataka, Tamil Nadu and Andhra Pradesh is repeated in a series of interviews conducted in Chennai, especially the interviews M1 and M2.
63. S. Gabriel, 'Social background to politics in Tamil Nadu', in *Encyclopaedia of India and her states*, vol. 8: *Karnataka, Kerala and Tamil Nadu*, Delhi: Deep & Deep Publications, 1998, p. 336.
64. R.L. Hardgrave, *Essays in the political sociology of south India*, Delhi: Manohar, 1993, pp. 81-91.
65. As for Tamil, it enjoys the status of a constitutional language like most regional languages: Y. Lacoste, ed., *Dictionnaire géopolitique des Etats 1998*, Paris: Flammarion, 1997, p. 261.
66. R.D. King, *Nehru and the language politics of India*, Delhi: Oxford University Press, 1997, pp. 73-4, 218-19.
67. M.R. Barnett, 'Cultural nationalist electoral Politics in Tamil Nadu', in *Electoral Politics in the Indian States—Party systems and cleavages*, ed. M.R. Barnett et al., *Studies in Electoral Politics in the Indian States*, vol. 4, Delhi: Manohar, 1975, p. 88.
68. *The Hindu*, 06/04/99.
69. *The Times of India*, 11/11/98 and 12/11/98.
70. Ibid., 17/11/98. *The Hindu*, 17/11/98.
71. *The Hindu*, 27/04/99.
72. *Frontline*, 26/05/2000, pp. 49-50.
73. *The Times of India*, 16/12/98; *The Hindu*, 02/06/97, 26/06/97.
74. S.S. Pandian, 'Crisis in DMK', *Economic and Political Weekly*, Mumbai, 29(5), p. 221.

CHAPTER 5

Portrait of Tamil Brahmins

Tamil Nadu has certain geographical and historical characteristics that contribute to the distinctive nature of the Tamil Brahmin identity. Separation from the major migration zones situated in the north, the peculiar nature of the regional caste structure and the socio-political situation explained earlier are the basic factors responsible for this distinctiveness.

Tamil Brahmins till now harbour attitudes based on these characteristics. When contemporary Tamil Brahmins express a feeling of separation, they are actually referring to their situation in different spheres and periods. However, it must be noted first and foremost that this notion of separation is inherent in the Brahmins' function closely associated with the sacred sphere. The term sacred itself means separated. This separation, necessary from the ritualistic and functional point of view, ended up functioning in the social sphere as well.

Firstly, the educational and professional conditions peculiar to Brahmins in Tamil Nadu explain the persistence of this feeling of being different. Secondly, only a close examination of the conscious and emphatic expression of identity among this group will enable us to understand the exact nature of this feeling. It is in fact the awareness of a unique identity built in relation to Brahmins outside Tamil Nadu or to non-Brahmins within the state, considered as the 'other' for purposes of reference.

As we have seen in the previous chapter, politics in Tamil Nadu revolved around the dichotomy between Brahmins and the rest of Tamil society. The implementation of reservation policies favouring non-Brahmins proved to be an effective method of putting an end to the social isolation of Brahmins by giving greater access to non-Brahmin communities to education as well as government jobs.

The distinctive nature of the educational and professional situation in Tamil Nadu is particularly noticeable in the regional difference between north and south India, as the south has always been the bastion of anti-Brahminism. The existence and furtherance of these policies opposed to Brahmin interests over a long period provoked reactions which gradually became a normal practice.

My own family, even in Madras, did not practice the kind of orthodox Brahminism that also exists even today. I became far more aware of Brahminism after coming here and after having two children and . . . as they grew up, they became very aware, because they were what was called forward castes and in Tamil Nadu, there is reservation for Scheduled Castes and backward castes, up to about 69 per cent. So, the remaining 30 per cent is opened to all castes, not just forward. So, you know, they grew up with lots of bitterness about it, because it was patently an unfair system and not only that. You see children who were getting very good marks, coming from homes where education, hard work was a tradition and not getting into college because of 0.5 per cent . . . after coming to Madras, I have been far more aware of it, because of these sociological problems.[1]

The regional situation in Tamil Nadu has had a strong influence on Brahmin identity. Brahmins feel that regional policies excessively favourable to underprivileged classes create obstacles in their path and disregard their excellence in a more obtrusive manner than in the north. Problems faced by young Brahmins during their schooling in Tamil Nadu is a topic broached by almost all the Brahmins we interviewed, and even those who were not directly affected referred to problems faced by relations and close friends.

There was no problem as far as I am concerned. I am very lucky. But lots of people are facing problems, some bright students do not get seats here . . . because of these reservations.[2]

The Dravidian movement, in its zeal to put an end to Brahmin predominance, fought for the introduction of policies to assist the advancement of non-Brahmins, especially in educational and socio-professional fields.

In Tamil Nadu, after the Dravidian party came to power, education . . . the particular situation in Tamil Nadu is no to Brahmins for education, no to Brahmins for government jobs.[3]

This tendency has made it extremely difficult for Brahmins to gain access to educational institutions funded by the government and afterwards to government jobs.

My son would have had some difficulty, but he got across (...). *Access to education is a problem for Brahmins for engineering, medicine, in government sponsored institutions.*[4]

As explained in the previous chapter, reservation policies have existed in Tamil Nadu for a long time ending up with a quota of 69 per cent after the adoption of the 85th amendment to the Constitution. These measures accentuate the precarious situation of Brahmins in this state, particularly in terms of access to careers such as medicine or engineering, but more generally in gaining admission to all institutions funded by the state.

Being a Brahmin today in India, they are branded as a forward community and many of our students belonging to this community are unable to get into very deserving colleges, though they have obtained high marks, because of cut-off points . . . and there are these only 31 per cent which go on merit. So the forward community has to compete with everybody else for these 30 per cent of seats in colleges. So, our Brahmin students who are passing out of the school are disadvantaged getting into engineering or medicine.[5]

Similar reservation policies were introduced in the north only after the implementation of the Mandal Commission's recommendations in 1990. But even the Mandal Commission, as already mentioned, proposed a reservation of only 27 per cent seats for Other Backward Classes in addition to the 22.5 per cent reserved for Scheduled Castes and Scheduled Tribes in government jobs. Discriminative policies favouring OBCs in government-aided educational institutions have still not been uniformly applied at the central level.

This difference in the situations prevailing in north and south India heightens the feeling of separation experienced by Tamil Brahmins and for some of them it even represents the basis of this feeling, as the ritual dimension of Brahmin identity has become marginal in urban areas. This institutional hostility is perceived by many Brahmins as a major restriction on their intellectual and professional development.

Today, someone takes birth and he goes to the school and he goes to the college, and he takes some profession, every step the man must have a stability. When you look at each and every step, it is not that if you are a Brahmin or not . . . but again, this excellence, the brains, he wants to go about each step 100 per cent, the goal is always in his mind, but in India, it is not possible (...). *Whatever the potential he is having, he is not being recognized.*[6]

In addition to issues of higher quotas, reservation policies favouring Backward Classes affect south Indian Brahmins more than those in the north because of the difference in the caste structure in the two parts of the country. In North India, Brahmins are not as isolated in the *varna* hierarchy as their counterparts in the south. North Indian Brahmins are closer to other social groups categorized as Forward Classes and do not see themselves, in terms of identity, as the only victims of reservations policies as I will explain in the last chapter.

In Tamil Nadu, on the other hand, one of the obvious results of the reservation policies favouring non-Brahmins is that for a long time, ever since the spread of the Dravidian Movement, young Brahmins have had to give up the idea of taking up careers that were once valued by members of their *varna*. Admission to engineering and medical courses has become difficult for young Brahmins because they are conducted mainly by institutions funded by the government thus putting an end to the Brahmin monopoly in these professions. However, it is interesting to note that a medical career, before it became a profession that gave the practitioner a place among the social élite, posed ethical problems for Brahmins because it involved impure contact with the human body.

But you know entry into the medical profession in what may be regarded as the period of anti-Brahminism, has been practically restricted to ridiculous small number of Brahmins. On the other hand, during the last few centuries, the Brahmin abstained from entering modern medical colleges, largely because they had courses of study which will entail contact with dead human beings, this was supposed to be polluting, in fact even the sight of it.[7]

Even where a teaching career is concerned, the situation appears to be more difficult than in north India. One of the Brahmin interviewees mentioned off-record that his son, an engineer, teaching in one of the Indian Institutes of Technology was subjected to pressure because he was a Brahmin and had to resign and find a job in the private sector.[8] Another denounced, also off-record, the particularly hostile policies followed by Madras University. He then added that the situation is quite precarious as far as the general level of higher education in Tamil Nadu is concerned because talented Brahmins wanting to teach or do research become frustrated. The teaching career is no longer very attractive in India in terms of remuneration as well as working conditions. This raises the more general question of the quality of teachers in the Indian educational system today and its harmful effect on future generations.[9]

The fall in the standards, in the university in Tamil Nadu has been phenomenal, lots of decline of standards, and it is evident from the percentage Tamil Nadu has in various competitive exams. Fall in the standards due to reservation that they follow in recruitment. Here I must point out that there is only one other factor, there are so many factors, multiplicity of colleges and all, among that is also the factor that the really talented ones do not enter the teaching line or we can put it this way, the talent is not a monopoly of the Brahmins, but the few Brahmins who are also talented do not have an access to employment in teaching.[10]

In south India, the situation is markedly more anti-Brahmin than in the north. The Mandal Commission Report did not harm the interests of only Brahmins in the north. But in south India, in addition to reservation policies targeting Brahmins specifically, the highly antagonistic social relations that have existed long between Brahmins and non-Brahmins have affected the perceptions of many.

Finally, some Tamil Brahmins wonder if quotas for Backward Classes are valid in the present context in view of the supposed disparity between the academic performance of upper class students and those belonging to Backward Classes.

For a Brahmin to come into a college, his or her cut-off has to be very high, say 98 per cent, 96 per cent, whereas for others it is less. All was started because they felt that opportunities were not given to others. But nowadays it is not like that, all communities are doing well in all fields. Many years back, it was only Brahmins who were good at studies, so they felt that other people were not given the opportunity.[11]

This statement is corroborated by two academics who believe that quotas for Backward Classes are no longer justified.

The person in charge of admissions at the Anna University in Chennai since 1979, declares that in terms of examination results, there is no disparity between the upper and lower castes (Backward Castes, SCs and STs not included).[12] An engineer, who is a professor in the Indian Institute of Technology, Chennai, shares his viewpoint:

My feeling is that definitely there has been a setback with the 69 per cent going against forward castes. That is definitely a setback for Brahmins, as far as their admission to professional colleges is concerned. If you look at engineering colleges and medical colleges, you will see that the gap between the forward and the backward castes is narrowing down. In other words, the situation today is that many non-Brahmins do as well as Brahmins. This is basically because of the increasing of awareness amongst people for the last thirty to forty years. Lots of non-Brahmins have realized the importance of education (...). If this gap is narrowing so much, I don't see the reason why there should be so much of reservation.[13]

In the southern part of the country, these positive discrimination policies are considered as a direct attack on Brahmins and their tradition of excellence, especially because in south India, the term Backward Classes refers essentially to non-Brahmins although the actual social situation is much more complex. This hostile trend has provoked typical reactions on the part of the affected Brahmin community. The most common reactions to these positive discrimination policies are professional reorientation and emigration. They represent the two major material aspects that crystallize the relation between Brahmin identity and hostile reservation policies.

You are expected to do these things and nobody really will violate these broad norms. If you are not supposed to go into business, you don't go. You either become a doctor, a professor, or an advocate. Now times are changing.[14]

Tamil Brahmins have a tendency to value some professions more than others. These are professions requiring a superior intellect, traditionally considered to be the monopoly of the Brahmin *varna*. North Indian Brahmins also prefer the same professions, as they are associated with financial stability and social prestige. A Kashmiri Brahmin mentioned that the practice of law, engineering, medicine and teaching are the most coveted professions.

Teaching, engineering, medicine, law . . . basically Kashmiri Pandits are a community based on . . . who concentrates on studies, whether pure sciences, pure arts, pure humanities, engineering, medicine, law . . . engineering, medicine, law was because that is a paying profession, not because of any love for that.[15]

The career of an advocate or judge is even now a symbol of intellectual and social achievement for Brahmins.

He (the Brahmin) has an advantage over others in terms of . . . he has held this thinking power and brain for a longer period than other communities and therefore he is certainly at an advantage today in terms of his ability to study, to think, to... explain in his subject, science, medicine, he has been in the forefront of all these professions, till twenty-five, thirty years ago, advocacy for instance if you take, the leading advocates, if you look back, if you go to the Bar Association CD, pictures of the presidents in the Madras Bar, you'll find 80 per cent will be Brahmins. So, we had that advantage (...). And, always, Brahmins have been a forward community in terms of their intellectual capacities, even in other communities they are good, I am not saying they are not, but if you take an average, that they have been ahead of others in academic pursuits and professions which are connected with academic pursuits.[16]

The sociologist, Yogendra Singh, describes south Indian Brahmins as 'pioneers'. They have always been at the forefront in new fields of knowledge. Involved for long with the social sciences, engineering and medicine, south Indian Brahmins nowadays stand out in the private sector because of their expertise.[17]

For some Brahmins in south India, entry into the private sector was a safety measure when faced by quotas in government jobs. Similarly in the north, after the implementation of the recommendations of the Mandal Commission, Brahmins were able to bypass the barriers raised by the government by joining the private sector.

To become an engineer or a doctor, there would have been problems with reservations. In business, there is no problem. And I managed with my sons. . . . [18]

This professional reorientation in south India started by moving away from government jobs to join the banking sector. But after the nationalization of banks in 1969 and the introduction of job reservations in the banking sector, the private sector became the principal option.[19] The development of the TVS group established in 1960 by the Brahmin industrialist, T.V. Sundaram Iyengar, with a loan from the central government is a good example of this shift to the private sector.[20]

It must however be pointed out that Brahmins have been active in commerce and industry in Madras city for a very long time. The areas of Kallidaikkuricci and Alvakkuricci in Tirunelveli district have a tradition of Brahmin bankers and traders going back three hundred years.[21] But in recent years more and more Brahmins, who do not belong to such a tradition, have been opting for careers in the private sector.

For upper middle-class Brahmins, this shift to the private sector is still a fairly unorthodox step which may be criticized within the community.

I am, in my family, first generation businessman. All of us have been advocates, in fact, we look down, with contempt on this businessman.[22]

But a real revolution has been brought about with the immense popularity of the information technology (IT) sector among young Tamil Brahmins. India is now recognized worldwide for its expertise in computer software. It is also trying to enter into wide-ranging cooperation agreements in this field with South-East Asian countries.[23] South India is leading in this field and Bangalore's success is a glowing example. But Chennai, ranked number two in the export of information technology, is not far behind Bangalore with Hyderabad occupying the third place.[24]

Training centres have mushroomed in Chennai and in cities and towns all over India. Newspapers are full of advertisements put out by these institutes, which being private are not subject to the problem of quotas, drawing attention to their educational and professional collaboration with institutions and companies abroad. But the glorious path to success is gaining admission in an Indian Institute of Technology. Directly funded by the central government, these institutes are not affected by reservations like the Regional Engineering Colleges. They do not have special quotas for Backward Classes but only for SCs and STs. Gaining admission into one of these institutes is extremely tough. Only 1 to 2 per cent of those who appear for the entrance exam are selected and their graduates are considered the cream of Indian engineers.[25] In IIT, Chennai, the number of Brahmins is definitely much higher than in other engineering colleges in the city. This Brahmin student of IIT, Chennai, testifies to the high proportion of south Indian Brahmins among the candidates selected on the basis of a national-level entrance examination.

My classmates in IIT, as far as Tamil people were concerned, there were lots of Brahmins, most of them. Same with people from Andhra, yes from Tamil Nadu, almost all of them were Brahmins.[26]

Success in this examination is a label that overrides all considerations of caste in the professional development of the successful candidates.

I cleared an exam, Indian Institute of Technology (...). *After that, this tag is there, IIT, this guy is from an Indian Institute of Technology. After that I went to IIM, Indian Institute of Management, so the IIT–IIM tag sort of transcends all these caste barriers.*[27]

The success of Brahmins in these highly competitive examinations is not surprising. Education continues to be a priority for middle-class Brahmins all over India. And the IT sector offering a combination of intellectualism and economic openings has now become the new preserve of Brahmins.

Brahmins, as a community, have a strength in intellectual areas. IT software is also an area which requires lots of intellectual abilities, as opposed to other activities, like business, or physical activities . . . so it is a natural thing which is happening… it is one of the reasons why lots of Brahmins are going into IT, especially on the software side.[28]

Professor P. Radhakrishnan explains that this sector has become a truly Brahmin speciality, especially in view of the large-scale emigration of Brahmins, which is the last stage of their reaction to hostile reservation policies.[29]

Given the educational and professional situation in Tamil Nadu, emigration is indeed the final solution to overcome constraints in the economic and political domains. There is nothing new about the migration of Brahmins. Part I described in detail the professional consequences of the forced migration of Brahmins in north India, first from religion to agriculture and then to the army. In the south, Brahmin migration triggered by professional motives can be divided into three phases, viz., from rural to urban areas, from towns and cities in Tamil Nadu to towns and cities in other parts of India and finally emigration to foreign countries.

The migration of Brahmins from villages to towns and cities to gain access to urban resources was largely motivated by considerations of employment and by the desire to acquire an élite status in both religious and economic spheres.[30]

The second phase involves migration from Tamil Nadu to other parts of India after the introduction of the reservation policies in the beginning of the twentieth century. This phenomenon is related to the field of education:

The entire world is their backyard. Comparatively, you will find more Tamil Brahmins in Delhi, in Jawaharlal Nehru University than in Madras University, because it is a more relatively open society.[31]

The Mandal Commission Report mentions in its analysis of the situation in south India that as far back as in the 1920s, following the Government Order of 1927 for giving greater opportunities to non-Brahmins, the Brahmins of Tamil Nadu realized that there were no professional opportunities for them in their native state and started migrating to the north and to other Indian metropolises, especially Bombay.[32] But this trend applied only to middle-class Brahmins who had the financial and intellectual means to leave their native environment.

From my perception, the problem is not the middle-class educated Brahmin families, because they have various options. Say, for example, if my daughter doesn't get admission in Madras, I can afford to send her to Delhi or any other place. Problem comes with the poor in rural areas, those who don't have the means.[33]

After Independence, Tamil Brahmins crossed the bounds of south India where they were already quite mobile, their preferred destinations being Bangalore in Karnataka and Trivandrum in Kerala. Delhi too has been a great favourite and 75 per cent of the south Indian settled in Delhi are Brahmins, Tamil Brahmins being the most predominant sub-group.[34]

But for these educated middle-class Brahmins, the most attractive option that has recently emerged is settling abroad where their professional excellence can find free expression without any constraints.

The question of Brahmins is not good. For example, even during their studies and profession there should be a normal channel, merit and all, it is not . . . so, the normal treatment which is supposed to be given, it is not given (...). It may not be the exact thing what it was a decade or two decades ago, now it is better, the reason being Brahmins, where they go to the school, or college, or their profession, they really excel. It is again a thing it automatically comes to their brain, because of . . . especially in villages, there are no Brahmins, they come to cities, the city is better. And from cities they go abroad. And abroad they prosper. So, the people who come with their advanced qualifications or engineering qualifications or any other profession with them, they prosper in other countries.[35]

The preferred destinations abroad are the United Kingdom and even more the United States, a country mentioned by all the Brahmins who referred to the issue of emigration. Apart from careers in law and medicine, it was information technology that opened the glorious path to success for these highly educated Tamil Brahmins, taking them directly to the Silicon Valley.

It is very difficult, that is why very well educated Brahmins they go out of this country, they settle down in United States.[36]

In fact, you can be sure that almost every upper middle-class Brahmin or even a very low middle-class Brahmin also has one person or another living abroad, because they studied hard, they went to good colleges and then they worked their way up and they do get good jobs abroad, go to the United States, UK, do their higher studies and settle down too.[37]

Today it is like, mostly if you are a Brahmin and you are twenty, they say, ah you are going to go to the US . . . for higher studies. If you see the number of Brahmin students who go abroad for higher studies, they are the largest. They are the ones who go abroad for higher studies (...) that is a new trend that has started. Because they are getting into IITs first, engineering colleges or medicine and then going abroad.[38]

What is happening, especially among Brahmins, is going to the US. It started in the early 80s. At that point, we were a closed economy, we did not have too many job opportunities in India. So, Brahmins wanted to use their intelligence and learn more. And avenues for higher education were in the US, and monetary prospects. So people, especially Brahmins started getting in good colleges in India, using that to then go to US, start a job and settle there, so this urge among Brahmins to go to US (...). Early 1980s, it was people from the IITs who would go to US, late 1990s, the IT sector is the new way to go to US. So, one of the major attractions in India to go to IT is that they want to go to the US. There is a large community of Brahmins in the US, who are working in the IT sector.[39]

In an article in the *Weekend* magazine, a journalist has quoted President Clinton's remark about the three symbols of the Silicon Valley, the red dot, the *lungi* and *chappals*, indicating the large presence of Tamil Brahmins.[40]

This dynamic corresponds to a real 'brain-drain' which did not start with the recent emigration of IT professionals. Indian scientists and engineers indeed have been playing a significant role in the American economy since the 1970s.[41]

The Indo-American Chamber of Commerce is very active in Chennai where it organizes frequent seminars on immigration procedures and commercial regulations in force in the United States. Even though Indians from all parts of the country have been successful in obtaining jobs abroad in the IT sector, Brahmins stand out because of their excellent qualifications and high level of expertise.[42]

The IT revolution has now acquired astonishing dimensions and it has incited the Indian government to regulate the migration of IT professionals to foreign lands, setting up a data-base in order to meet the demand in both national and international markets in a more rational manner.[43]

The idea of getting a highly qualified and relatively cheap workforce has seduced many countries and not just the United States. The new immigration policy introduced by the German government in August 2000 has opened the doors wide to Indian software engineers who represent the largest group among the new candidates of varying profiles and nationalities recently recruited by German companies.[44] However, salary scales and cultural adjustment are the two sour points in this otherwise pleasing situation of socio-professional success.[45]

Many people, in the 1980s and 1990s emigrated to the US. Now, people who are going are going for monetary matters. And the US ask for Indians these days, for software engineering especially (...). *Today, all my cousins and all have gone to the US and got married... a place of opportunity and ... for the quality of life* (...). *They feel lonely, but, with the cable TV the gap is filled.*[46]

It must also be noted that this migratory trend is essentially motivated by better career prospects which are usually central to the middle-class Indian identity.[47] But this motivation is more noticeable among Brahmins from Tamil Nadu because of the local socio-professional scenario.

A large slice of middle-class Brahmins from Tamil Nadu have gone abroad leaving behind Brahmins at the two extremities of the socio-economic scale, the very rich and the very poor. The majority of the real middle-class Tamil Brahmins has emigrated.[48]

Many Brahmins have gone away abroad, especially to the USA, because of some job opportunities, and today in Tamil Nadu especially, Brahmins are in two extremes, either you have the very well to do businessmen and industrialists and so on, like my husband, or you have the very poor Brahmins, who have not been able to get out of the country (...) *but even the ones in between have gone and have taken jobs in private industry, but most Brahmin families have several young people in the States today. In my own husband's family, he and his brother are the only two people, all the cousins, everyone is far.*[49]

The Brahmins of Tamil Nadu, who have turned in large numbers to the IT sector which often provides attractive openings abroad, constitute the vanguard of modern Brahmins who, with the onset of the new millennium, seem to have forgotten the dark period of the 1990s and the aftermath of the Mandal Commission Report.[50] Despite the bleak scenario they paint in their general remarks, the Brahmins of Tamil Nadu have managed to get away at the right time. In this very specific scenario, Brahmins have revealed their distinctive character by adapting themselves to the circumstances. This perception of the notion of distinctiveness, of separation with reference to the economic and political issues at stake should not eclipse the significance of cultural issues in which this notion has its roots.

North Indian Brahmins, when they talk of their counterparts in the south, maintain that their conservatism has a positive connotation. South Indian Brahmins, when talking about themselves, lay stress on the purity of their Brahminical traditions in addition to their strong social conscience.

Some of the Tamil Brahmins, who were interviewed, said that they feel that they belong in south India, an entity they would oppose to the north.

South India is . . . even in the habits if you see, you will find a divide between the north and the south. The four states of south, we have a lot of things, India, whatever you are, the culture is the same, but amongst the south, there is definitely a certain difference, between the south Indian and the north Indian. I am a Brahmin, suppose my daughter wants to marry, if she is marrying a Punjabi, it doesn't matter to me if he is a Brahmin or not. His way of life and thinking is so different. Because we are living in a different climatic condition, we are living in a different ambiance.[51]

A characteristic feature of south Indian culture is its attachment to the purity of traditions and its respect for the original teachings of the Shastras. This trend also applies to rituals and architecture.

If you go to any south Indian temple, the temple architecture, the worship, etc., it remained as it was prescribed in the shastras, whereas it has undergone drastic change elsewhere in the north, but in south it remains intact, this is even according to north Indian Brahmins, I toured all over India.[52]

It also affects their basic habits, vegetarianism being a common practice. The question of food habits came up in most interviews highlighting certain regional disparities, e.g. Bengali Brahmins traditionally eat fish while Kashmiri Brahmins eat meat. These cultural traits correspond to geographical conditions and climatic differences.

We live in a flat, with non-Brahmins also, so we are very disturbed by non-veg food, but no big issue.[53]

Orthodox Brahmins, basically they are all very strict vegetarians, whereas amongst the Bengali Brahmins in West Bengal, that tradition of taking fish is there in many families . . . they may not be taking mutton or chicken or anything of that nature, but fish culture is definitely there in many many Bengali families.[54]

Well, I made a marital choice . . . of somebody who was outside my community, I was the first person in my family to marry outside my caste. It's so happened that she's a Brahmin too. But everything about her is against . . . take the kind of purity, ritual purity I was raised on, she's a Kashmiri Brahmin, Kashmiris eat meat . . . and there is nothing more reprehensible to Tamil Brahmins than consumption of meat.[55]

This last point of view comparing Kashmiri and Tamil Brahmins would amount to claiming that the only true Brahmins today are those from south India, a claim, it should be noted, that goes against the Dravidian ideology. For according to this viewpoint, the Brahmin threat comes from the north, as we have stated earlier, in the form of Hindi and Sanskrit and the Congress's all-India outlook.

That's a lot of difference between north India and south India. We, in south India, especially, we are more particular than in north, for example a priest in north he might go and worship an idol on the one hand and he might go and light a bidi *in the other hand . . . which you will not find in south (...) if you take north, it's more for money, for money sake. Within the temples, you will see the money part more rather than what you call the devotion or Bhakti.*[56]

South Indian Brahmins, who are so proud of remaining faithful to their traditions, believe the north has allowed itself to be corrupted. They feel that south India has been able to preserve its culture while adapting itself without much difficulty to the changes that have taken place in India. This south Indian trait can be explained historically. All through history the north has been the scene of major overland invasions. It has therefore become a melting pot of cultures and has been affected by the inevitable ensuing changes.

Broadly these diseases affected the Brahmin community more in the north than in the south. Even today, somehow the Brahmin community in the south has been able to deal with the rest, Westernization, English. We are very good in handling this language, we never got anglicized. The trend is quite recent because of this globalization. But in the north, the deterioration has been much sharper, because of Islamic and Christian influences, we were much more protected.[57]

Communal conflicts are not as intense in the south as those in north India. Conflicts between Brahmins and non-Brahmins have occupied the centre of the political stage in south India as opposed to the Hindu-Muslim conflicts in the north. That is why Hindu extremism could be considered as something alien to south India. According to one of the Brahmins interviewed, the strong religious conservatism of this region has reinforced this phenomenon by preventing politicians from exploiting religion excessively.

The south Indians have always been liberal. They accepted things faster. You take for example even Hinduism, the VHP and all these things, the activity is all because the TV is percolating down. Otherwise, we have always lived in peace, with Muslims, with Christians; we have never known this (...). Pacifism has always been. Naturally also because, we have never seen tough times, real wars, ravages, the Muslim invasions, all these things have been only in the north. People have suffered more there and therefore they are I think (...) . . . we are traditionalists, much more than the north.[58]

But electoral alliances as well as the regressive tendency of some Brahmins in Tamil Nadu who bitterly resent the reservations policies in their state provide a fertile soil for the propagation of the Hindu nationalist ideology. In Tamil Nadu, Hindu revivalism could easily be equated with a Brahmin reawakening.[59]

All these elements, which constitute the Tamil Brahmins' attachment to a certain type of tradition, are responsible for their feeling of cultural isolation. Their awareness of this tradition sets them apart not only from Brahmins belonging to other regions but also from the rest of Tamil society. Many Tamil Brahmins associate this cultural isolation with a keener sense of patriotism and public-spiritedness. This attitude has been found among the closed élitist type of the classification presented in Chapter 1 and is the assertion of Brahmin supremacy as a reaction to a hostile socio-political environment. In other words, Brahmins continue to consider themselves as an 'enlightened élite' having a clear understanding of social dynamics.

A thirty-one-year old Brahmin lady working in the marketing division of a company indicates that she belongs to this type when she describes herself as 'superior', 'advanced', 'a cut above the rest' and claiming at the same time that she is 'broad-minded' and 'open-minded'. Her attitude can be summarized in the following terms: we are superior because we are more educated and thus better able to adapt ourselves of changes in society.[60] It is because of this keen awareness of their identity supported by unambiguous references that south Indian Brahmins can turn towards others and have very clear opinions about the functioning of society.

Some Tamil Brahmins believe that north Indian Brahmins have suffered more than Brahmins in the south throughout history because of their geographical location. But most of them lay stress on problems peculiar to south India that are more recent but affect Brahmins directly on account of the powerful non-Brahmin movement.

It is important in Tamil Nadu, because it is here that in the last fifty years, there has been a movement against the Brahmins. I don't think it was there in north, there was no specific movement. Here, there has been a specific movement targeting only the Brahmin community, because they were found to have discriminated, they have kept the others down, which is as usual only part of the truth.[61]

This type of attitude leads to a historical comparison of the condition of Brahmins in south and north India focused only on the twentieth century and gives rise to the feeling that north Indian Brahmins have not suffered as much as those in the south.[62] The virulent ostracism of Brahmins practised in south India is quite legitimate according to some in view of the élitist and non-egalitarian attitude of Brahmins all over the country.

All over India this has been so that Brahmins have considered themselves superior in so many forms, therefore it is very true. For example in the village, if you take, they had an agrahara where only Brahmins live, you can not enter it. These are all the sins committed by my forefathers for which we are paying now . . . this kind of a differentiation was there for a long time, even in the north, I think it was there.[63]

But in spite of these common attitudes in the past, it seems that today south Indian Brahmins react quite differently. Many of them believe that an exaggerated ostracism leads to greater awareness. Firstly, it is simply an awareness of their being Brahmins. Tamil Brahmins who were interviewed referred invariably to the ascendancy of the Brahmin identity in Chennai in spite of the unfavourable socio-political conditions.

For me Madras almost, it's almost saying that I am a Brahmin if I say I am from Madras (...). So, it's . . . in fact that's part of the reason that it has become so integrated to my identity, maybe, if I was born . . . I mean if I lived in Delhi, or lived in Bombay, or lived somewhere else, it wouldn't have been so . . . strong.[64]

Secondly, this keen awareness makes south Indian Brahmins criticize the arrogance of their counterparts in the north, who continue to ill treat members of the lower castes. South Indian Brahmins seem to have understood because of their past experiences the need to adjust and adapt to ensure greater social harmony.

Unfortunately, still, in some other states, northern states, like Bihar and U.P., they don't want to live in the society, they still think they are supreme. (...) Today, if somebody wants to live peacefully, he cannot live with all satisfaction, he has to totally depend upon others, that feeling, that thinking has to come in everybody's mind. I have to live with people. The others have to accept me also.[65]

They think that north Indian Brahmins still live in the feudal ages, especially where ownership of land is concerned, implying the attraction of money and a strong tendency to commit violence, both of which are against traditional Brahminical ethics.

There are few south Indian Brahmins who would be landowners and rich, but here, in the north, it is not the case, Brahmins are powerful (...). Being a landowner, simply by the need to maintain order, produces violence.[66]

Tamil Brahmins tend to stress the fact that they are culturally different from the rest of society claiming at the same time that they are fully assimilated. They feel that they are the repositories of pure traditions in their private sphere with a highly developed social conscience in the public sphere. The distinctive nature of their educational and professional problems also makes them pay particular attention to socio-political changes not only in Tamil Nadu but in India as a whole. Tamil Brahmins feel they are different, but they also believe that this difference is the basis and the justification of a socio-political awareness that can give rise to an altruistic attitude. According to some, this political awareness is accompanied by a willingness to commit themselves to various causes. And this sense of commitment is considered to be an expression of humanism.

Tamil Brahmins continue to be proud of their identity in spite of the historical turmoil that they have been through. This strong identity is often analysed as a feeling of superiority even though it may not be expressed overtly. However, this feeling of superiority does not imply a watertight social division. The fact that they are a separate entity because of hostile policies targeted against them and their distinctive cultural traits has not isolated the Brahmin community from the rest of Tamil society. Today in Tamil Nadu, except for the younger generation of Brahmins who are too involved in their professional lives, Brahminism is associated with social service organizations and other manifestations of social responsibility.

You are supposed to read, knowledge, help out other people with your knowledge, people with problems will come to you . . . that is the original, according to me, the starting point of the Brahmin (...). *I believe everyone should set aside, in a country like India, a certain percentage of whatever their earnings towards the betterment of others, not your own community. I mean really the people who are suffering, and this is again I would say the essence of Brahminism, it is also this, in my small way I want to do it.*[67]

Tamil Brahmins insist that being concerned about others, being aware of one's social responsibilities is an essential function of the Brahmin.

There are three classes of Brahmins, the upper, very rich, very well to do classes and then the upper middle-class and the lower middle-class. The very poor Brahmins are also there, now it is more. They are abandoned. Actually, the top-class Brahmins have become very cosmopolitan in their outlook and whatever they do, nobody questions it (...). In the upper middle-class and in the lower middle-class, things are still rigid because of the older generations, so that it becomes a handicap. They are not able to break away from the conventional way of life, they think they must do these things and if they don't they will be blamed or criticized or feel guilty.[68]

As we have already seen, in the framework of institutionalized response to reservation policies, Brahmins of Tamil Nadu have different attitudes depending on their socio-economic status. Since the real middle-class Brahmin tends to emigrate, that leaves us with the two extremes—the very rich and well-to-do at one end and the lower middle-class and the poor at the other. As far as engagement in social service is concerned, the élites do not act in the same way as the lower middle-class and do not have the same perceptions about such activities, as we will now see.

For Brahmins in Tamil Nadu belonging to the privileged classes social service is associated with activities of a cultural or educational nature. This type of activity, even if it is close to the traditional Brahmin sphere related to knowledge, spiritual matters and art, has been considered by our interviewees as a phenomenon that is not explicitly Brahminical.

My father built a music academy and it's a very prestigious institution, it's about seventy-two years old and it promotes south Indian classical music and dance and every year, during December we have a fifteen days festival.[69]

One Brahmin industrialist, a very rich and socially prominent personality in Chennai, declares that he is proud to be associated through his family with the promotion of classical Indian culture. But, at the same time, he does not want this activity to be labelled as Brahmin.

There again, I want to tell you that we don't differentiate Brahmin musicians from non-Brahmin musicians and even honouring an eminent artist, that is not coming into consideration, it is his qualification (...). Narrow-mindedness doesn't exist in this organization (...) it was a group of people of all communities who started this institution, in 1928.[70]

The fact remains that this devotion to classical dance and music is the preserve of the intellectual élite of which the Brahmins, in spite of all the hostile policies against them, are still prominent members.

A young Tamil Brahmin lady, who has recently joined a music production company, explains this cultural dimension of Brahmin culture in the following terms:

The main thing is I feel very comfortable being a Brahmin. I am into Carnatic music section now. And in this section, only Brahmins, most of them are Brahmins. I have the chance to mingle with Brahmins only, so I feel very comfortable to communicate with them. And Carnatic music, I don't say that non-Brahmins or any other people, they don't have the talent to sing Carnatic music, but mostly, Brahmins, they get the chance to get popular in this field (...) *because of the family background. Brahmin families, they want the children to learn music, dance* (...) *one thing, being a Brahmin is a plus point for me yes. I have chosen my career as entering the Carnatic field . . . my parents have given importance to this choice . . . we have moved to Madras for that.*[71]

Interest in matters related to education is a traditional means for Brahmins to show their concern for the proper functioning of society.

I took to this profession more to start as a community service, because I found that many of our children, especially the forward community children were becoming very very Westernized because most of them were going to missionary schools, and especially after independence, the teenagers and the younger generations took to a Western way of life, more than under the British. So I started this centre to Indianize the child, teach our classical music, make them take pride in our culture, our classical dance, our epics, and also the Indian way of life, it is full of culture (...). *Just Indianizing the child won't be enough, he has to survive in a competitive world. We have to think of that also.*[72]

The above view was expressed by the lady principal of a 'Brahmin school', as such schools which conduct educational courses in line with the great Hindu tradition are still named today.

I studied in a Brahmin school, for my last 4 years of schooling, in Madras (...). *My two sons also are studying in a school where there are more Brahmins than non-Brahmins . . . it is by practice that Brahmins come* (...). *I felt they will at least learn a little bit of all these* shlokas *and at least grow up in that atmosphere, because college is something that I have absolutely no control on them . . . So at least, the few first years of their life, if they come to know our tradition, our culture and all, probably they will not go haywire in college, that was the feeling I had (...). At least, they should know something. I am sure by the time they get married, they have children, there will be nothing left of Brahmins and all . . . our culture, our traditions.*[73]

This type of education aimed at preserving cultural traditions achieves its purpose by introducing children to the classical Indian arts at an early age. The Society for Promotion of Indian Classical Music and Culture amongst Youth (Spicmacay) is very active in this field. But this expression of cultural superiority is also coupled with a social conscience that urges Brahmins to work for the underprivileged.

Apart from activities aimed at promoting culture and education, Brahmins are indeed also aware of the help that they can provide directly to the poorest of the poor, whether Brahmins or non-Brahmins. The willingness of well-to-do Brahmins in Tamil Nadu to bring succour to the underprivileged classes can be viewed from different angles. In the first place, it may be an alternative for the purely religious services performed by Brahmins. A sixty-one-year old civil engineer who has always worked out of office hours for the temple, explains his views as follows:

As a true Brahmin, I feel that I have to live without hurting people, not to do bad things. You are supposed to be god fearing, you are supposed to do service to the god. Those things I believe very strongly in and I do them . . . . My daughters may differ, because they feel doing some service for the downtrodden and destitutes is a better way of doing it. But I feel, I have to do something on the spiritual side, should do more for the temple.[74]

Wanting to help the poor may also correspond to a deep awareness of society's needs or assuage a feeling of guilt, as we will explain later. It must however be noted that this altruistic perspective is often disconnected from any reference to the Brahmin identity. This approach has already been shown in the classification of Chapter 1, through the unconscious personalization of the Brahmin category made by 'natural' Brahmins.

Natural Brahmins have been shown as being prouder and more confident of their Brahmin identity without laying any explicit claims on it.

A thirty-seven-year old Brahmin lady, holding a doctorate in economics and working as a journalist for *Frontline*, believes that it is her Brahminical environment that has made her aware of social inequalities. That is why she concentrates on these subjects in the course of her work even though she refuses to define herself as a Brahmin.

You are asking the wrong person (...). I never look at myself as a Brahmin (...). I would just categorize myself as a human being, I never look at it as a Brahmin/non-Brahmin thing (...). I come from a very traditional family. And then this Brahmin element was very positive, very much there in my family. I was in a joint family also, so the older generations were also there . . . this was very strong in us. That is precisely why I also think that I was at a tremendous advantage. My colleagues and my friends who are around now . . . see I cover social issues and most of the time, I write on things which deal with deprivation of different sorts, education, health, wealth . . . so precisely because I come from a Brahmin family, a traditional Brahmin family, where I was always told that I am a Brahmin, I realized the advantage that I have had over my friends who do not have that.[75]

The lady director of a prestigious foundation in Chennai that coordinates programmes in the fields of education, environment and culture, also avoids explicit connections with her Brahmin family, which is however well known for its very high status in the socio-religious as well as the socio-economic hierarchies. On the other hand, a woman employee of the same foundation declares that she is happy as a Brahmin to belong to this institution which is for her the epitome of a 'Brahmin family'.

Most of my friends are Brahmins and now I am working in a Brahmin institution which is a completely Brahmin family, so I am very happy to work in the foundation, with Mrs. K., because she used to take only, give a chance to Brahmin people. You see, these days, people are having these BC, Backward castes and all that, these people can get a job, but not for the Brahmins. So she is helping in that case, she is taking Brahmin people, where you can get a chance in the foundation, and here we are all like a family, like a Brahmin family, we are used to work together.[76]

But upper middle-class Brahmins are not content to think of the problems faced by the members of their own *varna*—a notion that is fundamental, as we shall see later, to lower middle-class Brahmins. They can organize more general assistance networks, playing down at the same time the part played by Brahmins in such organizations as compared to other communities in Tamil Nadu.

I am very proud that we created opportunities for employment, for say, more than six to seven thousand families directly . . . and that does not mean this is only the Brahmin community who is contributing to the growth. No, there are so many communities who contribute to the growth of this country. So, I don't attribute anything extraordinary being a Brahmin or of an affluent status, I take a broader view. All right, in your life, what have you contributed to the community. That's why you see my involvement happening in music and public work, like being associated with an orphanage, four hundred children (....). *And then another thing I am proud is that we run a health centre for the lower and deprived communities, we started about 1953 and it has become a hundred bedrooms hospital, offering different services to the community. That's my philosophy.*[77]

Many Brahmins from this affluent social background are very conscious of the fact that social service is not the exclusive domain of the Brahmin community.

We do everything in the low profile and we try to do something else also which the business communities have been doing in a big way. See if you look at him (*a non-Brahmin friend of the merchant caste*) *. . . social service in certain areas, at the street levels, businessmen they have an excellent social obligation, the businessmen have it.*[78]

In the Indian context, all these activities have a highly spiritual value. This kind of social service, which involves giving large donations and engaging in charitable activities, is part of a long tradition traceable from the Roman times to the contemporary Hindu nationalist movement. It is the expression of a combination of devotion and aristocratic pride.[79]

Social service also exists among Brahmins belonging to a lower economic status but it is often of a demagogic and populist kind. This stratum of the population tends to use social service for strategic ends. Hindu nationalists are a characteristic example of people who engage in charitable work for strategic purposes. Whenever the government fails to take timely action, they use *seva* as a political tool, particularly to mobilize Untouchables, to compete with Christian missionaries and political movements working for their uplift.[80]

However, Tamil Brahmins belonging to the lower middle-class act in a different context. Instead of trying to exploit the shortcomings of the government, they seek to attract its attention to themselves by doing charitable work or *seva* in order to bolster their demand for policies that could be more favourable to their community. These lower middle-class Brahmins do social service mainly through the Tamil Nadu Brahmin Association (Tambras) which makes socio-economic demands that are hardly justified considering the general situation of Brahmins in Tamil Nadu.

Our association was founded about twenty years back. See what happened, the political development after Independence was that certain sections of the society felt that Brahmins were dominating and also wanted to gain an upper hand, but they could not come up on their own. Unless Brahmin community is suppressed, others can not come up. So, these sections got political support also, with the result that Brahmins did not find a place which they normally deserve, so we were subject to suffering all over, employment, education, all over. So, we want to safeguard our section of the community. It means that we Brahmins are not ready to see our brothers suffer like this, that's why we started this association, working towards this goal.[81]

Set up in Coimbatore on 16 November 1980 by N. Narayanan, Tambras seeks to satisfy the economic demands of the poorer strata of the Brahmin community in the hostile environment in Tamil Nadu. The majority of its actions are meant to help Brahmins. It organizes training programmes and employment for young Brahmins from the lower socio-economic strata. Private institutes have been set-up to provide technical training as well as professional courses in management and information technology. Classes are conducted to prepare candidates for entrance examinations to engineering colleges. In addition to these activities, the association also organizes cultural programmes and activities. For example, it has created a data bank of marriageable young Brahmins together with computer horoscopes and it regularly organizes thread ceremonies. Apart from these activities meant specifically for Brahmins, Tambras claims in the opening lines of its brochure that it was set-up to help the poor and the destitute. The association's president estimates that twenty-five of its activities benefit society as a whole.[82] These activities generally focus on medical and educational assistance for children and the aged of all castes. It must be noted that similar activities are carried out by Brahmins also through other institutions like the Probus Club, an offshoot of the Rotary Club, or more often through temple trusts.[83]

But unlike the Brahmins belonging to higher classes, the activities of these poorer Brahmins are accompanied by specific claims provoked by the anti-Brahmin context in Tamil Nadu as well as demands for recognition. This approach is based on the self-proclaimed openness and kindliness of Brahmins as a whole and their desire to contribute to social harmony by accepting one and all, irrespective of origin, which is not the case with non-Brahmins.

In ancient times, we lived in absolute harmony with all other sections of the society, the rest of other religions, castes, creeds, languages, we have no barriers, we have brotherly, sisterly affection towards all others. We treat everybody as human beings, not only here, even abroad, our people are living abroad, any human being is same for us, that's why we treat all people equally, but some people are not reciprocating that.[84]

Given the political situation in Tamil Nadu where deep-rooted anti-Brahminism is a historical reality going far back in time, the Brahmin members of Tambras have developed a logical argument that tends to consider in relative terms the élitism practised by Brahmins throughout history. The association's president even proclaims that it was the Brahmins who opened the doors of temples to Untouchables.[85]

Tamil Brahmins are isolated from the mainstream for the reason that the government says that Brahmins were dominating the society for so long, for this and that. In retaliation, they want to curb the influence of Brahmins in the present days. In the present time, Brahmins have nothing to do with what happened in the past. According to us, nothing has happened, whatever has happened through the Brahmins is good for the society (...). If the Brahmins had dominated the society for five thousand years, all the Brahmins would have been millionaires, in the economic sense. But that is not so. As a matter of fact, people from other communities, they are holding the economy only in their hands.[86]

The Tambras want to highlight that it is a fact that Brahmins have been social benefactors, guides and spiritual teachers and if they have occasionally been guilty of atrocities against the poor and oppressed classes, so have non-Brahmins.

We had so many gurus, so many highly religious people, but today we have to concentrate on the material aspects of the Brahmin community. The other communities highlight the fact that Brahmins were practising untouchability. Yes, it is true that it was practised by our forefathers, but we were the ones to shelve everything and started to be rationalist in mind, modern, in our practice. Untouchability is also very much practised by non-Brahmin high castes. So the aim of our association is to help poor Brahmins in whatever way, education, profession, marriage.[87]

But this approach is based on the image of the model Brahmin, an altruistic, devotional person ever willing to serve society and on the notion that Brahmins are willing to accept everybody as equals even though non-Brahmins are not willing to reciprocate.

Brahmins were leaders of the society because they were living virtuous lives which made others proud of them. They made ethical codes for themselves (...), lived in harmony with all others and helped others. I would like to follow Brahminism, to live the way it has been prescribed. But in the modern days, I cannot escape being a little bit materialistic at least. Still I have my own way of acquiring money, in a legitimate way to get what I require (...). I love to help people. Though our association works for the welfare of Brahmins, we also give support to people from other communities. Brahmins are meant for the service of humanity, not only for Brahmins.[88]

As far as socio-economic issues are concerned, Brahmins, members of Tambras do not want to be described as a 'forward community'. They claim, and they are justified in doing so, that there are considerable economic disparities within the Brahmin community and that many of them face serious economic difficulties. One of the active members of the association gave me the example of Brahmin priests whose living quarters around the temples of Mylapore in Chennai are comparable to slums.[89]

But their demand that they should be given a minority status does not have a solid legal base. After the demand submitted by Kashmiri Pandits to the National Minorities Commission that they should be treated as a minority, press articles stated that an organization of south Indian Brahmins made a similar demand towards the end of 1998. Even though this particular demand was not made by Tambras, it had voiced such an opinion during the interviews I conducted in Chennai in early 1999. The chairman of the National Minorities Commission replied that being a part of the Hindu community, Brahmins did not come under the Commission's jurisdiction and were not entitled to a minority status.[90] Today, Tambras has given up its claim and its president has turned his attention to demanding a list of the exact parameters defining social and educational backwardness.

On this reservation issue, we are going to make a very basic plea. The constitution speaks of socially and educationally backward citizens. . . . It is seven months I hold this post, I went through all the things and I discussed with lawyers from various communities . . . what is social backwardness, what is educational backwardness, it is not written there in black and white, it is not quantified. There are no parameters laid for that. So we are going to plead, you lay parameters for what is that, apply it not to caste, apply it to candidates. Even if you are a Brahmin, if your father was not educated, you must be given the reservation. If you apply this to the candidates, problems will be avoided.[91]

General critics of the manner in which reservation policies function at present, outside the strictly Tamil Brahmin context, are asking for an enumeration of Backward Classes as it was done in the case of Scheduled Castes and Scheduled Tribes, especially in the post-Mandal scenario.[92] Tambras, on its part, has demanded that positive discrimination policies should fulfil a list of qualitative conditions and that they should be implemented, taking individual circumstances into account and not the caste factor. In such a situation, Brahmins having a lower economic status would also have a right to reserved seats. With the intention of justifying a government policy favourable to Brahmins, an active member of the association points out that Brahmins as a whole are a dedicated and disinterested community.

Social service is inbred in Brahmins. Social work is part of a routine for them, like prayer and puja (...). *I feel I am an Indian, I mean I am for the upliftment of the whole population. Brahmins are almost all in this spirit, so why should there be reservations against us?*[93]

By insisting that positive discrimination policies are justified if they are based on economic status instead of caste, this demagogic statement actually conceals the desire of these Brahmins for government aid in the form of economic support. Tambras is a Brahmin association, but it wants to emphasize the benefits it can bring to society as a whole. It does not want to project a narrow-minded, sectarian and communal image of itself. It is keen on justifying its demand for an end to reservation policies hostile to Brahmins and, if that is not possible, the inclusion of deserving Brahmins in reserved quotas.

However, the situation of Brahmins in Tamil Nadu is not so alarming that the government should take particular note of their case. The social decline of Brahmins in Tamil Nadu has often been overestimated. It is true that the formulation of reservation policies favouring non-Brahmins has had far-reaching consequences in terms of attitude and social dynamics. But Tamil Brahmins have been able to adapt themselves, as we have seen, by changing their attitude to suit the new circumstances.

If you examine the situation closely, especially the so-called sensitive areas from where they have been evicted, you realize that, even today, Brahmins are not all that badly off. Going in for medicine and engineering and joining private institutions has borne fruit.[94] Further, outside Tamil Nadu, Tamil Brahmins are still considered to be the most brilliant and the most likely to succeed.[95] Even within the Indian Administrative Service (IAS), the proportion of Brahmins is very high. During the period from 1941 to 1959, almost 90 per cent of the IAS trainees selected from Tamil Nadu were Brahmins. From 1960 to 1992, their number declined but even then they accounted for at least 50 per cent of the members of this service.[96]

Brahmins, who have been affluent and influential for centuries and who, for this very reason, have had to face political hostility in Tamil Nadu, continue to be powerful and cannot really justify their demand for government assistance even though it is made by the poorest sections of the community. Apart from these strategic demands, Tamil Brahmins continue to be proud and fully aware of their distinctive traits and comfortable with their identity. It is due to this strong identity that Tamil Brahmins have been able to define Brahminism as an expression of humanism, attitude that has been presented in the classification of Chapter 1, through the case of 'responsible' Brahmins.

We, Brahmins from south India, are catholic in our outlook, very tolerant towards other communities.[97]

The 'responsible' type tends to take into account the interests of underprivileged classes. This is the result of a process of deep introspection and a liberal outlook. As a matter of fact, 'responsible' Brahmins avoid any compartmentalization of their Brahmin identity and generally insist on the importance of linking together the different spheres of their life.

This approach seems to me to have a 'Christian' connotation in many respects, not in terms of direct influences but more as an association of ideas. The 'responsible' type, as the epithet indicates, values the notion of responsibility finding its roots in a sense of guilt, a typically Christian sentiment.

For this matter, it is interesting to take note of an aspect of Mahatma Gandhi's works. The Mahatma, who came into close contact with Christians, was profoundly influenced by the 'Sermon on the Mount'. He said that he perceived the spirit of the *Bhagavad Gita* in it. Renunciation, as the supreme ideal of all religions, and moral and dualistic values are tenets that make Gandhi's philosophy the preferred reference base for a comparative study of Hinduism and Christianity.[98]

Further, this sense of guilt grows according to a pattern that is very similar to a model of contemporary French Catholicism as analysed by Jean-Marie Donégani in his extremely fine work published in 1993. Model 'C', as he calls it, is one of the 'integralist' models defined by the author and conceptualized in the following terms: 'Being a Catholic means committing oneself to building a world'.[99]

My comparison is first based on the dual principle of marginalism and integralism used by J.M. Donégani to explain the place occupied (either at the centre or on the periphery) by religion in the attitudes of French Catholics who were interviewed by him. In the integralist models developed by the author, the entire perception of the world is centred around a religious reference which corresponds in our classification to 'neo-Brahminism', where belonging to the Brahmin category is meaningful both in the private and public spheres as well as in the cultural and political domains.

For a forty-year old Brahmin lady advocate this means, in addition to the personalization of her *varna*, the impossibility of thinking of the issues raised by the Mandal Commission without acknowledging her position as a Brahmin.

To think, as a non-Brahmin, not to be a Brahmin, I find it's very tough because many of the issues were, one has to think, on these issues, on things like reservations . . . which have to do with the fact of being Brahmin or not being Brahmin. I can't think without acknowledging that I am Brahmin.[100]

On the other hand, Model 'C' gives rise to a way of thinking and a series of themes that are close to those concerning Brahmins of the 'responsible' type. J.M. Donégani explains that there are two main lines in this model, viz., the feeling that 'I' is part of a 'we' and a collective history and the conviction that this history in the making calls for personal commitment.

Following these lines, the attitude presented here expresses a sense of belonging to the Brahmin *varna* by denouncing its long history of élitism. Positive discrimination policies are seen as a necessary development that will lead to the restoration of social justice in some measure. Being a Brahmin, individually, is intrinsically connected to the awareness of a collective history. Brahmins expressing such an attitude believe that they are the inheritors of the history of past generations.

While criticizing this long history of injustices, the Brahmins are quick to point out the tendency of members of their community to abuse power and take advantage of the existing system and its structural imbalances without any justification other than that they were exercizing their privileges. When they managed landed properties in rural areas, there was a lot of discrimination against the lower castes who were thoroughly exploited by the Brahmins. This situation still persists in India which is essentially a rural country.[101]

It's like Ambedkar saying, well, how can you speak for us . . . I think there are some points in it, in the sense that, till we sensitize ourselves, and we're able to acknowledge that there is an ascendancy because for being there for such a long time . . . and . . . there is a responsibility . . . which we have not undertaken well, whether the bureaucrats, or the people at large, maybe not me, but, those who have large plots of land and who have been landlords or . . . I don't think we . . . we have been good human beings . . . not even good, I don't feel we even feel responsible for these days . . . we haven't really had a goal beyond perpetuating all this.[102]

Another expression of this phenomenon is that Brahmins too can be associated with corruption, particularly because they hold strategic positions in the administration.

All this major, you know, Brahmin Brahmin break, in these crimes and this corruption thing, every time it's . . . it's Brahmins who are in it, and still, the community is still not willing to accept that it is . . . you know . . . it's a problem.[103]

When individual Brahmins criticize their community they also express its excessive monopoly of knowledge. Brahmins who adhere to this belief become, like the Catholics in the model proposed by J.M. Donégani, fervent enemies of egoism in society and in themselves.

Being a Brahmin means that you've started with lots of advantages and being a Brahmin from a middle-class educated household means you start with enormous advantages. So that, that thing, you know, that you can be unselfish, so when you don't have at all it's very difficult to be unselfish, when you have so much, then you feel that it's absurd not to be unselfish.[104]

This awareness of their privileged position has prompted some Tamil Brahmins to take part in the struggle to establish a more just society, out of a need to commit oneself. In the contemporary social context, Brahmins can play a significant role. The attitudes we expose now are based on the principal points mentioned in most of the interviews about society's expectations from

Brahmins. As mentioned in Chapter 1, society expects a Brahmin to be honest, polite and to observe the principles of morality. Reference values mentioned in relation to Brahmins are generally purity, truth, honesty and sincerity. A Brahmin must command respect by his very behaviour. But unlike the majority of persons interviewed, Brahmins of the 'responsible' type do not want these principles to be disregarded. Being a Brahmin means committing oneself to the creation of a better world by accepting differences.

This means opposing tendencies that have firmly established themselves in a community bent on preserving its monopoly of knowledge and power.

If we have failed as a community, if we have been . . . invited the hate of many other communities, it's because of this, that we kept too many things to ourselves, we've privatized very much and we have held that, as a position of power, to then control others. I think that's what has been a major failing. I think we have already lost our relevance, because we refused to come down from that position . . . of sharing, we are, I think, we are essentially meant to share what we have . . . and we don't do that.[105]

Like Model 'C' Catholics, Brahmins of the 'responsible' type adopt a positive and deliberate manner, which is not, however, exultant. They find themselves in a paradoxical situation for, in spite of claiming to be normal by saying, 'we are human beings like all others', they want to be seen as different. Brahmins of this type are quite willing to accept the negative traits associated with the Brahmin community for they consider themselves responsible for them.

We would never say he's Muslim that's why he's bad or he's Scheduled Caste that's why he's useless, but we would say these Brahmins are like this. Somehow it's because it's a responsibility that you feel within your own community.[106]

They feel that they are responsible for bringing about social equality and, to achieve this objective, they are prepared to give up certain privileges.

I don't think that equality has come . . . and I really, personally I feel responsible of bringing that . . . no for . . . which means giving up, which means like, which is like appropriating or stopping to appropriate and to give up, you know . . . I don't know how I will do it but that's what it means to me.[107]

Their responsible attitude is also evident in their willingness to put their public convictions into practice in their private lives. This tendency is a result of their complete integration in the Brahmin category just like J.M. Donégani's integralist model where 'faith encompasses the totality of life'. But these two contexts are different as far as some of the consequences of this integration are concerned. The Catholics coming under this model relate their 'integralism' to their willingness to live intensely through their faith all by themselves. They also tend to be active members of religious associations of a militant nature. Brahmins of the 'responsible' type, on the other hand, refuse to interact with Brahmin associations of the Tambras type. The latter are more concerned with the staunch defence of Brahmin interests instead of trying to set right the social inequalities pointed out by the Mandal Report.

Being a Brahmin, who is conscious of the moral responsibilities that are a part of his or her Brahminical tradition, is synonymous to being a good, sincere human being who lives by the principles and values he or she defends in public and practises in private. These 'responsible' Brahmins equate Brahminism with humanism.

I have a private life and I have a public life. I believe that the public is private and the private is public. . . . So you have to, it has to be free, I mean, it has to be known. There should be nothing that I'm ashamed . . . which I would do in private which I would not let the public know then . . . . But, I wouldn't clip my Brahmin identity . . . . In fact it doesn't, it doesn't affect either the compassion or the empathy which I believe is, has to be integral to human natures.[108]

Tamil Brahmins, because of their wide range of attitudes towards the present situation in their home state, constitute a classic example of 'cultural mobility' to borrow an expression coined by Milton Singer in his study of Brahmins in the industrial milieu.[109] The Brahmin category has always had a special significance in Tamil Nadu but its substance has changed considerably in recent years. Their feeling of being 'separated' taken together with their peculiar educational and professional situation and distinctive cultural traits must be considered in terms of three major changes, viz., modernization, restructuring and adaptation.

Tamil Brahmins, taken as a whole, reveal their strong identity even in ultra-modern professions like information technology. They willingly restructure their way of life, especially in terms of time set aside for ritual observances. This process of change can be attributed to the ability of the Brahmin community to adapt itself to the changed circumstances.

Adaptability has been a classic trait of the Brahmins' distinctive nature all through history.[110] As a matter of fact, adaptability has been a means of exercizing control over society or at least of maintaining their high social status. Just as Hinduism is known for its ability to assimilate external influences, Brahmins too have manifested this quality in the face of change.

In their private lives, Brahmins all over the country have had to restructure their way of life and they will continue to do so in the future. As far as their public lives are concerned, there are regional differences. In the face of government policies hostile to their interests, south Indian Brahmins, have devoted themselves to the betterment of their individual interests in terms of careers while their counterparts in the north has responded by launching a political counter-offensive at the collective level, particularly through the Hindu nationalist movement. Even if Tambras expresses its vague desire to create a Brahmin vote bank in Tamil Nadu, the question of having sufficient numbers is one of the most decisive variables.[111]

As a social, cultural and political minority, Tamil Brahmins do not have the numbers to impose a collective political viewpoint that makes sense. Brahmins as a group have never been involved in any of the numerous caste conflicts in Tamil Nadu.[112] In north India, on the other hand, the nebulous cultural identity of Brahmins among the urban middle-classes and the presence of vote banks representing upper castes, OBCs and Dalits leave the door wide open for a collective political discourse by the Brahmins, as we shall see now.

NOTES

1. M6.
2. M13.
3. M11.

4. M12.
5. M14.
6. M2.
7. M3.
8. M12.
9. 'Who opts for teaching?' *The Hindu*, 23/02/2001.
10. M16.
11. M24.
12. Interview with Dr. Shankar Narayanan, Chennai, 16/02/2001.
13. M28.
14. M1.
15. 16.
16. M1.
17. Interview with Yogendra Singh, Delhi, 16/01/2001.
18. M13.
19. C.J. Fuller, 'The Brahmins and Brahminical Values in Modern Tamil Nadu', in *Institutions and Inequalities—Essays in honour of André Béteille*, ed. R. Guha and J.P. Parry, Delhi: Oxford University Press, 1999, p. 33.
20. K.S. Chalam, 'Caste and economic reforms', *Seminar*, Delhi, no. 471, November 1998, p. 35. The group first concentrated on the manufacture of automobile parts and diversified during the 1980s into consumer durables like mopeds and washing machines. It later divided its assets among three branches the most important of which is TVS with an annual turnover of Rs. 8.7 billion in 1995-6. B. Dorin et al., eds. *Le Patronat en Inde*, Delhi: Centre de Sciences Humaines, June 2000, p. 23.
21. M. Singer, *When a great tradition modernizes—an anthropological approach to Indian civilization*, New York: Praeger Publishers, 1972, p. 299.
22. M1.
23. *Hindustan Times*, 30/07/2000.
24. Ibid., 22/01/2001.
25. Out of the 150,000 candidates who appear for the entrance examination about 2,000 to 2,500 are selected. (Interview with Dr. R. Krishna Kumar, Professor, IIT, Chennai, in Chennai, 20/02/2001.)
26. M25.
27. M22.
28. M25.
29. Interview with Dr. P. Radhakrishnan, Madras Institute of Development Studies, Chennai, 16/02/2001.
30. M.R. Barnett, 'Cultural nationalist electoral Politics in Tamil Nadu', in *Electoral Politics in the Indian States—Party systems and cleavages*, ed. M.R. Barnett et al., Studies in Electoral Politics in the Indian States, vol. 4, Delhi: Manohar, 1975, pp. 75-6.

31. M16.
32. *Reservation for Backward Classes, Mandal Commission report of the Backward Classes Commission*, Delhi: Akalank Publications, 1980, p. 279.
33. M16.
34. C.J. Fuller, 'The Brahmins and Brahminical Values in Modern Tamil Nadu', in *Institutions and Inequalities—Essays in honour of André Béteille*, ed. R. Guha and J.P. Parry, Delhi: Oxford University Press, 1999, p. 34.
35. M2.
36. M13.
37. M14.
38. M24.
39. M25.
40. Article by Omesh Saigal, 'Tamils ride the "IT" wave in US', *Weekend*, Chennai, 14/10/2000.
41. K.N. Kabra, *Political Economy of brain drain—reverse transfer of technology*, Delhi: Arnold Heinemann, 1976, pp. 19-21.
42. Interview with D.V. Venkatagiri, Regional Secretary of the Indo-American Chamber of Commerce, Chennai, 20/02/2001.
43. *Financial Express*, 08/09/2000.
44. *Statesman*, 03/10/2000.
45. See the article on Indians employed in the Silicon Valley and problems regarding visas and general financial and social conditions in *Economic Times*, 06/09/98. As regards the cultural adjustment of Indians abroad, see the study conducted in Canada by G. Kurian and R.P. Srivastava, *Overseas Indians—A Study in Adaptation*, Delhi: Vikas, 1983.
46. M20.
47. C.P. Bhambhri, *Indian Politics since Independence*, Delhi: Shipra Publications, 1999, pp. 222-6.
48. Interview with Malini Parthasarathy, Chief Editor of *The Hindu*, Chennai, 19/02/2001.
49. M6.
50. Interview with Dilip Padgaonkar, Chief Editor of *The Times of India*, Delhi, 17/01/2001.
51. M2.
52. M9.
53. M24.
54. 19.
55. 5.
56. 14.
57. M15.
58. M1.
59. Malini Parthasarathy, Chief Editor of *The Hindu*, is trying her utmost

to combat this tendency. She herself is a Brahmin born in the family which established this newspaper and could be categorized as a 'natural Brahmin'. She does not have to flaunt her caste but is implicitly and naturally steeped in the Brahmin ethos. She makes a clear distinction between this personal image of herself and her newspaper, an intellectual and serious publication which is undoubtedly the most 'Brahminical' Indian newspaper, and her opposition to Tamil neo-Brahminism associated with the ideology of the Bharatiya Janata Party and its sister organizations (Interviewed in Chennai on 19/02/2001).

60. M18.
61. M18.
62. M5.
63. M1.
64. 6.
65. M2.
66. 5.
67. M1.
68. M14.
69. M5.
70. M5.
71. M19.
72. M14.
73. M18.
74. M26.
75. M27.
76. M7.
77. M5.
78. M1.
79. C. Jaffrelot, 'La stratégie de bienfaisance des nationalistes hindous—conjurer l'aspiration égalitaire des basses castes', *Critique Internationale* (4), Paris: Presses de Sciences Po, Summer 1999, pp. 151-2.
80. C. Jaffrelot , 'La stratégie de bienfaisance des nationalistes hindous—conjurer l'aspiration égalitaire des basses castes', *Critique Internationale* (4), Paris: Presses de Sciences Po, Summer 1999, pp. 142-8. See Chapter 6 for the strategies employed by the BJP in relation to Untouchables to prevent the formation of a strong Dalit identity, which go against the *Hindutva* ideology of a single undivided Hindu community.
81. M9.
82. Interview with N. Narayanan, president of Tambras, Chennai, 17/02/2001.
83. A medical centre, which treats 300,000 patients per year without charging them any consultation fees and providing free medicines, was opened by a temple trust in an area where one of our interviewees, also

a Tambras member, lives. Every year, in the month of June, Tambras distributes books and stationery as per the list given by the school to poor children in the same area (M17).

84. M9.
85. Interview with N. Narayanan, president of Tambras, Chennai, 17/02/2001.
86. M11.
87. M10.
88. M9.
89. M12.
90. *Statesman*, 06/11/98; 10/11/98.
91. Interview with N. Narayanan, president of Tambras, Chennai, 17/02/2001.
92. *The Hindu*, 21/02/2001.
93. M17.
94. G. Guru, 'The shifting sites of reservations', *The Hindu*, 02/12/97.
95. C.J. Fuller, 'The Brahmins and Brahminical Values in Modern Tamil Nadu', in *Institutions and Inequalities—Essays in honour of André Béteille*, ed. R. Guha and J.P. Parry, Delhi: Oxford University Press, 1999, p. 3.
96. B. Arora and B. Radin, eds., *The changing role of the all-India services, an assessment and agenda for future research on federalism and the all-India services*, Delhi: CASI/UPIASI-CPR, 2000, pp. 76-9.
97. M17.
98. See his autobiography which abounds in examples of this outlook: M.K. Gandhi, *Expériences de vérité ou autobiographie*, Paris: Presses Universitaires de France, Quadrige, 1994.
99. J.M. Donégani, *La liberté de choisir—pluralisme religieux et pluralisme politique dans le catholicisme français contemporain*, Paris: Presses de la FNSP, 1993, pp. 244-59.
100. 6.
101. See the articles in the series 'Caste Off', in *The Hindu* on the deplorable social situation of Untouchables. The articles in this series refer, for example, to the practice still followed in Andhra Pradesh of having separate glasses for Dalits in tea-stalls. The article dated 27 December 1998 talks of the attempts of high caste landlords to break the unity between Dalits and Backward Classes working on their lands, on caste considerations in a conflict about the minimum salary to be paid to agricultural workers.
102. 6.
103. 6.
104. 12.
105. 12.
106. 6.

107. 6.
108. 6.
109. M. Singer, *When a great tradition modernizes—an anthropological approach to Indian civilization*, New York: Praeger Publishers, 1972, p. 365.
110. B.N. Nair, *The dynamic brahmin*, Bombay: Popular Book Depot, 1959.
111. Interview with N. Narayanan, president of Tambras, Chennai, 17/02/2001.
112. See article on caste-based organizations that serve as a support base for various political parties in Tamil Nadu in *Frontline*, 02/03/2001.

PART III

DIALOGUES ON IDENTITY AND OTHERNESS IN THE 1990s

Brahmins and the Underprivileged

In a round-table discussion on 'The Rewriting of History: Intellectual Freedom and Contemporary Politics in South Asia' during the International History Congress in Montreal in August-September 2000, the Indian historian, K.N. Panikkar, spoke of the concept of the 'outsider' or the 'other' as an enemy and an ideological cement in the Hindu revivalist movements that had taken place since the late nineteenth century.[1]

The fact that the 'other' has cultural roots different from those of the community is used to justify the latter's possible decline. Hence Muslims and foreign colonizers were represented as the 'other' in the socio-religious reform movements that formed the basis of Hindu nationalism.[2]

From the very beginning of this study, I have taken account of this strategy of using the 'other' to strengthen identity, for example, Brahmins in the armed forces who use civilians or the police and Tamil Brahmins who use non-Brahmins from the same state or north Indian Brahmins. In the 1990s, the dialogue between identity and otherness came into the limelight in north India with two major issues: the political assertion of Dalits in Uttar Pradesh and the implementation of the recommendations of the Mandal Commission.

'Dalit politics' or the assertion of the Dalits through politics was one of the most striking elements in the political scene during the 1990s. This strategy, which lumps together all the underprivileged classes for political purposes without taking account of their cultural differences, is seen as a dangerous expression of otherness by most Brahmins. The latter are held up as negative references of identity—since from the Dalit viewpoint Brahminism is an ideological base to be deconstructed—and are thus constricted in their attempts to re-establish a hierarchical social order through the nationalist Hindu movement in particular.

The implementation of the Mandal Commission's recommendations was also perceived as a violent expression of antagonism by a large number of Brahmins. It gave rise to heated controversies in student and intellectual circles voicing the discontent of the upper castes in north India. South Indian Brahmins had experienced this kind of antagonism for many years and for them the Mandal affair was only the final outcome of a long series of similar measures operating at the regional level. This development highlighted reservation policies as measures stimulating identities.

Finding themselves face to face with other identities, which had remained in the background for a long time but which have been representing a kind of negative pole for their age-old supremacy, contemporary Brahmins are now forced to reconstruct their identity. Confronted with anti-Brahmin identity processes and social schemes engineered by the Dalits who became quite vociferous in the political arena of the 1990s, the Brahmins, especially in north India, are worried by the threat to their superiority in the post-Mandal era.

CHAPTER 6

Construction of Anti-Brahmin Identities by Untouchables

Placed at the opposite ends of the religious and ritualistic hierarchy, Brahmins and Untouchables share a history of hatred and hostility on account of discriminatory practices arising from the segregation of different castes in Hindu society. Since Brahmins are perceived as the keepers of sacred knowledge and were entrusted with the supervision of social codes, the Untouchables tend to consider Brahmins as a class to be censured, avoided or changed to create a more liveable environment for themselves. The archetypal Brahmin is the 'other', central to the construction of an Untouchable identity.

This notion of an Untouchable identity is quite recent but is the result of a long process which involved rather scattered cultural approaches as compared to its radical political assertion which led to its crystallization.

Generally portrayed as negative when compared to Brahmins, the Untouchables, always a heterogeneous and unstructured group, have finally started a process of search for an identity. Rich of varied regional and cultural references, Untouchables all over India tend to centre this search around ideological and terminological debates that have created a special space favourable to the development of Ambedkar's ideology.

The search for an Untouchable identity tends to go against the closed Hindu structural model that assigns them a fixed status on the lowest rung of the social ladder. That is why this search is associated with a variety of ideological movements that make the expression of specific interests possible.

When you look at the cultural heritage of the Untouchables, you realize that it is not uniform because of the varying regional and socio-historical influences in different parts of India. But what is common to all Untouchables is their desire for a reinterpretation of Hinduism. When he explains the notion of untouchability in his study of the Chamars, an Untouchable community of Uttar Pradesh, R.S. Khare wavers between a general cultural construct and more specific references to the Chamars of Lucknow. So he takes note of the tendency of Untouchable theoreticians to found this notion of untouchability on the existing differences between Untouchables and caste Hindus.[3] And as Bishnu N. Mohapatra observes in an issue of *Seminar* entirely devoted to this topic, it is this marked separation from a world shared by others, viz., the upper castes and Brahmins in particular who constitute this otherness, that gives rise to a sense of humiliation.[4]

From this viewpoint, Hinduism is seen as a social and ideological yoke whose mechanism must be carefully analysed to be able to neutralize it. It is quite obvious that contemporary Hinduism is the fruit of a long evolution, even though some of its more striking traits are of recent origin. It is an accepted fact, as we have explained earlier, that colonial rulers and Orientalists have transformed Hinduism into a rigid series of scriptural principles to create what is known as the 'Great Hindu Tradition' and placed the Brahmin and the Untouchable at the two ends of a holistic hierarchy.

The different ideological streams in modern India have also had serious repercussions on the ways of understanding and interpreting this socio-religious ideology. The Hindu nationalist movement, for example, has based its efforts at social reform on the platform of the Great Hindu Tradition. And even though Nehru and Gandhi had different views about the ideal Indian society, they both envisaged a Hinduism built around what could be called a 'Brahmin nucleus'.[5]

The Shudra activist, Kancha Ilaiah, vehemently condemns in his writings the violence of the Brahminical model imposed on the underprivileged classes. Criticizing Brahmins in the harshest terms for having defined knowledge in their own image, he denounces all the values and practices dictated by them, especially through their educational institutions, to communities who do not define themselves as Hindus or live like them.[6]

Way back in the nineteenth century, Jyotiba Phule opposed the prevailing ideological interpretation of Hinduism and condemned it as an instrument of Brahminical domination. He launched his social reform movement in Maharashtra and was willing to support the British to put an end to Brahmin hegemony in terms of socio-economic advantages and control over social norms amounting to a veritable 'Brahmin colonialism'.[7]

In the same vein, radical *adi* (derived from the Sanskrit root meaning 'origin') movements developed during the 1920s in various parts of India such as Uttar Pradesh, Andhra Pradesh and Punjab. In their fight against discrimination born out of caste distinctions, the Untouchables involved in these movements claimed that they were the descendants of the original 'non-Aryan' Indians. They were keen on reviving the *Bhakti* cult which, they believed, was the original form of worship.[8] These radical movements took advantage of the momentum gathered by the anti-Brahmin revolts in Bombay and Madras, creating a new way as compared to more moderate trends which remained within the conceptual framework that accepted Hindu structures and limited themselves to demands such as the entry into temples. It must be noted that between Phule's time and the 1920s, there was a marked difference in the spread of the Hindu nationalist ideology. A large number of Untouchables allowed themselves to be seduced by references to illustrious persons of a low ritual status like Valmiki and Vyasa, deemed to be the respective authors of the *Ramayana* and the *Mahabharata*, and began to lay claim to a Kshatriya ancestry.[9]

This latter tendency is characteristic of the Sanskritization process theorized by M.N. Srinivas in which people of a lowly status tend to associate themselves with the higher castes and appropriate their practices and symbols in a bid to improve their own status. Eleanor Zelliot notes that the decision of two Untouchable communities to change their names from Bhangi to Balmiki and Chamar to Ravidas (after a sixteenth century saint poet) is not a sign of revolt, but only an affirmation of their pride in their identity and a reaction to the humiliation heaped on them by the upper castes.[10]

This led to the development of a radical viewpoint focused on Untouchable interests outside the social structure deformed by Brahminism and insisting on a change in nomenclature from Untouchable to Dalit. This change was a decisive phase for Brahmins as it made them aware of the resolve of the Untouchables to assert themselves, as we shall see in the next chapter.

The Untouchables struggled to break the social codes of the Hindu system and put an end to the ideological and cultural domination of the Laws of Manu which, for example, denied the lower castes access to learning.[11] This is what the activist and research scholar Kancha Ilaiah condemns when he describes his approach as a challenge to 'Brahmin historiography' which prevents the oppressed classes from asserting their culture and their consciousness.[12]

Today Untouchables want to affirm their role in history by using their own references and viewpoints. They are no longer willing to be subjugated by the upper castes and suffer their insults and ostracism, nor do they want to be subjected to studies in an outdated mould that are not at all inclined to upset the *status quo*. Viewed from this angle, the Marxist ideology could have provided an outlet to the Untouchables for expressing their frustrations, but nothing did materialize. On the other hand, the construction of a Dalit identity allowed them to express their cultural and political aspirations.

Embracing Marxism was one way of getting out of the Hindu reference system. As a matter of fact, there are two major approaches to the study of Untouchables or the underprivileged classes as a whole. Firstly, there is the caste-based approach, dealing with the repercussions of the caste system on social hierarchy and ritual pollution, as I have extensively explained earlier. Secondly, the class-based perspective, and this is where Marxism could have played a role, could define Untouchables as a body consisting of groups of peasants, workers and others employed in similar socially and economically disadvantaged spheres.[13] In the Indian context, Untouchables could well be defined as the archetypal 'proletariat'. But the struggle launched by young socialist and communist activists during the pre-Independence era had no reference base and did not recognize caste divisions. It was simply a part of the larger theoretical and ideological class struggle that eliminated traditional identities instead of reinterpreting them.[14]

Further, political movements of this kind did not lead to ideological emulation among the concerned communities. Divided by internal factions to the point of losing their revolutionary fervour, entering into alliances based on compromise, especially with the Congress, these movements gave up their aspirations of becoming mass movements to become a part of the classic parliamentary system. Finally, as Kancha Ilaiah has rightly pointed out, these movements are mostly dominated by the upper castes.[15] Even the more radical Maoist wings of these leftist movements remain, according to Rajni Kothari, 'Brahminical in their style and intellectual approach'.[16]

The Marxist approach has been a convenient ideological tool for some Brahmins in south India to combat the anti-Brahmin diatribes of the Dravidian Movement. In spite of its egalitarian ideology, a powerful force in Indian society, Marxism has been used to reinstate Brahmins in their positive historical role against rampant anti-Brahminism. The achievements of E.M.S. Namboodiripad, a Malyali Brahmin, in the 1940s and 1950s is quite characteristic of this approach. He reinterpreted the institution of caste according to the Marxist philosophy as a key to a progressive system of production. The elaborate division of work under the caste system enabled Brahmins to devote themselves to intellectual and artistic pursuits. They were thus able to take up in earnest the harmonious development of society in Kerala by supporting the patriarchal system as opposed to the matriarchal system traditionally followed by the rival Nair community. At the same time, they strove to create a cultural and political cement to set-up a democratic government and establish a strong regional unity.[17]

These Marxist-inspired movements did not really bring succour to the oppressed nor did they prepare the ground for a real social transformation. As for denomination, this tendency is visible in the choice of the name *Harijan* (God's child) used by Mahatma Gandhi and adopted in their turn by the Communists, without bothering to find out the feelings of those who were given this name. The term *Harijan* is often considered condescending and originating from the upper caste ideology. It even has a suggestion of illegitimacy for people belonging to these underprivileged communities. But more than anything else, it has no discursive power, no substance nor any value as a tool of ideological conflict unlike the term Dalit.[18]

The more militant Untouchables tried to develop references that were different from Brahmin symbolic references and create their own cultural domain. There is no doubt that many groups resorted to the reinterpretation of the Great Hindu Tradition and, despite their desire to deviate from it, they remained within the Brahmin mythical and symbolic frame of reference. The traditional songs sung by the Marathi women as they grind grain on their grinding stones are characteristic of this kind of approach. In their songs, these women identify themselves with Sita, from the *Ramayana*, and sing of her fears, her doubts and her suffering caused by her husband Ram, brother-in-law Lakshman and mother-in-law Kaikeyi. These family references become figures with a polyvalent status reflecting the tensions prevalent in their own underprivileged rural environment.[19]

But the most militant and purist movements would like to avoid this type of approach and find original references. The path of *Bhakti* in Maharashtra is quite characteristic. It has become the historical and symbolic heritage of the Untouchables since most of the medieval saint-poets were Untouchables and expressed themselves in Marathi, the language of the common people. They could thus avoid two essential Brahminical practices, viz., the use of Sanskrit and the rituals of the Great Hindu Tradition.[20] There is also a direct relationship with God with no hierarchy separating him from ordinary mortals, nor is there any hierarchy among humans, which eliminates the Brahmins as an institution. The fourteenth-century Marathi poet Chokhamela describes a reversal of social codes when a divine being diligently takes care of a young servant girl and is willing to perform even the most demeaning tasks generally performed by Untouchables. This form of expression, a blend of devotion and poetic refinement stirs up Brahmins attempt of reappropriation, like in the story of the medieval saint Namdev and the creations of his young maidservant Janabai.[21]

The Untouchables claim that they have created their own culture and they would like to project it as a distinctive and original one that is not just a counter-culture or a parallel culture stemming from the Great Hindu Tradition. If one were to look for the ancient roots of the distinctive artistic traditions of the Untouchables, one could cite the example of the Mahars of Maharashtra known for their musical talents and their active participation in *tamasha*, the popular folk theatre of this region dating back to the sixteenth century. But the Untouchable militants want to affirm their 'folklore of pride', as Eleanor Zelliot puts it, by projecting their contemporary creative energy.[22]

In the last two decades indeed a new school of militant Untouchable literature has emerged using the term Dalit as a means of revolutionary expression. Dalit, which means 'broken' or 'downtrodden', is a reference to the discriminatory practices underlying the Brahmin hierarchy. It is nevertheless totally opposed to the Dalits' past docility. The term was first used in journalistic writings in the 1930s and it gained popularity with the spread of the Untouchable movement in the 1970s to become a positive term expressing pride in the Untouchable heritage and the rejection of oppression.[23]

The Dalit category has moved away from distinctions such as 'forward' and 'backward', 'privileged' and 'underprivileged'. It does not derive its substance from relations of patronage nor from the official recognition of the 'Scheduled Castes' as a special category. It does not have the impersonal character of legal classifications nor the metaphysical, albeit passive, connotation of the Gandhian term *Harijan*. It is not a category that exists in principle but it has to be negotiated in various socio-political spaces.[24] The Dalit must be accepted as a symbol of change and revolution, driven by a humane discourse that must denounce and make public, especially through literature, the atrocities perpetrated on the Untouchables.[25]

Dalit literature was a result of this political awareness linked with the literary fervour seen among the Untouchables from the 1970s.

There was absolutely no relation between the house where I was born, the village where I grew up and literature. At home, there was the most abject poverty and the terrible blinding of ignorance (...). *I told myself it would be better to read books than to sit with the men and talk. I enjoyed reading* (...), *I read anything and everything that I could lay my hands on* (...). *I just had to see a book and I would forget everything else. I even forgot to eat and drink* (...). *I was obsessed by a deep regret for not having been able to pursue secondary or higher education. I wanted to make up for this lapse. So, I began to read like a man possessed, bewitched by reading* (...). *I always told myself that if I wanted to rid myself of my ignorance, I had to read a lot* (...). *Then I showed the lines on my hand to an expert palmist. He said, 'You will become a painter, an artist, but you must first fast on Saturdays and give alms to Brahmins'* (...). *This convinced me that saintly men were useless when it was a matter of putting an end to poverty, ignorance, suffering and inequality. I started reading again wholeheartedly (...). I became aware of the fact that I had something different to say and that it was worth the effort. Encouraged by this notion, I began to write poems, short stories and then novels (...), I love books, I worry about the fate of my fellow-beings, I try to explore the human spirit. And the words rush to my help, I want to use them to capture the world of my experiences. I have become a writer. That is the place occupied by literature in my life.*[26]

As these lines written in 1984 by Madhav Kondvilkar,[27] an award-winning writer from Maharashtra, indicate, literature became a favoured weapon of the oppressed classes to defend their rights, their interests and more over their dignity. The first stirrings of this Dalit identity constructed through the literary medium were felt with the birth of the Dalit Panther movement in Bombay in 1972. This group was set-up by the new generation of writers and poets in a context marked by tremendous changes: the rise in the level of education among the Dalits, the economic crisis in the latter half of the 1960s and the rebellious mood prevalent on the international stage embodied in the protest movements in China, Vietnam and Cambodia and above all the Black movement in the United States.[28] Directly inspired by the Black Panthers, the Dalit Panthers proclaimed in their manifesto in 1973 the need to destroy ancient writings and customs. 'We do not want a little place in the Brahmin Alley. We want the rule of the whole lane'.[29]

This spirit of revolt, which took shape in Maharashtra, soon influenced literary activities among Untouchable activists in Gujarat and in the Dravidian world. In Tamil Nadu, the bastion of anti-Brahminism, there was an attempt to look for symbolic ancestral figures and develop close-knit networks among the Untouchables.[30] The Untouchables strove to destroy one of the main pillars of Brahminical ideological supremacy by creating their own space in the literary world. The cultural aspect of Dalit identity is based on the negation of symbols and references defined by the Brahmins. But it is when they have to face the Dalits' assertiveness in the political domain that many of the Brahmins I interviewed expressed a real anxiety.

The political dimension of the Dalit identity is associated with Ambedkar's actions. The Untouchables started expressing themselves through literature only after the disillusionment caused by the political blunders of the Ambedkarite movement which seemed to have somehow lost the vigour of its master's message. However, the cultural and ideological contribution of Ambedkar's writings continues to be a major factor for understanding contemporary Dalit identity. By assessing the scope of his writings, we can also understand the principal debate among the Untouchables which is, in effect, a complex dialogue between cultural demands and political representation.

Bhimrao Ramji Ambedkar (1891-1956) is one of the legendary figures of Indian political history. Although Gandhi and Ambedkar were both keen on improving the condition of the oppressed classes, Ambedkar was known for his opposition to Gandhi in the 1930s. He subsequently gave up the policy of reformism and in 1935 adopted a radical approach by declaring that though he was born a Hindu, he would not die as one, proclaiming himself to be an ardent champion of Buddhism. His two main enemies were Brahminism because it supported the caste system and capitalism because it was based on the class system. His ideology, nurtured by his anti-Brahmin sentiments, inspired him to launch a strong political movement in defence of the Untouchables.

Ambedkar's ideology was buttressed by significant events in his public and private life, especially his political altercations with the Mahatma and his attraction to Buddhism.

Mahatma Gandhi, the revered leader on the Indian nationalist movement known for launching mass actions and for his interest in problems of the common man, was a controversial personality as regards his attitude towards the Untouchables. He could not break away from the upper-caste mindset and was therefore unable to take a radical decision in their favour in the name of preserving Hindu unity. His social ideas were actually the result of a political reinterpretation of religious considerations based on the Great Hindu Tradition and a blend of instrumentalism and faith in the original Hindu precepts, both in his public and private life. And the concept of non-violence was the most important of these reinterpreted notions.

Non-violence, which has become a household word all over the world because of the Mahatma's social and political actions, actually refers to the notion of *ahimsa* which literally means 'non-desire to do any harm'. This notion is central to the conflict between Brahmin domination and anti-Brahmin reactions such as Buddhism. The notion of *ahimsa*, which is the basic principal of the heterodox Jain and Buddhist doctrines, was initially opposed to Vedic sacrificial rites performed by Brahmins.[31] The institution of renunciation based on the ethic of non-violence was a result of this process and soon became the archetypal Brahminical function.

Gandhi who belonged to the Great Hindu Tradition was deeply inspired by the ideal of the Brahmin-renouncer. His choice of strict vegetarianism and his campaigns of passive resistance or *Satyagraha* were influenced by this tradition.[32] But more than anything else, it was through his 'political fasts' that Gandhi showed his adherence to the Great Hindu Tradition.

Going back to the ancient Brahminical practice of fasting to attain certain ends, Gandhi used it as a tool for exerting political pressure. In ancient times the Brahmins used the fast as a means to protest against the abuse of kingly powers or to settle private disputes.[33] In the latter instance known as the 'creditor's fast', Brahmins would put their life in balance to resolve difficult problems that concerned them directly or when their help was solicited.[34] Gandhi used similar processes: persuading the adversary to convert to his own views, emotional blackmail because there was a strong possibility that the fast would lead to death, self-inflicted violence to avoid open violence in a process of settling disputes.[35] Gandhi indeed borrowed this ancient practice and using it at a larger scale involving the whole Indian society, elevated the fast into a traditional method of expressing political discontent.

And Gandhi used this tool to oppose Ambedkar's views on the creation of a separate electorate for Untouchables, a major stumbling block. The 1930s witnessed a fierce struggle between these two great leaders on this sensitive topic. The Mahatma warned the British rulers against introducing separate electorates by putting his life at stake. He believed that this decision would bring to nought the attempts to maintain Hindu unity as well as the efforts of many Hindu reformers to improve the condition of the underprivileged classes.[36]

This idea, which was put forward in the Communal Award of August 1932 keeping in mind the future Constitution of India, crystallized the divergent approaches of the two leaders. Gandhi considered the fast as a means of purification intended to purge Hinduism of the misdeeds associated with untouchability and to urge the upper castes to give up the practice. But Ambedkar was convinced that the fast was directed against the Untouchables and their cause and was a form of moral blackmail because there would be violent reprisals against them if Gandhi were to die. The Poona Pact signed in September 1932 put an end to this altercation. Owing to the pressure exerted by Gandhi, the idea of a separate electorate was given up in favour of a few reserved seats. This blackmail, which can be perceived as an expression of Brahminism considering the pattern of action and the objective, viz., maintaining the cohesiveness of Hinduism to the detriment of the political rights of Untouchables, was too strong, even for Ambedkar.[37] The final decision taken by the two men set the seal on their conflict by the establishment of a *de facto* relationship between Gandhi as the representative of the upper castes and Ambedkar as the spokesman of the Untouchables.[38]

Finally, there was a clear demarcation between their respective approaches. Ambedkar insisted on using political weapons for the socio-economic advancement of the Untouchables and the establishment of social equality. Gandhi, on the other hand, continued to adopt a reformatory approach wanting to maintain the conceptual framework of the *varna* system but removing, at the same time all traces of untouchability.[39] Ambedkar was also opposed to the judicial settlement of the problem of untouchability because it seemed quite futile. He believed that it was necessary to abolish the caste system because outcastes and castes are consubstantial. Gandhi, for his part, was looking for unity in this diversity, that is to say, he did not condemn the caste system and believed that the natural law of reincarnation would set the imbalance right. So, according to him, all members of society should remain united. He also believed that they all had specific places and should continue to occupy them, thus advocating what Christophe Jaffrelot called an 'ecumenism having organicistic tones'.[40]

So, Gandhi's approach remained Brahminical for he supported the continuance of a social hierarchy for the sake of complementarity. And it is precisely this aspect of Hinduism that Ambedkar wanted to eradicate because of his opposition to

Brahmins and Brahminism. Through his writings and his social and political activism, Ambedkar tried indeed to devise a suitable approach to find a better place in Indian society for the people described as 'untouchable'. The social order built around the Hindu matrix does not propose a road to salvation for these people because it is not based on fluid social dynamics but constitutes a rather strongly stratified hierarchy where Untouchables are placed at the very bottom as per the Brahminical perception.[41]

Ambedkar was determined to fight against inequality which formed the very essence of the cultural and socio-economic structure of Brahminism. But after the Poona Pact, Ambedkar realized that this struggle could not be conducted on a small scale. The example of Christian missionaries, if we leave out the controversies relating to proselytism and their links with the colonial power, is very similar. Their intervention gave rise to a lot of criticism in Indian society and even in the ruling circles because of their education policy regarding Untouchables.[42]

Ambedkar wanted to carry out a true cultural revolution in order to eradicate the non-egalitarian attitudes deeply rooted in the Hindu mentality. He was keen on continuing Jyotiba Phule's work by criticizing the wrong-doings of the Brahmins. To pursue this end, he launched a desperate struggle against untouchability, Hinduism and the Brahmins as a caste, three facets of the non-egalitarianism that plagued Indian society. He believed that the caste system was not only unjust but also immoral. To destroy the institution of caste, identified as the source of all suffering, he wanted to destroy its foundations, i.e. the religious teachings justifying its existence in the sacred books of the Great Hindu Tradition like the Vedas and the Shastras.[43]

As a matter of fact, Ambedkar was convinced that the institution of caste was based on religious and ideological norms rather than on racial or economic factors. So it was social conflicts or the forces of civilization that had given birth to the caste system, as he understood it in his time, through religious and ideological factors. And it is precisely the succession of the three historical phases of Vedic Brahminism, the Buddhist anti-Brahmin revolution and the Brahminical counter-revolution of the *Manusmriti* which forms the matrix of the caste system. The 'Laws of Manu' represent the period when the castes were crystallized as hermetically sealed groups organized in a systematic hierarchy.[44]

Fretting under the yoke of Brahminical Hinduism, Ambedkar was driven by a feeling of frustration and revolt to express himself in the following words in his famous speech in 1935:

Because we have the misfortune of calling ourselves Hindus, we are treated thus. If we were members of another Faith, none would dare treat us so. Choose any religion which gives you equality of status and treatment. We shall repair our mistake now. I had the misfortune of being born with the stigma of an Untouchable. However, it is not my fault; I will not die a Hindu, for this is in my power.[45]

After his critical analysis of the non-egalitarian motives of Hinduism, Ambedkar felt that conversion to another religion was the only path to salvation available to Untouchables to put an end to their enslavement to Brahmins. The only path that leads to egalitarianism in Indian society is following the teachings of the Buddha, even though his message of hope was subverted in India by the Hindu counter-attack. Conversion to Buddhism theoretically opens the door to a more humane social system. This argument is still advanced by activists supporting the cause of the Untouchables even though social reality may not conform to this idealism. Kancha Ilaiah analyses the Buddha's basic ideas regarding the concepts of caste and class and shows us how Buddhism puts an end to the caste hierarchy. The Buddha, he says, did not practice any kind of caste discrimination—he did not despise the lower castes nor did he show any favouritism to his own Kshatriya community; the only discrimination he permitted was on the basis of actions and not of birth.[46] With a praise of Buddhism, Ambedkar put forward the opposition to Brahmins, the principal target of this movement, as the ideological basis of his conception of the Untouchable identity.

It may be your interest to be our masters, but how can it be ours to be your slaves?.[47]

It was with this quotation from Thucydides that Ambedkar began his famous diatribe, 'What Congress and Gandhi have done to the Untouchables' against the Congress and against Gandhi, proclaiming his conviction that it was necessary to assert the rights of the Untouchables. After denouncing Brahmin domination in the social and religious sphere, he turned his attention towards defending the interests of the Untouchables in the political domain. During his lifetime, and later in his name, the Ambedkarite vision of politics held sway for many years.

Gandhi believed that the problem of untouchability was essentially 'moral and religious' and not 'political'. That is why he was so opposed to the creation of separate electorates, which, he was sure, would not solve the problem but only affect Hindu unity, his prime concern.[48]

Ambedkar, on the other hand, held that political weapons were indispensable to defend the Untouchable cause. His political activism began in the 1920s with a group of Mahars and some upper caste sympathizers who formed the Bahishkrut Hitakarini Sabha. With the help of this group, Ambedkar organized demonstrations, lectures and direct action programmes to make the Untouchables aware of their plight and mobilize them against the social, religious and political domination of the Brahmins. For these despised people, this domination consisted of refusal of access to temples and roads in their vicinity and sources of water like wells and tanks. The temple and water were both symbols of the supremacy of Brahmins, considered the repositories of knowledge and the enemies of all kinds of pollution, and they became the main targets of the political struggle launched by Ambedkar. The agitation in 1926 for access to the water-tank in Mahad, in the Konkan region of Maharashtra, is a good example of this activism, especially since it ended with the burning of the *Manusmriti*, the ultimate symbol of Brahminism.[49]

After his confrontation with Gandhi, Ambedkar's radicalism became stronger and in 1936 he founded the Independent Labour Party (ILP), a party of workers and peasants to oppose the 'Brahmin-bourgeois' Congress. His new strategy was directed against the institution of private property and he launched attacks against landowners, most of whom belonged to the upper castes, especially Brahmins, simultaneously targeting two enemies of the Untouchable cause, Brahminism and capitalism.[50]

Although he was convinced that a political struggle was justified, Ambedkar asked himself whether the Untouchables constituted an easily distinguishable category in the Indian nation to merit a separate identity. The responses of Gandhi and Ambedkar to this crucial question represented two antithetical and incompatible approaches. Ambedkar did not want the Untouchables to be defined in negative terms in relation to Brahmins standing at the other end of the socio-religious hierarchy. Instead, he wanted their rights to be restored to them as an independent category.

The Scheduled Castes Federation set up in 1942 was asked to do the spadework for arguing and justifying these demands. Ambedkar wanted the Untouchables to be officially recognized as a minority in need of protection, especially in view of the insistent demands for such protection from the Muslim community. The Muslim demand for separate electorates gave a fresh impetus to the assertion of the Untouchable identity.[51] It was extremely important to ensure that the Constitution of independent India would protect the fundamental rights of the Scheduled Castes. Ambedkar made sure that these underprivileged classes were adequately represented in the central and state legislative bodies as well as in various administrative services. He also saw to it that they were given preference for admission to educational institutions.[52]

Ambedkar emphasized the distinctive nature of the Untouchables who, according to him, were a 'separate element' in India's national life that the Constitution was duty-bound to protect.[53] Ambedkar's spadework in this respect was responsible for the momentous decisions included in the Constitution of Independent India which came into force in 1950.

These crucial measures appear quite paradoxical when compared to the predominant ideology of that time. Nehru, who advocated a secular vision of Indian society based on his Western ideas on citizenship, considered caste an injustice and wanted to avoid any policy that used caste as a reference. Article 17 of the Indian Constitution declared that untouchability was abolished and illegal. But on the other hand, owing to Ambedkar's efforts there is a reference to Untouchables in the Constitution as it guarantees them access to public places (Article 15) and reserved seats in legislatures (Articles 330 and 332). This major paradox continues to this day and critics point out that the implementation of positive discrimination policies based on caste is detrimental to society: though intended to oppose caste-based discrimination, these policies actually reinforce identities based on caste.[54]

In addition to the movement led by Ambedkar during his

lifetime, certain principles he formulated came to be accepted as the essence of 'Ambedkarism' or the ideology of Dalit liberation as perceived by him. As we have already seen, Ambedkar devoted his whole life to the Dalit cause and put together an ideological system with social, economic, religious and political dimensions. Basing his approach on rationalism and economic radicalism, Ambedkar devoted himself primarily to a critical analysis of Hinduism. This led him to embrace Buddhism because he was convinced of the necessity of getting rid of the caste system, especially since it conferred a superior status on the Brahmins.[55]

Ambedkar's death caused a vacuum and raised numerous doubts regarding the ways and means of asserting a Dalit identity distinct from the Brahminical hierarchy. Were conversion to Buddhism and Ambedkarization the only ways of building and asserting Dalit identity? Should the struggle against inequality be pursued in the social, religious, economic or political domain? These were some of the questions that Dalit activists and Ambedkar's admirers asked themselves when he was not there any more to guide them.

The cultural struggle gathered strength in the 1970s with the rise of the Dalit Panthers and their literary and social contribution to the betterment of the Untouchables. The post-Ambedkar period was also characterized by debates on the Dalits' desire to pay tribute to their 'Mahatma' by renaming the Marathawada University in Aurangabad after him and the controversy about the publication of his works.[56] But what interests me more is his political heritage.

The Republican Party, which inherited Ambedkar's political mantle, found itself in a dilemma having to choose between an ideological position and electoral demands. Desirous of widening its base, the party tended to lay greater stress on socio-economic issues and organize campaigns in rural areas to bring succour to the poorest peasants. Still inspired by the Master's spirit, the party was particularly active in the 1960s and won a number of seats not only in Maharashtra but also in Andhra Pradesh, Punjab and above all in Uttar Pradesh. The 1962 elections witnessed an alliance between Untouchables and Muslims, a coalition of two oppressed communities against upper caste Hindus, in accordance with Ambedkar's stand. But as a result of internal factions and political takeovers by other parties like the Congress, the movement lost its representative character and its electoral and ideological strength.[57]

Ambedkar's political legacy is quite widespread today even though it did not give rise to a unified movement or a single organization that could claim to be the sole heir to the legacy of this proud champion of the oppressed. The voice of the Untouchables, though loud and rebellious in the literary sphere, was stifled and exploited and even distorted by various actors on the Indian political stage. In the following pages I will analyse this difficult relationship between Dalit identity and party politics for a better understanding of the Brahmin identity in relation to such dynamics.

Owing to the cultural domination of the Brahmins in a Hindu system founded on this supremacy, some Untouchables have become aware of the need to mobilize their community politically to put an end to upper caste hegemony in politics. The Untouchables had to come a long way before they were accepted in political parties and organizations as activists, party cadres and finally as candidates in elections in various parts of the country. This political mobilization, the visible element of an identity in full bloom, has made the Brahmins anxious. Facing this assertion of a strong 'otherness', Brahmins had to assess the political dimension of their own identity, as we shall see later.

Various parties have been trying since Independence to control the vast vote bank constituted by Untouchables, but with sporadic success. It is mainly during the last two decades that the Untouchables have acquired importance as a major force in the political domain. Through various broad-based political programmes, which try to include Untouchables as pawns on the political chess-board intertwined with movements specifically meant for the uplift of the oppressed, political mobilization in India has radically changed.

Firstly, it is important to understand how the 'Untouchable' variable is considered by the two major national parties, the Congress and the Bharatiya Janata Party (BJP), in order to understand the reasons behind the growing visibility of the Untouchable 'otherness' strengthened by politics, from the Brahmin point of view.

The Congress is traditionally presented as a party that is not concerned about class and caste differences and has an electoral base covering all social strata. But, at the same time, it has some special vote banks, especially mong the Untouchables. From being almost the only significant political party in India at the time of Independence, the Congress lost its stature, from the late 1980s to the late 1990s, in a fast-changing political scenario. The study of this decline in the Congress's political strength will enable us to understand the reasons underlying the Untouchable vote.

As the inheritor of the nationalist movement and the legacy of great men like Gandhi and Nehru, the Congress party founded its ideology on the promotion of secularism and the protection of the rights and interests of all Indian citizens, irrespective of caste and creed. The Constitution of Independent India, which came into force in 1950, reveals this approach to society and includes, as I have mentioned earlier, a series of guarantees to protect the rights of the section of people branded as 'Untouchable'.

At the time of independence, the Congress projected itself as the sole champion of the oppressed and the minorities in order to ensure the country's unity by protecting its weakest citizens. But even though the leaders and party cadres belonged to the élite classes, the party's electoral base was traditionally very extensive. It was in effect a paradoxical coalition between the two extremities of the social scale with the ruling classes aligning themselves with the lower castes, underprivileged classes and minorities. The Congress therefore attempted to devise specific policies to satisfy the needs of these different groups. Its social programme thus consisted of policies aimed at combating poverty and maintaining the Muslim Personal Law.[58]

The Congress was thus able to develop an effective electoral machinery covering the whole gamut of society to form what was called the 'Congress system'. As during the Independence movement, its leaders continued to belong to the upper castes, mainly Brahmin, with populist views and not been inclined to disturb the existing Hindu social hierarchy. The lower castes remained faithful to their 'benefactors' belonging to dominant upper castes and constituted a dependable vote bank for them. This was the 'Congress system'. During the golden age of the Congress, the lower castes were a crucial factor in terms of influence and electoral success. Efforts had to be made to obtain their votes without giving them the status of potential electoral candidates. After the long struggle for independence, the Congress finally understood the intricacies of power and the advantages of a coalition between élite groups comprising the bourgeoisie and the landed aristocracy and of working in close collaboration with business circles to maintain a 'conservative democracy' ruled by the upper castes.[59]

As mentioned earlier, many persons and movements within the Untouchable community were trying to make the Untouchables politically aware and put an end to their docile acceptance of the symbolic, cultural and political supremacy of the Brahmins. The Congress, which had inherited Gandhi's ideology about the oppressed classes, was strongly criticized by Ambedkar and his followers as well as by the Dalit Panthers. In their 1973 manifesto, the latter condemned the Congress for its inability to bring about social changes because of the continuation of the old Hindu feudal system which left the Dalits devoid of power, wealth and status for thousands of years.[60]

Since its grand old days in the 1950s the Congress has suffered many reverses. In the case of Untouchables, there is no doubt that Ambedkar's actions made a considerable impression. The Republican Party of India, which had inherited Ambedkar's mantle, was very active in Maharashtra and also in some districts of Uttar Pradesh during the 1960s. But the Congress suffered a real crisis in the late 1980s with a steep decline in its popularity after its peak in 1984. This was due to a large extent to the growing popularity of the Hindu nationalist forces, following a process of communicating vessels. The Congress itself brought communalism into politics and created a strategic space on the right side of the political chessboard. It soon found itself unable to control the growing attraction of the upper castes, especially Brahmins, for the more radical version of communalism proposed by the Bharatiya Janata Party.[61]

The dynamics of these changes can be analysed by studying the evolution of the Untouchable vote in Uttar Pradesh. As the biggest and the most populous state of India and due to the importance it gives to caste and politics, Uttar Pradesh is the ideal setting for observing this phenomenon. After the 1960s and 1970s when the Ambedkarite movement was particularly active, the Congress lost its traditional electoral base in this state. From the late 1980s, it found itself facing a stiff competition from upcoming political parties like the Bharatiya Janata Party and the Bahujan Samaj Party, the two main players responsible for the changes in the Untouchable voting pattern of which we shall discuss later. This period marked the end of the Congress's hold, as noticed during the elections of 1996 and 1998 and confirmed by those of 1999. The process of vertical integration started by the upper castes does not function as a basic system any more and marks the end of populism as the dominant scheme between the upper castes and Untouchables in the electoral process.[62]

The Untouchables were keen to assert themselves as an independent entity in the fast-changing political scene. These political changes were particularly noticeable in Uttar Pradesh, once the Congress's strongest bastion and a typical example of the success of its traditional strategies. The decline of the Congress in Uttar Pradesh started at the junction of the 1970s and 1980s.

The repercussions of the Green Revolution and the rise of peasant movements gave considerably more power to rich farmers and members of the Other Backward Classes who began to defend their specific interests as opposed to the policies practised by the Congress. As for the Untouchables, the disillusionment caused by the anti-poverty programmes alienated them from the Congress. On the other hand, the Brahmin influence in the state did not decrease, but quite the reverse. The Brahmins of Uttar Pradesh, who represent 40 per cent of the country's total Brahmin population, had considerable clout among local Congress leaders, so much so that the Brahmin representation in the Congress headquarters rose in the early 1980s, going against the general trend of growth in political influence of the Untouchables and OBCs.[63]

The 1990s witnessed the total collapse of the Congress, its decline in Uttar Pradesh being the principal symbol of this phenomenon. In terms of image, it was the end of the 'catch-all' party with a wide electoral base that won votes on a national scale unaffected by divisions of caste and class. And the rise of parties dependent on the support of specific sections of Indian society and advocating particularistic ideologies, was a total negation of the strategies practised by the Congress and disturbed the traditional voting patterns. As Mark Tully observed, 'The Congress has been nowhere since this caste politics began ten years ago, they don't have castes of their own.'[64] However, the loss of its vote banks is not the sole explanation for the Congress' decline and it would be particularly interesting to have a look at the study undertaken by Anthony Heath and Yogendra Yadav.

Their study published in the *Economic and Political Weekly* looks at the social profile of people who vote for the Congress. It refutes the general impression that the Congress is a 'catch-all' party and reveals the fluidity of the Congress vote-bank that changes before every election according to the nature of its principal rival. The study, though largely based on the results of the 1996 and 1998 elections, remarks that the same pattern has been evident since 1967. Heath and Yadav describe the Congress as a party that resorts to four main strategies. When there are several parties contesting an election, as in Uttar Pradesh in the 1990s, the Congress is a loser, especially when the other parties have a strong base among a particular caste or community. However, it is a 'catch-all' party when it has to compete with regional parties. The Congress becomes the party of the élite when it has to confront the Left, since the Untouchables opt for the latter's radical views rather than the sweeping outlook of the Congress. Finally, the Congress is the party of the underprivileged when it confronts the BJP, a party keen on defending the interests of the upper castes, and thus manages to win the Untouchable votes.[65]

We will now look at this confrontation between the Congress and the BJP and find out what the low caste Hindu vote means for the BJP. This is a subject particularly dear to Brahmins, many of whom discern their legitimate representative strength in this political trend. But the BJP strategy to win over the support of the Untouchables is somewhat confused with a noticeable difference between its official image and pronouncements, its electoral strategy and its ideological convictions.

As the predominant party of the post-Congress era, the BJP is yet to consolidate its Untouchable electorate. Torn between its electoral ambitions and a rigid Brahminical ideological framework, it has not yet been able to mobilize support among the Untouchables.

The rise of the Bharatiya Janata Party, which was largely responsible for the decline of the Congress, is the most striking political phenomenon of the late 1980s. Its rise to power was a result of a drastic change in the voting pattern due to distinct ruptures in the social fabric. The use of the Untouchable vote to establish the Untouchable identity in the face of Brahmin domination, is one of the principal manifestations of this new political situation. As Yogendra Yadav puts it, the period marks the advent of the 'India's third electoral system' when Congress ceased to be a dominant political force.[66] On the socio-historical plane, this period is associated with three main themes 'Mandal, Mandir and Market'.[67]

This period of major social, economic and political upheavals led to a readjustment and the realignment of political mobilization processes. The BJP took advantage of the situation to modify its strategy and wage a successful battle against the Congress which brought it to power at the centre. The Hindu nationalist movement, which seeks to protect the interests of the upper castes within the framework of the traditional caste hierarchy and the Great Hindu Tradition, realized that there was a dichotomy between its ideology and the electoral strategy it would be obliged to adopt to attain the status of a national party. Even as it continued to defend the cause of the Hindu élite through its Ayodhya plank in particular, the BJP had to think of ways and means to enlarge its electoral support base.[68]

When you look back at the BJP's progress during the 1990s, you see it as an attempt to expand the social, regional and political reach of the party. The BJP thus extended its sphere of influence to new areas lying beyond its strongholds in the Hindi Belt and won over the support of communities other than those belonging to the upper castes. The Untouchables too increased their share in the BJP's vote-bank at the national level during the 1990s. The BJP managed this amazing feat by forming electoral alliances with other parties in order to tap their electoral resources.[69] We must also take into account various differentiating factors like rural and urban electorates and disparities in socio-economic levels. Among the Untouchables, the sections that were more disposed to vote for the BJP were the more affluent groups in urban areas.[70] But the relationship between the political organization of the BJP and the Untouchable electorate continues to be problematic because the BJP's ideological outlook is basically opposed to the latter's real interests and remains 'Brahminical'.

The Hindu nationalist organization is quite aware of the significance of the Scheduled Caste vote and it tries to reconcile its ideological principles with the need to win over Untouchable voters. The contemporary Indian political scene, as mentioned earlier, is characterized by the reinforcement of caste solidarity which prevents the development of a comprehensive Hindu identity. The BJP, the great winner of the 'third electoral system' based on mobilization of votes on the basis of caste differences, has suffered due to the success of rival political parties whose political ideology consists of helping groups placed at the bottom of the social ladder to build their own distinctive identity. The tendency to form alliances between castes, with the idea of forming bigger blocs runs counter to these casteist programmes. The idea at the core of the Hindu nationalist ideology is to form a union bringing all castes together as a single Hindu community opposed to other religious communities.[71] The promotion of Hinduism as a militant political doctrine results in this case in negating the hierarchical caste system.[72] The BJP's political platform thus aims at bringing the Untouchables into the fold of the great Hindu family.

Many strategies have been devised to achieve this objective. The first one is to co-opt Ambedkar in order to prevent specifically Dalit movements from becoming stronger. By adopting slogans like 'You will save Hinduism if you put an end to Brahminism', the BJP has been trying to appropriate this great Untouchable leader as one of the great Hindu reformers. By including books like *Dr. Ambedkar—A True Aryan* in the library at the party's headquarters, BJP ideologues have shown that they are keen on including this eminent leader in the party's official pantheon. The author of this book has twisted Ambedkar's sayings and writings to suit the main points of the BJP's programme and show that the Untouchable cause coincides with the party's objectives. So, Ambedkar's statements disparaging the Muslims are highlighted together with respectfully critical commentaries on his stand on the caste system and Hinduism. For example, the author focuses on his observation about the cultural unity of all Hindus and his rejection of the racial theory of caste. This rejection is interpreted as a negation of the strategic and calculating attitude of Brahmins most of the time held responsible for the caste hierarchy. And even though it does not make sense when confronted with the essence of Ambedkar's beliefs, it fits in with the BJP's views and interests.[73]

At the same time, Ambedkar could be severely criticized by others in the BJP movement, like Arun Shourie who believes that he was a British agent as he helped to further the colonial divide and rule policy. Shourie does not question the validity of the Untouchable cause, also dear to Hindu nationalists, but wants to highlight Ambedkar's egocentric tendency to identify this cause with himself, an approach that is dangerous for *Hindutva* as it seeks to split the Hindu community.[74]

In order to win the allegiance of the lower castes, the Hindu nationalist group is firmly opposed to their conversion to other faiths. The Vishva Hindu Parishad, in particular, has officially declared itself against all such attempts and denounced foreign agencies for alienating these classes from the great Hindu family through monetary rewards.[75]

The BJP's strategies also include the exploitation of Dalit icons. Educational institutions are an ideal setting to carry out this task. In a blend of mythology and history, the debate between Brahminical Hinduism as an ideological base and the exploitation of Dalit idols for electoral purposes can also lead to the creation of a pan-Indian pantheon that includes figures other than those belonging to the Great Hindu Tradition. That is how, for example, Valmiki, a Dalit, can be shown teaching two orthodox Brahmin students.[76]

One of the ways of winning over these underprivileged classes at the school stage is the old but tried and tested method of Sanskritization. To forestall the demands of the lower castes, the Hindu nationalists try to instil Brahminical values in them. In schools run along the lines prescribed by the movement, the observation of Hindu rites is compulsory for young Untouchable students who must feel honoured to be admitted in the great Hindu family. But though these practices may not succeed among all Untouchable communities, this strategy serves the BJP's interests as it prevents the crystallization of a strong Untouchable political identity that would thwart its plans of uniting all Hindus.[77]

The Hindu nationalist movement is too constricted by its Brahminical ideology to be able to draw up a political scheme to mobilize the majority of Untouchables. The 'Brahmin lobby' within the BJP is always ready to denounce any transgression of this kind. So in 1999, Kalyan Singh, the then Chief Minister of Uttar Pradesh, was accused of adopting an 'anti-Brahmin style of functioning' by the Brahmin lobby in the party.[78] The party's Brahmin cadres were against the 'Dalitization' of politics in Uttar Pradesh by tilting the political balance in favour of the communities described as 'backward'.[79] Kalyan Singh, recognized as the champion of the 'backward classes', strove hard to contain the winds of opposition. During the first few months of 1999, he made numerous visits to holy places with the idea of winning the support of the *sadhus* of Ayodhya who were hostile to his politics harmful to the interests of the upper castes.[80] Though he was expelled from the party at the end of November 1999, he remained one of the major political players in the state. He claimed that his devotion to the cause of the lower castes was aimed to promote the Hindutva doctrine, which seeks to unify all Hindus irrespective of their status, and that this cause was not the monopoly of any one person.[81]

The lower caste vote in Uttar Pradesh is a very sensitive topic. A case study of the state is very useful to understand the characteristics of the Untouchable vote. Built around caste polarization, elections in this state are problematic for the BJP because it is restricted in its approach to the OBCs and Dalits, who on the other hand are mobilized by caste-based political parties fighting for their specific interests, as we shall see in the following pages.[82]

The definition of their interests on the basis of independent cultural references gives the Untouchables the will and the strength to participate fully in the political domain. The development of a party like the Bahujan Samaj Party which is totally consistent with this dynamic raises the crucial question, 'Who is a Dalit?'

The BSP's strength lies in its efforts to crystallize a strong Dalit identity by involving this section of the population in politics. However, these efforts have suffered a setback because of the need to form strategic electoral alliances.

During the 1990s, the Untouchable electorate became very vocal and this, together with the repercussions of the Mandal Commission Report, convinced the Brahmins that Indian society was undergoing a radical transformation.

As we have just seen, the Untouchable vote is one of the factors responsible for the Congress's decline and an obstacle for the BJP's strategy of Hindu unification. Although Indira Gandhi had projected herself as a protective mother figure to the Untouchables, the subsequent governments of Rajiv Gandhi and Narasimha Rao, with their economic policies aimed at the full-scale expansion of the middle-class, made the Dalits sceptical and see the government's anti-poverty programmes just as an electoral bait.[83] As far as the BJP is concerned, being fully aware of the importance of Untouchable vote to come to power, it took a lot of interest in their welfare. Consequently, out of the 179 seats it won in the 1998 Lok Sabha elections, 24 were from constituencies reserved for Untouchables. Nevertheless, it continues to be highly Brahminical in spirit and unlikely to adopt a radical attitude in favour of these people.[84]

It was only during the 1996 and 1998 elections that the Dalits asserted themselves fully in the political domain and this period represents a new phase in their organization, mobilization and political awareness. This stratum of the Indian population did make a conscious effort to assert itself as a single political bloc in spite of numerous internal rifts, particularly among the various socio-economic classes. These internal rifts had indeed severe repercussions on their identity and ultimately gave rise to divergent political attitudes hampering their efforts to form a united bloc. This made, as I have already shown, many Untouchables from the middle and higher classes to cast votes in the BJP's favour.[85]

The Bahujan Samaj Party played a major role in the unification and the consolidation of the political identity of the Untouchables. Founded in 1984 by Kanshi Ram, a Punjabi Untouchable, the BSP has its origin in a government employees' union, created in 1976. Kanshi Ram, who had closely followed the Ambedkarite movement in the 1960s, left it later to join the Congress. He subsequently took up Ambedkar's message and emphasized the need to suppress the caste system.[86] But his ideological stand has always been rather ambiguous playing second fiddle to his electoral priorities.

Kanshi Ram declares that he respects the Indian Constitution and Dr. Ambedkar, one of its principal architects, who fought to include provisions in favour of the Untouchables but he remarks that in actual fact social disparities have not only persisted but they have increased over the years. In the fields of education, health-care and safety as well as in working conditions in rural areas, the stigma of untouchability is as strong as ever. And more than social or economic justice, it is necessary to fight for political justice so that the Dalits can attain full power in accordance with the spirit of the Constitution of Independent India.[87]

Dalit empowerment is Kanshi Ram's ultimate goal and for that he is willing to agree to any compromise. The party's activities can be analysed according to successive phases. From 1985 to 1989, the BSP claimed to be a radical movement adopting strategies for socio-cultural mobilization through agitation and activism at the time of elections. Later, from 1989 to 1995, the Ambedkarite influence became evident as the party came closer to the Shudras or OBCs as they were called in official and political terminology.[88]

It was during this second period that BSP won its historical victory in Uttar Pradesh in the 1993 elections. Kanshi Ram's BSP joined hand with Mulayam Singh Yadav's pro-OBC Samajwadi Party to form a government without the participation of the Congress. But this strategic alliance did not take into account the latent animosities between the two groups. The atrocities perpetrated by the OBCs on the Untouchables increased with the conflict of socio-economic and political interests. The OBCs, who had Untouchables working for them in rural areas, were against giving them too much freedom or the space to improve their status. In response, the Untouchables made every effort to increase their political and social visibility and in an attempt to increase the political awareness of their fellow-beings, they erected numerous statues of Ambedkar. This climate of tension led to the withdrawal of the BSP from the coalition government in June 1995 after being in power for sixteen months.[89]

This strategy of forming tactical alliances increased during the third phase, after 1995, when the BSP became a really opportunistic party. It then formed alliances with the Congress, and even the BJP representing totally antagonistic interests. This last alliance brought Brahminism and anti-Brahminism together in a comprehensible electoral pact between two parties bent on furthering their interests—the BJP looking for anti-Congress regional allies and the BSP wanting to empower the Dalits at any cost—but in a rather striking ideological incoherence.[90]

Is acquiring power by any means, even at the cost of ideological compromises the ultimate goal and expression of Dalit identity? Some political observers tend to view the BSP as a political party guided solely by electoral gains. Consequently, it occasionally neglects the essential interests of the Dalits, unlike the movement led by Ambedkar which emphasized pure ideology and the betterment of the condition of these oppressed peoples. It must also be pointed out that Dalit political awareness in western UP existed long before the birth of the BSP. Ambedkar had taken note of this region and its numerous social and cultural organizations. The latter seemed to be the keystone of the cultural foundation of Dalit identity. Dissociated from the issue of political power, these cultural organizations concentrated on the social problems central to the day-to-day existence of these people.[91]

So the crucial question is 'Who is a true Dalit?'. The term 'Untouchable' has a socio-religious connotation while 'Scheduled Caste' is a legal term. Even if we were to ignore semantic differences, do they refer to the same strata of the population covered by the term Dalit? There have been many attempts to give a broader definition to the term Dalit and the possibility of covering a large number of social groups has seduced many a man devoted to the cause of the Untouchables. The term Dalit could encompass all the oppressed peoples as well as minorities in addition to the simple category consisting of the Untouchables themselves. Carried away by his passionate zeal of the 1930s as well as during the last years of his life, Ambedkar believed that this idea would help him realize his dream of creating a united anti-Brahmin and anti-Hindu front.[92]

In the same spirit, the BSP selected the term Bahujan, the majority, to denote the gathering of all the oppressed classes. This term is also commonly found in the writings of intellectuals and research scholars sympathetic to the Dalit cause, especially Kancha Ilaiah. Kanshi Ram brought under the Dalit umbrella the Scheduled Castes, Scheduled Tribes, all educationally and socially backward classes, minorities, artisans and manual workers. The one thing that all these categories have in common is exploitation by the upper castes. They constitute the majority of the population or the 'majority community' (Bahujan Samaj).[93] In his numerous books and articles, Kancha Ilaiah defends the rights of the *Dalitbahujans* or Scheduled Castes and OBCs who have long suffered discrimination at the hands of the Brahmins. His reasoning is based on the fact that these classes, of whom he is a member, do not feel that they are Hindus as they are alien to the Hindu social references such as religion, symbols, way of life and education.[94] He criticizes the *Hindutva* plan of unifying all Hindus as it tends to spawn a cultural nationalism and impose norms based on the great Brahmin tradition.[95]

This dogmatic scheme is aimed at standardizing all aspects of cultural and social life among the Hindus and also dragging in the Dalits who are, however, strangers to the Great Brahmin Tradition. Kancha Ilaiah points out the dangerous consequences of this endeavour, especially when it tries to mystify history and control state power.[96] The danger of this attempt at cultural homogenization seems all the greater when it is in a position to disseminate its views through official institutions as the embodiment of truth. Television and radio programmes sponsored by the Departments of Culture and Education in Maharashtra under the Shiv Sena-BJP coalition government abound in references to divinities of the Great Hindu Tradition and to the moral code to be followed to conform to the 'Hindu way of life'.[97] Similarly, the RSS supported by the BJP minister Murli Manohar Joshi declared its intention to control the nation's conscience through education. A series of booklets entitled *Sanskriti Gyan* containing fudged historical facts were distributed to the six thousand schools run by *Vidya Bharati*, the educational wing of the Hindu nationalist organization, to glorify the greatness of Hindu India and the activities of this organization.[98]

The Dalit revolt against this socio-political plot should have brought together all Indians who do not belong to the *Dvija* or twice-born category. But in terms of identity, the socio-political interests of the Scheduled Castes and the OBCs differ from one another, as seen in the failure of their coalition government in Uttar Pradesh after their joint victory in 1993. Throughout history, the conflicts between Scheduled Castes and OBCs were no less violent than those between Brahmins and Untouchables. Their hierarchical relationship in rural areas as well as the recent attempts of Dalits to assert themselves and their identity through the symbolic action of erecting statues of their icons has not improved the situation.[99]

The real Dalit prefers to remain faithful to his Untouchable community while revolting against Brahmin oppression, proud of his distinctive culture and keen to work for the improvement of his living conditions. This noble enterprise is complex and fraught with danger. Striving for Dalit empowerment at any cost may lead to an ideological vacuum dangerous for the cause, as seen in the actions of the BSP. Similarly, adopting a cultural policy that is too radical can lead to excessively narrow views and the creation of a 'Dalit history' based on factual aberrations as in the case of the Sangh Parivar.[100]

One of the core issue remains political representation. The definition of specific interests in various fields, ranging from culture to politics entails the promotion of these interests. This approach is central to the relationship between identity and otherness for both Brahmins and the underprivileged classes. Having witnessed the expression of interests leading to the implementation of political programmes coming directly from these classes, the Brahmins have to take a definite stand.

The failure of Congress and BJP policies targeting a wide spectrum of interests also represents the failure of the upper castes, and particularly Brahmins, to keep the lower castes in a situation similar to the one that existed when traditional hierarchies were still operational. On the other hand, the assertion of a strong Dalit identity poses a threat to Brahmin identity in the contemporary political situation where caste plays a crucial role.

The different facets of the Dalit identity are actually a mirror image of the various facets of the feeling of threat experienced by the Brahmins. The rejection of the Brahmin ideology as a system of social control at the junction of the cultural and political spheres prompts Brahmins to question their present status in modern Indian society. The desire of Dalits to bring together diverse interests to build a strong and united identity makes Brahmins question the problems peculiar to their own group as well and its coherence. The tendancy among Dalits to keep away from political programmes having too wide a scope makes Brahmins reflect on current social projects and on the strategies necessary to maintain their central position in society. We shall take up in the next chapter this complex process of social positioning operated by Brahmins, especially in the view of debates on social justice.

NOTES

1. K.K. Panikkar, 'Outsider as enemy—The politics of rewriting history in India', *Frontline*, 19/01/2001, pp. 73-8.
2. C. Jaffrelot, 'Des nationalistes en quête d'une nation: des partis nationalistes hindous au vingtième siècle', Ph.D. thesis, Paris, 1991, pp. 54-8.
3. R.S. Khare, *Untouchable as himself: ideology, identity, and pragmatism among the Lucknow Chamars*, Cambridge: Cambridge University Press, 1984, p. 29.
4. B.N. Mohapatra, 'Understanding indignities', *Seminar*, Delhi, no. 471, November 1998, p. 46.
5. T.N. Madan, 'Whither Indian Secularism?', *Modern Asian Studies*: Cambridge University Press, 1993, 27(3), pp. 675, 683-4. C. Jaffrelot, 'L'émergence des nationalismes en Inde—Perspectives théoriques', *Revue Française de Science Politique*, Paris, August 1988, pp. 572-3.
6. K. Ilaiah, *Why I am not a Hindu—a sudra critique of Hindutva philosophy, culture and political economy*, Calcutta: Samya, 1996, pp. 6-17.
7. M. Gavaskar, 'Colonialism within Colonialism: Phule's Critique of Brahmin Power', in *Dalits in Modern India—Vision and Values*, ed. S.M. Michael, Delhi: Vistaar Publications, 1999, p. 88.
8. R. Kamble, 'Dalit interpretations of society', *Seminar*, Delhi, no. 471, November 1998, p. 21.
9. G. Omvedt, *Dalit Visions: the anti-caste movement and the construction of an Indian identity*, Hyderabad: Orient Longman, Tracts for the Times (8), 1995, pp. 39-40.
10. E. Zelliot, 'The roots of Dalit consciousness', *Seminar*, Delhi, no. 471, November 1998, p. 29.
11. B.R. Joshi, *Untouchable!: voices of the Dalit liberation movement*, Delhi: Selectbook Service Syndicate, 1986, p. 83.
12. K. Ilaiah, 'In search of the roots of anti-caste stuggle: a dalitist reading of the buddhist reading', *Research-in-Progress Papers, History and Society*, Nehru Memorial Museum & Library, Third Series, no. 1, Delhi, March 1996, pp. 165-8.
13. J.C.B. Webster, 'Who is a Dalit ?' in *Dalits in Modern India—Vision and Values*, ed. S.M. Michael, Delhi: Vistaar Publications, 1999, pp. 68-9.
14. G. Omvedt, *Dalit Visions: the anti-caste movement and the con-*

struction of an Indian identity, Hyderabad: Orient Longman, Tracts for the Times (8), 1995, p. 40.

15. K. Ilaiah, *Why I am not a Hindu—a sudra critique of Hindutva philosophy, culture and political economy*, Calcutta: Samya, 1996, pp. 50-1.
16. R. Kothari, *Communalism in Indian Politics*, Delhi: Rainbow Publishers, 1998, pp. 184-5.
17. D.M. Menon, 'Being a Brahmin the Marxist way: E.M.S. Nambudiripad and the pasts of Kerala', *Research-in-Progress Papers, History and Society*, Nehru Memorial Mnsoum & Library, Third Series, Delhi, January 1998.
18. G. Guru, 'The politics of naming', *Seminar*, Delhi, no. 471, November 1998, p. 16.
19. G. Poitevin, *The Voice and the Will, Subaltern Agency: Forms and Motives*, Delhi: CSH-Manohar, 2002, pp. 46-68.
20. G. Poitevin and R. Rairkar, *Stonemill and bhakti: from the devotion of peasant women to the philosophy of swamis*, Delhi: D.K. Printworld, 1996, pp. 245-50.
21. G. Poitevin and R. Rairkar, *Stonemill and bhakti: from the devotion of peasant women to the philosophy of swamis*, Delhi: D.K. Printworld, 1996, pp. 254, 261-2.
22. E. Zelliot, *From Untouchable to Dalit: Essays on the Ambedkar Movement*, Delhi: Manohar, 1992, pp. 317-20.
23. S.M. Michael, 'Dalit Vision of a Just Society in India', in *Dalits in Modern India—Vision and Values*, ed. S.M. Michael, Delhi: Vistaar Publications, 1999, p. 99. B.R. Joshi, *Untouchable!: voices of the Dalit liberation movement*, Delhi: Selectbook Service Syndicate, 1986, p. 3.
24. G. Guru, 'The politics of naming', *Seminar*, Delhi, no. 471, November 1998, pp. 17-18.
25. B.R. Joshi, *Untouchable!: voices of the Dalit liberation movement*, Delhi: Selectbook Service Syndicate, 1986, pp. 79-81.
26. G. Poitevin, tr. and comp., *Maharashtra: paysans et intouchables de l'Inde occidentale*, Paris: Lieu Commun, 1987, pp. 29, 144-56.
27. From the French translation by Guy Poitevin.
28. G. Omvedt, *Dalit Visions: the anti-caste movement and the construction of an Indian identity*, Hyderabad: Orient Longman, Tracts for the Times (8), 1995, pp. 73-6.
29. B.R. Joshi, *Untouchable!: voices of the Dalit liberation movement*, Delhi: Selectbook Service Syndicate, 1986, p. 146.
30. M. Kannan, 'Les *dalit* tamouls en quête d'une littérature', *Bulletin de l'Ecole Française d'Extrême Orient*, Paris, 1996, vol. 83, pp. 125-53.
31. The two main trends that emerged at that time were the spread of this notion in Indian society and its adoption by the Brahmins. According to Dumont, it was a strategic assimilation by the Brahmins who were

afraid of losing their supremacy, while Hans Peter Schmidt believes that this process was a result of internal changes in the Hindu ritual theory, as we have pointed out in our first part. I am of the opinion that it was a combination of both the strategies.

32. M.K. Gandhi, *Expériences de vérité ou autobiographie*, Paris: Presses Universitaires de France, Quadrige, 1994, pp. 404-5, 435-7.
33. C. Malamoud, 'Remarques sur la dissuasion dans l'Inde ancienne', in *Violences et non-violences en Inde*, ed. D. Vidal et al., Paris: Editions de l'EHESS, Purusartha, 1994, pp. 58-9.
34. L. Renou, *L'Inde fondamentale*, Paris: Hermann, 1978, pp. 164-9.
35. E.F. Irschick, 'Gandhian non-violent protest: rituals of avoidance or rituals of confrontation?', *Economic and Political Weekly*, Mumbai, 21(29), 1986, pp. 1279, 1283.
36. H.H. Dodwell, ed., *Cambridge History of India: the Indian Empire, 1858-1919*, Delhi: S. Chand & Co., vol. 6, p. 637.
37. B.R. Ambedkar, *Babasaheb Ambedkar writings and speeches*, comp. V. Moon, Bombay: Education Department, Government of Maharashtra, 1989, vol. 5, p. 341.
38. G. Omvedt, *Dalits and the democratic revolution: Dr. Ambedkar and the Dalit movement in colonial India*, Delhi: Sage Publications, 1994, pp. 173-5.
39. E. Zelliot, *From Untouchable to Dalit: Essays on the Ambedkar Movement*, Delhi: Manohar, 1992, p. 105.
40. C. Jaffrelot, *Dr. Ambedkar, Leader intouchable et père de la Constitution indienne*, Paris: Presses de Sciences Po, 2000, pp. 105-17.
41. S.M. Michael, ed., *Dalits in Modern India—Vision and Values*, Delhi: Vistaar Publications, 1999, p. 28.
42. The Dharwad case in 1856 reveals the difficulties associated with the implementation of reforms favouring Untouchables. An Untouchable boy, who had been educated by Christian missionaries, was refused admission in a government school in Dharwad, then in Bombay Presidency and next in Karnataka. The government admitted that the applicant had 'abstract justice' on his side, but his admission to the school would lead to the automatic withdrawal of all caste Hindu students which would affect the functioning of the school and the cause of education as a whole: A. Pinto, 'Education and democracy in India: contribution of the Christian missions', Seminar on *Education and Society in India*, organized by the International Centre and the Centre de Sciences Humaines, Delhi, India International Centre, 29-31 March 2000, p. 7.
43. S.M. Michael, 'Dalit Vision of a Just Society in India', in *Dalits in Modern India—Vision and Values*, ed. S.M. Michael, Delhi: Vistaar Publications, 1999, p. 109.
44. G. Omvedt, *Dalit Visions: the anti-caste movement and the con-*

struction of an Indian identity, Hyderabad: Orient Longman, Tracts for the Times (8), 1995, pp. 49-50.

45. E. Zelliot, *From Untouchable to Dalit: Essays on the Ambedkar Movement*, Delhi: Manohar, 1992, p. 206.
46. K. Ilaiah, 'In search of the roots of anti-caste stuggle: a Dalitist reading of the Buddhist reading', *Research-in-Progress Papers, History and Society*, Nehru Memorial Museum & Library, Third Series, no. 1, Delhi, March 1996, pp. 19-24.
47. B.R. Ambedkar, *Babasaheb Ambedkar writings and speeches*, comp. V. Moon, Bombay: Education Department, Government of Maharashtra, 1991, vol. 9, flyleaf.
48. B.R. Ambedkar, *Babasaheb Ambedkar writings and speeches*, comp. V. Moon, Bombay: Education Department, Government of Maharashtra, 1989, vol. 5, p. 333.
49. B.R. Ambedkar, *Babasaheb Ambedkar writings and speeches*, comp. V. Moon, Bombay: Education Department, Government of Maharashtra, 1989, vol. 5, pp. 247-58. G. Omvedt, *Dalit Visions: the anti-caste movement and the construction of an Indian identity*, Hyderabad: Orient Longman, Tracts for the Times (8), 1995, p. 44.
50. G. Omvedt, *Dalit Visions: the anti-caste movement and the construction of an Indian identity*, Hyderabad: Orient Longman, Tracts for the Times (8), 1995, pp. 44-7.
51. C. Jaffrelot, *Dr. Ambedkar, Leader intouchable et père de la Constitution indienne*, Paris: Presses de Sciences Po, 2000, pp. 132-3.
52. B.R. Ambedkar, *Babasaheb Ambedkar writings and speeches*, comp. V. Moon, Bombay: Education Department, Government of Maharashtra, 1989, vol. 1, pp. 401-4, 422-4.
53. B.R. Ambedkar, *Babasaheb Ambedkar writings and speeches*, comp. V. Moon, Bombay: Education Department, Government of Maharashtra, 1991, vol. 9, pp. 181-98.
54. S. Bayly, *Caste, Society and Politics in India from the eighteenth to the modern age*, the New Cambridge History of India, IV(3), Cambridge: Cambridge University Press, 1999, pp. 268-78.
55. G. Omvedt, *Dalits and the democratic revolution: Dr. Ambedkar and the Dalit movement in colonial India*, Delhi: Sage Publications, 1994, pp. 223-4.
56. E. Zelliot, *From Untouchable to Dalit: Essays on the Ambedkar Movement*, Delhi: Manohar, 1992, pp. 180-1.
57. C. Jaffrelot, *Dr. Ambedkar, Leader intouchable et père de la Constitution indienne*, Paris: Presses de Sciences Po, 2000, pp. 222-7.
58. P.R. Brass, *The politics of India since Independence*, The New Cambridge History of India, Cambridge: Cambridge University Press, 1990, pp. 69, 191-2.
59. C. Jaffrelot, *La démocratie en Inde*, Paris: Fayard, 1998, pp. 163-70, 213.

60. B.R. Joshi, *Untouchable!: voices of the Dalit liberation movement*, Delhi: Selectbook Service Syndicate, 1986, p. 141.
61. Zoya Hassan, 'Congress and "consensus" II', *The Hindu*, 07/01/97.
62. Pushpendra, 'Dalit assertion through electoral politics', *Economic and Political Weekly*, Mumbai, 34(36), 1999, pp. 2612-14.
63. Z. Hasan, 'Communal Mobilization and Changing Majority in Uttar Pradesh', in *Making India Hindu*, ed. D. Ludden, Delhi: Oxford University Press, 1996, pp. 84-7.
64. *Outlook*, 27/09/99, p. 24.
65. O. Heath and Y. Yadav, 'The United Colours of Congress, social profile of Congress voters, 1996 and 1998', *Economic and Political Weekly*, Mumbai, 34 (34 and 35), 1999, pp. 2518-28.
66. Y. Yadav, 'Electoral Politics in the Time of Change—India's Third Electoral System, 1989-1999', *Economic and Political Weekly*, Mumbai, 34 (34 and 35), 1999, pp. 2394-5.
67. Mandal refers to the implementation in 1990 of reservation policies in the public sector in favour of the OBCs in accordance with the recommendations of the Mandal Commission made ten years earlier. Mandir (temple) refers to the construction of a Ram temple in Ayodhya. It is believed that during the Mogul era a mosque was built on the site of the original temple. This was the main plank of the Hindu extremist policy of the BJP from the 1980s to the 1990s. Market is a reference to the economic liberalization process launched in India in 1991.
68. S. Bayly, *Caste, Society and Politics in India from the eighteenth to the modern age*, the New Cambridge History of India, IV(3), Cambridge: Cambridge University Press, 1999, pp. 296-300.
69. O. Heath, 'Anatomy of BJP's rise to power—social, regional and political expansion in 1990s', *Economic and Political Weekly*, Mumbai, 34 (34 and 35), 1999, pp. 2513, 2516.
70. Pushpendra, 'Dalit assertion through electoral politics', *Economic and Political Weekly*, Mumbai, 34 (36), 1999, pp. 2614-15.
71. P. van der Veer, *Religious nationalism: Muslims and Hindus in India*, Delhi: Oxford University Press, 1996, pp. 52, 134-6.
72. S. Patel, 'On the discourse of communalism', in *Region, Religion, Caste, Gender and Culture in Contemporary India,* ed. T.V. Sathyamurthy, Social Change and Political Discourse in India: Structures of Power, Movements of Resistance, vol. 3, Delhi: Oxford University Press, 1996, pp. 145-79.
73. K. Elst, *Dr. Ambedkar—A True Aryan*, Delhi: Voice of India, 1993, p. 15.
74. See two articles by Arun Shourie, 'Some antidotes to passionate devotion', *The Asian Age*, 08/12/95 and 'No reservations in this game of divide and rule', *The Asian Age*, 05/01/96.

75. See the campaigns launched by the VHP in Bhopal, *The Hindu*, 13/01/97.
76. See the fieldwork done by G. and J. Chatruvedi in the schools of Agra and their paper on *The Construction of Saraswati—Formation and transformation of saffron identity in contemporary Uttar Pradesh*, for the seminar on *Education and Society in India* organized by the India International Centre and the Centre de Sciences Humaines, Delhi, 29-31 March 2000.
77. C. Jaffrelot, 'La stratégie de bienfaisance des nationalistes hindous—conjurer l'aspiration égalitaire des basses castes', *Critique Internationale* (4), Paris: Presses de Sciences Po, Summer 1999, pp. 145-51.
78. *The Hindu*, 'BJP Brahmin lobby to "take on" Kalyan Singh', 02/02/1999.
79. *The Pioneer*, 'Simmering discontent', 04/01/99.
80. *The Indian Express*, 'With rebels on his heels, Kalyan woos sadhus', 28/03/99.
81. *Frontline*, 24/12/99, pp. 36-7; *Frontline*, 07/01/2000, p. 13.
82. V.K. Rai, 'In search of a new balance—caste, region and community in Uttar Pradesh', *Economic and Political Weekly*, Mumbai, 34 (34 and 35), 1999, pp. 2405-6.
83. See Siddharth Dube's book, *Words like Freedom: The Memoirs of an Impoverished Family, 1947-1997*, Delhi: Harper Collins India, 1998. Retracing the history of an Untouchable family, the author criticizes the failure of the successive campaigns launched by the Congress to free this neglected majority from poverty.
84. See article by C.P. Bhambri, 'The Empowerment of *Dalit* Civilization', *The Hindustan Times*, 09/07/98.
85. Pushpendra, 'Dalit assertion through electoral politics', *Economic and Political Weekly*, Mumbai, 34 (36), 1999, p. 2609.
86. S. Pai, 'The BSP in Uttar Pradesh', *Seminar*, Delhi, no. 471, November 1998, p. 39.
87. K. Ram, 'Why is Bahujan Samaj Dependent in Independent India?', Delhi: Bahujan Samaj Party, 1997.
88. S. Pai, 'The BSP in Uttar Pradesh', *Seminar*, Delhi, no. 471, November 1998, p. 40.
89. C. Jaffrelot, *La démocratie en Inde*, Paris: Fayard, 1998, pp. 163-70, 222-3.
90. S. Bayly, *Caste, Society and Politics in India from the eighteenth to the modern age*, the New Cambridge History of India, IV(3), Cambridge: Cambridge University Press, 1999, p. 302. After several tactical alliances with the BJP, Kanshi Ram could still say, at a time when the two parties were estranged, that Aryans like Vajpayee and Advani, senior BJP leaders, are the real foreigners who should be

expelled from the country and not Sonia Gandhi (*Outlook*, 06/09/99, p. 54). Also see the article by Asghar Ali Engineer on the recent tendency of Indian political parties to neglect ideological principles in favour of opportunistic electoral strategies, *The Hindu*, 12/11/97.

91. J. Singh, 'Ambedkarisation and assertion of Dalit identity, socio-cultural protest in Meerut district of western Uttar Pradesh', *Economic and Political Weekly*, Mumbai, 03/10/98, pp. 2614-16.
92. G. Omvedt, *Dalit Visions: the anti-caste movement and the construction of an Indian identity*, Hyderabad: Orient Longman, Tracts for the Times (8), 1995, pp. 46, 51.
93. K. Ram, 'Why is Bahujan Samaj dependent in Independent India?', Delhi: Bahujan Samaj Party, 1997.
94. K. Ilaiah, *Why I am not a Hindu—a sudra critique of Hindutva philosophy, culture and political economy*, Calcutta: Samya, 1996.
95. K. Ilaiah, 'Cultural nationalism', *The Hindu*, 26/05/98.
96. Ilaiah refers to the BJP's electoral success in the latter half of the 1990s and to the attacks against Ambedkar, the revered symbol of a separate Dalit identity, particularly in the writings of Arun Shourie. See 'Attacks on Ambedkar', *The Hindu*, 30/08/97 and 'The meaning of the 1998 elections', *The Hindu*, 17/03/98.
97. Gopal Guru, 'End of the Hindutva Ideology?', *The Hindu*, 03/02/98.
98. Anitya Katyal, 'RSS propagating Hindutva through textbooks', *The Times of India*, 25/10/98.
99. Krishna Ananth, 'Isolation forces Dalit consolidation', *The Hindu*, 14/11/97.
100. Gopal Guru, 'Bahujan politics in UP', *The Hindu*, 11/11/97; Akshaya Mukul, 'I, me, myself: the Dalit writes his story', *The Hindustan Times*, 04/04/99.

CHAPTER 7

Brahmins and Social Justice: Who are the Underprivileged?

The 1990s, apart from being the decade of Dalit politics, also witnessed to stormy debates on social justice following the adoption of reservation policies in favour of the underprivileged classes. There was nothing new about these policies in south India where the anti-Brahmin and Dravidian movements had started in the first quarter of the last century. But when the Mandal Commission, appointed in the late 1970s, got its report finally implemented in 1990, the phenomenon met with an unprecedented intensity.

The anti-Brahmin movement in south India gave rise to widespread intellectual debates in the artistic, legal and political spheres. This phase marked the beginning of legal discussions on the identification of disadvantaged groups needing protection and the definition of criteria for their selection. This led to the official recognition of Scheduled Castes and Scheduled Tribes. The Constitution of Independent India, under the influence of the Untouchable leader, Dr Ambedkar, reflects this urge to fight caste discrimination. It has specifically designated this category of Scheduled Castes and Tribes for preferential treatment. The Dalit movement emerged from these sections of the Indian population with the aim of building a strong political identity that became particularly visible in the political scenario in Uttar Pradesh in the 1990s.

However, the Indian Constitution refers very vaguely to other underprivileged classes belonging to the Shudra category who are placed higher than the Untouchables in the caste hierarchy. The Mandal Commission was thus appointed to go into the condition of these disadvantaged classes since there were no policies at the centre until then for the betterment of their condition. So, in addition to the 22.5 per cent seats reserved for the Scheduled Castes and Tribes in government jobs, the Mandal Commission Report recommended the reservation of another 27 per cent seats for the intermediate castes, or 'Other Backward Castes' (OBCs). This momentous event in the Indian socio-political scene assumed the proportions of a scandal and triggered a stormy debate between intellectuals and politicians followed with the utmost interest by all Indians.

So, north India, in the 1990s witnessed the socio-political rise of the lower castes as a result of the positive discrimination policies of the post-Mandal era and the spread of the Dalit movement. Putting forward issues of caste and social justice, this political context gave rise to very specific reactions among the Brahmins.

The decision to implement the recommendations of the Mandal Commission was given unprecedented publicity by the media and produced a backlash that was much stronger than expected in the socio-political arena. There was a spate of ideological debates on the concept of social justice as well as on the issue of using caste in politics.

The concept of social justice is central to any democratic society. The French revolutionary slogan 'Liberty, Equality, Fraternity' is a typical example of the philosophical principles associated with social justice. The concept remains quite vague as it is based on such grandiose principles whose interpretation allows a wide margin of manoeuvre. In the Indian context, we will assess the general significance of this concept—its theoretical substance as well as its use in politics.

The debate on social justice in India is based on the principles defined in the Indian Constitution that have given rise to numerous discussions and interpretations, especially in the context of the Mandal affair.

In its Preamble, the Indian Constitution declares that the principle of justice in its social, economic and political dimensions should be defended, before using the universal trio of liberty, equality and fraternity. These three great principles are then discussed in detail, especially in the third part of the Constitution dealing with fundamental rights guaranteeing among other rights, the right to freedom and especially the freedom to profess the religion of one's choice, the right to equality, the right against oppression as well as cultural and educational rights.

Going beyond these general categories, a detailed analysis of questions related to social justice has given rise to a series of debates of a fundamental nature on legal and sociological issues of concern to Indian society. In his numerous writings on inequalities in India, Professor Amartya Sen, winner of the Nobel Prize for Economics, asks some crucial questions: why do we look for equality? What equality are we talking about? As a matter of fact, whenever the issue of equality is raised, it is defined with reference to a particular space and in relation to social, economic and political spheres. Absolute equality is no more than an idealistic concept. Stressing on a particular type of equality such as equality of opportunity, equality of treatment or equality of results inevitably implies inequality in another space.[1] This paradox is central to the pursuit of social justice in India.

The five articles of the Indian Constitution referring to the right to equality define the different ways of approaching the concept of equality. Article 14 guarantees equality before the law. Article 15 forbids any form of discrimination on the basis of religion, race, caste, sex or place of birth. Article 16 takes into account the equality of opportunity in government jobs. Article 17 abolishes untouchability while Article 18 abolishes all titles with the exception of military or academic honours.

But the authors of the Constitution realized that given the essentially hierarchical context of Indian society, these fundamental rights should be accompanied by directive principles on state policy to fully ensure individual dignity. In the Indian context, the equality of opportunity is a fine principle, but it has no real value because there is no equality of status.[2] This issue is central to the arguments relating to the recommendations of the Mandal Commission.

Equality before the law, as proclaimed in Article 14, is one of the most precious democratic rights of an Indian citizen. But equality of opportunity in the educational and professional fields is an utopian concept given the ancient and deep-rooted disparities in Indian society. Simply proclaiming the rights to freedom and to equality does not automatically lead to an equitable society. The Mandal Commission was entrusted with the task of finding ways and means to ensure social equality in order to protect the rights of the underprivileged classes other than the Untouchables known as 'Other Backward Classes'

(OBCs). As a matter of fact, treating persons of unequal status on an equal footing in the name of equality amounts to perpetuating inequality. To ensure real social justice, there should be positive discrimination policies for the benefit of the underprivileged sections of society.

Articles 15 and 16, mentioned above, and Article 29, which protects the interests of minorities, give the impression that there is equality of opportunity in the fields of education and employment. But Clause 4 of Article 16, read with Clause 4 of Article 15, makes special provisions for the advancement of all underprivileged classes in social and educational matters.[3]

This antithesis between the right to equality and the urge to assist the most destitute forms the core of the debate. The contradiction arises from the conflict between individual and social interests. Articles 15(4) and 16(4) define the principle of the right to social advancement embodied in the recommendations of the Mandal Commission, but they violate the general principle of equality that every individual has the right to claim. There is nothing unusual about this conflict of principles and the problem was raised as far back as in 1951, during the debate on the first amendment to the Constitution.[4]

By asking for a reservation of 27 per cent in educational institutions and government jobs in favour of OBCs, the Mandal Commission emphasizes the importance of the principle of social advancement in relation to individual claims because of the essentially hierarchical nature of Indian society. Despite the strength of the non-Brahmin movement in south India, born as a result of the Brahmin monopoly in education and government jobs, the central government took no action in this respect.

The over-representation of Brahmins among the professional élite was quite evident at that time. In his study of the urban élite focused on government officials, industrialists and university professors, conducted in the latter half of the 1960s, Suren Navlakha points out that Brahmins alone represented almost 50 per cent of the Hindu members of these privileged bodies.[5] The much coveted Indian Administrative Service is one of the Brahmin citadels where 38 per cent of the posts were held by Brahmins against 2 per cent by OBCs in the late 1970s.[6]

The implementation by the central government of reservation policies favouring OBCs, in accordance with the recommendations of the Mandal Commission, could be considered a triumph of positive discrimination first introduced in south India following protests by the non-Brahmin and Dravidian movements. This decision, an important milestone in terms of identity for contemporary Brahmins, is considered by many south Indian Brahmins I interviewed as the first really hostile measure against north Indian Brahmins.

The debates on social justice are not new in India, as evidenced by the first amendment to the Constitution. But the Mandal Commission Report attracted a lot of attention from the media that led to the politicization of the issue. Social justice, apart from being a philosophical concept having legal and social consequences, is an important strategic tool in the political arena in India today.

The implementation of the recommendations of the Mandal Commission Report came in for severe criticism on various counts, especially on the protection of the right to equality, but also because of the accompanying circumstances. Issues related to the OBC category and the social dynamics of 'Mandalization' were raised in the name of social justice.

During the 1977 elections, the problem of the underprivileged classes was an important point in the political agenda of the Janata Party, a coalition of anti-Congress parties that came to power after the withdrawal of the state of emergency declared by Indira Gandhi. Prime Minister Morarji Desai gave top priority to this question and in February 1978 a commission was appointed under the chairmanship of B.P. Mandal. But with return to power of the Congress, the Commission's report submitted in 1980 was put in cold storage and revived only when another anti-Congress coalition, the National Front, was voted to power. The Janata Dal, an offspring of the Janata Party, was the main constituent of the National Front. Prime Minister V.P. Singh was certainly not prompted by ideological considerations. He used the Mandal Commission Report purely as a short-term political weapon to oppose the growing clout of Devi Lal's peasant movement which was gaining popularity among the OBCs in north India.[7]

From then on, the OBC category became a major electoral issue. This phenomenon was undoubtedly the result of the growing political awareness among these underprivileged classes who had lived as a silent majority for a long time. Although no clear social policy was formulated in favour of the backward classes, the appointment of the first Backward Classes Commission and the fact that their common interests were being discussed and could be defended by the introduction of reservation policies made the political leaders of these communities take greater interest in the subject.[8]

Further, the development of peasant movements led to a more precise definition of their common interests that formed the basis of their nascent political identity. As a result of agrarian reforms and the Green Revolution, an intermediate class of peasants became quite affluent and this brought about a change in their socio-economic condition and also in their strategy. They gave up their demand for the redistribution of land and asked the government for measures to lower production costs and raise the price of their produce.[9]

As observed during the census operations, the issue of quotas stimulated the formation of a separate identity and a change in their position in the social hierarchy. In the early stages of their economic growth, these rural classes tended to distinguish themselves clearly from the Untouchables during events like marriages and other social interaction involving pollution. Family or community reputations based on the ownership of landed property played an important role in this process. These communities also started laying claim to a Kshatriya ancestry although the general trend followed the logic of 'Mandalization'.[10]

In the newly defined context, moving up the social scale through Sanskritization was less advantageous than following the path of Mandalization, i.e. claiming a 'backward' status to gain access to reservations recommended by the Mandal Commission. The case of Jats is quite characteristic of this change. Excluded from the OBC category and opposed to the dynamics of Mandalization, the Jats built the identity of their community on the basis of their Kshatriya ancestry, in order to gain easy access to the army, within the ideological framework of the Arya Samaj movement.[11] But after the implementation of the Mandal Commission Report, the issue of access to quotas became important in many different ways.

Today, it serves as a reference point for demands in power structures. It also plays a leading role in electoral dynamics. The community's leaders, who are fully aware of these interests, now tend to negotiate favours in exchange for Jat votes. They have thus succeeded in getting the Jats included in the list of 'backward' classes, not so much to reap the benefit of reservations but to ensure the social and political development of their people.[12] But despite these political moves, not only the Jats but similar other communities continue to claim an affiliation to the symbolic Kshatriya heritage in their private lives.[13]

The OBC category has become a prized vote-bank and hence a major political category in contemporary Indian society. It is an important turning point in the socio-political history of independent India. As I have already pointed out in relation to the rise of the Dalit movement, the political assertion of classes having a low social status signifies the end of the populist system practised by the Congress based on the support of local élites. And this has led to the birth of a real 'OBC front'.

As a proof of this development, we can cite the change in the sociological profile of elected leaders in the northern Hindi belt. From the 1970s onwards, the share of OBCs rose substantially, particularly when anti-Congress coalitions came to power in 1977 and 1989. But it was only in the 1990s that the OBC caste front established itself firmly without any likelihood of a reversal, despite regional disparities.[14]

The issue of reservations, bolstered by the implementation of the recommendations of the Mandal Commission, which was a key factor in the quest for social justice, has now become a central reference for identity and a major political weapon in Indian society. This process denotes one of the principal trends in the contemporary political scenario, viz., the use of caste as a means of political mobilization and for the fulfilment of communal demands. But the debate on the consequences of this trend continues, especially in view of the condition of the lower classes.

As explained in the Introduction, the institution of caste has undergone significant changes during the evolution of Indian society. Caste, once the basic unit of the socio-religious hierarchical system, has now become an essential element of political discourses and practices. As a result of the Mandal affair, this trend is visible in the crystallization of the identities of various castes around political issues. With the introduction of numerous schemes to provide assistance to underprivileged classes, there has been a marked increase in questions and opinions regarding the exploitation of caste during debates on rights, justice and merit. I will successively take up the unfavourable and favourable opinions about this phenomenon.

The institution of caste is used most frequently to analyse social phenomena in India. This tendency is especially noticeable in the works of Orientalists who adopt an essentialist approach giving prominence to the hierarchical structures of the *varna* system in accordance with the sacred books of the Great Hindu Tradition. The social system was based on rules of purity and pollution controlling all social activity. In this context, caste was a symbol of the essentially non-egalitarian nature of Indian society.

The emphasis on the political dimension of caste reopened the debate on a different level. In the Indian political scene there are innumerable references to caste through the mobilization of communal networks and vote banks. The use of caste is also central to the ideology of positive discrimination. From this viewpoint, there was a lot of protest against the predominance of caste in political debates and practices.

The decline of the Congress and the aggravation of social rifts for the purpose of political mobilization during the 1990s placed the caste factor at the centre of electoral strategies. Uttar Pradesh is a typical example of this new 'logic of fragmentation'.[15] The present phase of caste-based political activity is interpreted by some analysts as a negation of the forces of modernism and secularism in society and the political system. Caste-based reservation policies in favour of underprivileged classes have only served to strengthen the institution of caste and its inherent inequalities. A political system based on caste affiliations cannot but lead to the crystallization of caste identities and, even if there is a certain amount of reconfiguration, to the continuation of social differences that these policies are meant to eradicate. Those who deprecate the use of caste in politics also point out that political awareness is not synonymous with an improvement in living conditions.[16]

The well-known sociologist, André Béteille, has been against such reservations. He has compared the situation in India and in the United States with regard to positive discrimination policies. While the United States formulates programmes keeping in mind efficiency and public policy, the Indian approach is based on the defence of rights and the pursuit of justice. André Béteille criticizes this insistence on rights because it leads to radical and clear-cut positions based on narrow identities. Further, the provision of reservations in government jobs does not have a very extensive reach in an essentially rural country like India. The quest for equality in the name of distributive justice, though it does not directly imply socio-economic equality, can harm the functioning of the state machinery due to lack of competence and negation of individual merit.[17] The Indian and American examples also differ from each other because of the difference in social conditions in the two countries. In the United States, there are individual problems concerning race while in India there are communal problems related to caste. Reservation policies applicable to groups have been adopted in India but they are treated with scorn by the Americans because they do not conform to their philosophy of 'self-made men'.[18]

But even if conditions in India were considered favourable for this type of system, many people voiced opinions against this trend after the recommendations of the Mandal Commission were implemented. The well-researched article on this subject by N.B. Dirks recounts the intellectual debates in several newspapers with a profusion of anti-Mandal diatribes. Apart from André Béteille and Veena Das who saw in this reservation policy a return to the colonial strategy of 'divide and rule', other scholars like M.N. Srinivas, A.M. Shah and B.S. Baviskar pointed out that they would widen social rifts.[19]

The last argument against caste as a tool in policies providing assistance to the underprivileged has been that class inequalities within the different communities were not taken into account.[20]

But in this stormy social debate, the use of caste in political activities in the country has also been appreciated by some and presented as a force that can help to improve the lives of the poorest of the poor. The political scientist Rajni Kothari is among the most ardent advocates of the politicization of caste. Long before the implementation of the Mandal Commission Report, Rajni Kothari had developed an argument based on the very concept of the politicization of caste. In his well-known book *Caste in Indian Politics*, first published in 1970, he has defined the positions that he was to take later in the debates of the 1990s.

He believes there is no sense in complaining about casteism in Indian politics. Politics is essentially a competitive game. Its object is to win power to achieve certain goals by identifying and manipulating incipient and existing allegiances in order to mobilize and consolidate one's position. From this perspective, the basic element is organizing and gathering support. It therefore follows that when the caste structure provides an organizational network covering a large part of the population, politics must try and make the most of the available structure. This so-called casteism in politics, according to Kothari, is no more nor less than the politicization of caste.[21]

This point of view is shared by many other intellectuals. Asghar Ali Engineer, a specialist in Indian Islam, explains that caste conflicts are a part of the democratic system involving a confrontation of identities, be they religious, regional or related to caste.[22] Similarly, Harold A. Gould, in his study of the relations between caste and politics points out, as soon as the introduction, that conflicts and adjustments between particular interest groups are not the result of partial modernization or its failure but a logical process that is part of the formation of a modern state. Especially in India, particularities of caste, religion and region are functional and entirely part of the contemporary social dynamic.[23]

Seen from this angle, caste may change from an instrument of oppression into a weapon used in the struggle against oppression. The BSP's strategy, explained in the previous chapter, is based on this viewpoint. The BSP aims at grabbing state power because it represents the key position in the existing non-egalitarian system. It believes in total revolution through the electoral process and it wants to succeed by mobilizing the Dalits.[24]

In the process of the politicization of caste, *jatis* having common interests try to unite and form larger groups for purposes of political mobilization as in the case of the Dalit movement or the OBC front. This political use of caste is then a means of destroying the traditional hierarchical relations of the *varna* system.[25]

Rajni Kothari has used the same approach to explain his views on the changes brought about by the implementation of the Mandal Commission Report. In 1990 itself, he advocated the use of caste as a tool of social justice in a violent controversy with sociologists whose approach has been explained above. He believes that caste has the potential to carry the social dynamic to both the extremities of the absolute hierarchy and the challenge of it. He bases his argument on the failure of the attempts after Independence to do away with the caste system. It is actually wrong, he says, to repose one's trust in an automatic diminution of communalism and casteism with an increase in secularism and egalitarianism. Movements based on caste mobilization can work for the spread of secularism and democracy by promoting the concept of pluralism.[26]

However, Rajni Kothari does not justify any particular movement but only defends the legitimacy and the usefulness of this dynamic. We are still far from reaching an ideal situation, but by adopting a vigilant approach, caste can be used as an effective instrument for bringing about important social changes. By giving due importance to ideological, ethnic and socio-economic factors that are also a part of the caste system, identity and dignity can be combined to attain true social justice.[27]

Putting on blinkers and refusing to recognize the significance of the caste factor is not a viable solution, given the persistence of the institution of caste and its ability to adapt itself to the prevailing circumstances. Debates on the reintroduction of caste criteria in the census data are a part of the same problem. The opponents of this idea brandish caste as an instrument of backwardness not to be mentioned under any circumstances. But it seems more realistic to consider the usefulness of this information that can be collected without any extra effort to launch a real struggle against inequality.[28]

In this interminable debate on social justice, the Brahmins adopt various positions, particularly with reference to the Mandal affair. The politicization of caste is a process that brings to light the way developing identities operate in the political sphere. The discourses of the Brahmins on social justice that I am going to analyse now actually highlight clearly the strong political dimension of caste.

The majority of interviewees do not fail to mention the implementation of the recommendations of the Mandal Commission, which constituted a significant landmark in the political developments in the 1990s. Along with the assertion of Dalit identity, the Mandal affair became the most recent and also the most significant point raised by Brahmins in arguments on their contemporary identity. We will look first at responses coming from Brahmins to policies favouring an improvement of the status of OBCs, before analysing discourses on the issue of fragmentation in the context of the assertion of Dalit and OBC identities.

Brahmin reactions in terms of identity to the political situation in north India in the 1990s correspond in general to the attitude of the closed élitist type of Brahmin described in Chapter 1. It is true that we remarked on the openness of some Brahmins, for example in the framework of the responsible type, who were from north India, but what struck me most about north Indian Brahmins was their feeling of threat, which has forced them to adopt a control mechanism to maintain the cohesion of their threatened identity. Distressed by the Mandalization of Indian society, Brahmins expressed their anxiety about a wide variety of issues ranging from the reassertion of their superiority to the low socio-economic status of some members of their community.

Brahmins, who value merit and other Brahminical qualities, tend to avoid any explicit reference to the feeling of being threatened, even though they covertly express their fear when they talk about their identity.

We are dealing here with Brahmins who are against positive discrimination policies and see them as a temporary phenomenon arising from prevailing political circumstances but not likely to affect their élite status based on their unique qualities. They have in effect developed an élitist view of politics.

You know, in Congress regime, Brahmins were in a dominant position and as long as the Brahmin element was dominant in any government, (...) some values were maintained in Indian politics.

This kind of attitude tends to propagate the idea that Brahmins are real experts in politics. In accordance with a personalized category, they insist that for generations they have been the keepers of the values that society needs to cultivate and advisers to kings and rulers. The logical conclusion is that their political role has a strong historical legitimacy.

If you see during the independence movement, most of those who were in the foreground were the Brahmins. One reason they were . . . Brahmins, if you notice . . . were not a majority part of the government service, they were also not the rulers. . . . So, they had really nothing to lose from the British government, and they were the only ones who could come out very openly, and since they had the intellectual background, they knew how to counter-argue and how to fight it all. So, by and large, most of those who were into the independence movement were the Brahmins. So, when it took over, when the independence came in, all those who were there, they were obviously to come into power.[29]

This type believes that since Brahmins have participated actively in public life for a long time, they are more inclined to look after general interests and are aware of what is beneficial to the general public. They are supposed to be a part of the 'enlightened élite' with a strong civic conscience and concerned about the common good. This is clearly akin to the social conscience mentioned by Tamil Brahmins quoted in Chapter 5.

As I said, India is a country of many castes as you make a bouquet. So, in a bouquet there are Brahmins and other castes, but above all, we are Indians. This is how we exhibit unity in diversity, and this thinking of mine is because I am a Brahmin.[30]

Brahmins who have developed this type of attitude are not carried away by egoistic views, they do not try to promote the interests of their own community. Unlike other social groups, they are not in a position where they need to prove something to society. This is particularly true of upper middle-class Brahmins whose attitude is based on an exaggerated awareness of the fact that they fully belong to the élite and are placed at the top of both the economic and the socio-religious hierarchies. So these Brahmins do not have to stoop to protect the narrow interests of their community like others following casteist movements.

This type of attitude is similar to the one expressed by Tamil Brahmins, who are members of Tambras, when they project Brahmins as being deeply involved in social service for the advancement of society as a whole.

When a Scheduled Caste, Scheduled Tribe comes into politics, or bureaucracy, he's over-obsessed with the feelings that he and his kinsmen have been deprived, have been kept away from certain things. So, his zeal for putting that right takes precedence over his general doing the right and doing the wrong. And then he tends to do wrong things.[31]

Brahmins expressing such opinions generally project themselves as moralizers and tend to highlight the incomparable qualities of Brahmins.

The Brahmin brain (...), the excellence and being at the top, that can not be diminished by laws, or constitutional amendments.

According to this type, regardless of the socio-political context, Brahmins remain at the top because of their superior qualities. Having been educated for innumerable generations and armed with solid professional qualifications, they have no reason to feel threatened by periodic reservation policies. On the contrary, the underprivileged classes need to be protected because they have been deprived in the socio-economic and educational spheres. But the government's decision to give a more equitable representation to these classes in the educational system and in government jobs does not always take into account the realities of the situation.

You can never build up a whole society overnight by doing reservations. (...) Most of the professional work will still be in the hands of the Brahmins (...). By reservation, the UP government was able to give admissions to the Roorkee University to a child with 0 per cent marks, just because the Chief Minister at that time said no there are seats that all those OBC who have applied must seat there. But then, when he went to the university, he would not just understand.[32]

Brahmins are fully aware of the paradoxical situation caused by the blind application of reservation policies, as I mentioned earlier in relation to André Béteille's analysis. These policies are meant to create a more harmonious society, but there ought to be compatibility between social justice and institutional functioning. Any society, even if it is to be founded on the ideology of social justice, must take individual capabilities into account and give due importance to merit.

Brahmins following this approach feel that they structurally belong to the élite. They have a natural intellectual superiority nurtured over several generations and it has now become a part of their genetic makeup.

They are born Brahmins, which possibly gives them a slight genetic advantage, slight because their forefathers got classified as Brahmins because they had a certain inherent intellectual ability which has filtered down.[33]

I do believe the discipline, the hard work of the Brahmins is also an explanation of their being at the top, it is not luck, it is not manipulativeness.[34]

They have many intrinsic qualities that justify and will continue to justify their dominant position. Reservation policies are confined to the political sphere and cannot raise any doubts about the natural talents of Brahmins because 'only persons with talent will survive'.[35] In fact, it is their intellectual superiority that justifies the absence on any specific policies in their favour. This is a reversal of the arguments forming the basis of positive discrimination policies in favour of underprivileged classes.

I'm still proud of being a Brahmin, because I am there, out of my own merit. I have not been privileged because I was born in a particular caste.[36]

This notion of merit is central to debates on reservation policies. In the late 1960s, Ghurye, the well-known Brahmin sociologist from Maharashtra, declared that he was totally opposed to such policies in theory because they go against the principles of social justice. As a matter of fact, such actions tend to penalize people just because they belong to a particular caste. This argument is a reversal of the argument against the Brahmins who treat the caste hierarchy as an instrument of domination.[37] Caste can indeed either be a source of oppression or of social advancement.

The notion of merit was also considered during the discussions held by the Mandal Commission, as it is one of the major arguments against positive discrimination policies. In response to this criticism, those who drafted the Commission's report cited the fictitious but realistic example of two children belonging to very different social backgrounds appearing for the same examination. They finally came to the conclusion that the merit touted by the privileged classes opposed to reservation is an 'amalgam of privileges acquired by birth and those related to the environment'. Talking of equality among unequal persons will only perpetuate inequality.[38]

When the report was implemented, a violent backlash happened. There were numerous arguments and demonstrations among intellectuals and students bringing into the open the dissatisfaction of the upper castes. The latter were against the report because it would limit their access to government jobs. They also rejected it because it implied a drastic change in the established social order. The new social scenario focused on the formation of a new aggressive class that questioned the socio-economic status of the Brahmin *varna*.

The most violent reaction to the implementation of the Mandal Commission Report was undoubtedly the decision of young Brahmins to immolate themselves to express their total opposition. Rajeev Goswami, the only son of a Punjabi Brahmin family started this trend. A highly politicized young man, who was disappointed by the failure of the nine-day hunger strike he had undertaken with his friends, he decided to stage a suicide attempt to attract publicity. But due to undue haste and the confusion around him, something went wrong with the stage-managed immolation and Rajiv Goswami suffered severe burns.[39] This single act of despair triggered a string of suicides by students all over the country, especially among Brahmins and upper castes. At the end of October 1990, there were hundred and fifty-nine attempted suicides by students of which sixty-three ended in death.[40]

The abrupt change in the social situation brought about by the implementation of the Mandal Commission report explains the change in Brahmin reactions. As M.S.A. Rao observed in 1987 in his analysis of backward class movements before the Mandal affair, what distinguished upper class social movements from those of the lower classes was the presence of an element of protest in the latter because of their underprivileged status.[41]

But, according to many Brahmins, the implementation of the Mandal Commission Report changed the situation completely by reversing the existing social hierarchy. The socio-religious hierarchy of the caste system that guaranteed Brahmin superiority was often despised but rarely questioned. Added to this feeling of superiority was a clear conscience based on by the conviction that it was a self-regulated system that took care by itself of the underprivileged. Indologists like Louis Dumont supported this idea since they believed that the caste system was essentially a holistic expression rather than an institutionalization of inequality.[42]

It is therefore necessary to question the intensity of Brahmin reactions to reservation policies in favour of OBCs, especially the difference in their attitude to similar reservation policies in favour of the Untouchables. Policies formulated to benefit the latter did not provoke such strong reactions in terms of identity. It is important to remember that the struggle for improving the conditions of the Scheduled Castes and Tribes was a part of the nationalist movement and that this improvement is visible only now after several generations.[43] The mixture of various factors like the latent guilt of many upper castes, reinforced by Gandhi's support to the cause and the evident identification of these people as historically oppressed made policies in their favour appear 'politically correct'.

Many Brahmins feel however that the OBCs are the ones truly responsible for the oppression and persecution of Untouchables.

Actually, if you find in such states like Bihar, UP, the maximum atrocities on the scheduled castes and scheduled tribes in India now, they are committed by the Yadavas, Jats, etc., you know, and that it is not the other higher castes. They had committed atrocities in the centuries gone by, but not now. Now in India you'll find these other intermediate castes and OBCs, they are the biggest perpetrators of crimes against the Scheduled Castes and Tribes.[44]

There were numerous reports about such incidents caused by the conflict of interests between the *Dalits* and OBCs, especially in Uttar Pradesh in the early 1990s. The OBCs are not considered a minority, but are perceived more as an ill-defined group used only to satisfy the exigencies of electoral vote-bank politics.[45]

The recommendations of the Mandal Commission thus appeared to challenge the Brahmin status. Brahmins saw this type of politics as a sign of the social decline of the upper castes, particularly of their own varna, who are no longer at the centre of the social dynamic.

We were taught when we were young, by our elders that as Brahmins we were the best. However, as the social processes and the political and economic processes have developed in India subsequently, the Brahmin finds that he is encountering a very different kind of reality, which is very different from the self-perception which he has internalized.[46]

The sociologist Dipankar Gupta points out that the notion of hierarchy is relative. There is no universally accepted position. The arguments on hierarchy depend on the relation of the person who is speaking to the hierarchy in question.[47]

The interviewees who feel threatened by positive discrimination policies are aware of the élitist image of Brahmins everywhere and of the unrealistic nature of the demand for reservations in their favour. But according to them, this type of policy is a social offence.

Quite obviously, there is not and there cannot be any quota or reservation in jobs, in the employment market for Brahmins . . . who are perceived as the perpetuators of an unequal and unjust social system. . . . Therefore, the reservation system for the Scheduled Castes and later on, the reservation system for the OBC, it is widely perceived as an economic, social offence against the Brahmins and in a lot of Brahmin families, the daily evening discourse over meal time is a whole range of debates on this issue.[48]

Such a pessimistic and defeatist attitude to these policies is based on economic considerations. The affected Brahmins generally belong to the lower middle-class and for them the term 'Brahmin' is not entirely synonymous with 'élite'. The Brahmin does not belong any more to a social mould that is synonymous with hierarchical supremacy. Sociologist Jagpal Singh was remarking that a Dalit in Uttar Pradesh, while commenting on the validity of reservation policies in his village, expressed the opinion that in view of their extreme poverty, Brahmins should have been the beneficiaries of these reservations.[49]

The poor Brahmin, specially the middle-class Brahmin, specially the . . . intelligent articulate educated but lower middle-class Brahmin, specially their girls, their daughters, they find themselves in a great upheaval, and they have great difficulty in deciding whether they are the best, they continue to be the top or that the processes have brought them down together, in the political, social and economic level.[50]

Their precarious economic situation is responsible for their demand that the government should take care of their needs, just as in the old days when Brahmins devoted themselves to religious matters and were looked after by society. These Brahmins with a low social status justify their need for assistance because, unlike other Brahmins who are well-to-do but dissociated from traditional Brahminical functions, they are the 'true' Brahmins concerned at their level with the spread of knowledge. This approach is similar to the populist attitude of the Tambras in Chennai.

Brahmins should not have so much money because it was the duty of the society to give them finance, to give them food, to facilitate them. But the duty of Brahmins was to get knowledge and give that knowledge to other people. Now, there is no such work for Brahmins. He is doing business, he is holding money, other things that he should not do.[51]

These demands raise the problem of caste-based reservations which cannot include members of the upper castes even if they are part of the economically weaker sections of the population.

Brahmin is generally avoided in the government policies. There is reservation on the basis of caste. . . . There should be reservation on the basis of economic conditions. If a person is weak economically, he should be given reservation to get admission, and starting from the primary school, whatever caste, Harijan, or Brahmin.[52]

This controversy about the criteria for selecting people who need protection under positive discrimination policies is not new and has always been raised during debates preceding the formulation of such policies. Today, when defining the sections protected by the Mandal Commission, the term class—not caste—is used in the expression 'other backward classes' (OBCs). However, when selecting the criteria that set apart these people, caste continued to be the basic unit for the legal classification of 'classes' needing protection and for the determination of the level of backwardness. This trend was deeply rooted in central government circles, despite many opinions to the contrary, notably coming from local state governments.[53]

But the Mandal Commission Report advances different justifications for this reference to caste. Referring to studies by well-known sociologists, it points out that caste is the basic factor of 'natural' mobilization in India. Quoting Rajni Kothari, the Commission declares that 'Those in India who complain of "casteism" in politics are really looking for a sort of politics which has no basis in society.'[54] Later, after a survey conducted in the states, it was seen that a majority of them were in favour of using caste as an important criterion for determining social and educational backwardness.[55] Similarly, three-fourths of the people polled to ascertain public opinion on this subject were in favour of the caste criterion.[56] Finally, it is very important to remember that in Indian society there have always been strong links between an individual's caste and his economic, educational and social status. As a matter of fact, the Brahmins had every reason to maintain a dominant and rigid caste system to ensure and justify the supremacy of the upper castes.[57]

Some sections of the Brahmin community nevertheless continue to demand government assistance. Apart from social groups who insist that sections needing protection should be selected on the basis of economic criteria, there are also those willing to be labelled 'backward' to gain access to existing reservations. This could be described as 'downwards social climbing' where the desire to gain access to social advantages is so strong that the group is prepared for the devaluation of its officially recognized status, as in the case of the Jat community seen earlier in this chapter.

But Brahmins suffer because there is no ambiguity about their classification and they cannot resort to such manipulation.[58] The situation is changing however, and the government agreed in August–September 2000, to enlarge the official list of Other Backward Classes to include among others the Nayee Brahmins of Andhra Pradesh.[59] The Tambras of Tamil Nadu is also fighting for a clearer definition of criteria relating to educational and social backwardness that should be made applicable to individuals instead of communities.

Brahmins, who insist on their economic weakness, also raise the question of affluent classes among the OBCs. This type of argument led, as early as 1992, to the exclusion by the Supreme Court of India of the 'creamy layer' among the OBCs, from privileged access to government jobs.[60]

Further, these reservations deprive Brahmins of their traditional jobs, particularly in government service, and oblige them to turn to the private sector, as mentioned in our study of Tamil Brahmins.[61] The drastic conditions that were once peculiar to the south have now spread to the rest of the country.

Reservation policies at the central government level have put an end to one of the professional traditions of Brahmin communities.[62]

I feel good to be a Brahmin, but . . . today, S.C. and other people like this get more advantages. Brahmins have problems in service jobs. Education was their priority. But today's situation is very bad for Brahmins. Access to service must be by the level of education, not by castes. For Brahmins, it is difficult . . . no promotions for them. So, we went into business.[63]

But adopting non-traditional professions often raises the problem of social acceptance in circles that are still imbued with traditional ideas, especially in the case of 'going into business' which is often looked down upon in India, in non-business communities.[64]

We have observed that the expression of Brahmin identity as a direct reaction to the implementation of the Mandal Commission Report has raised problems similar to those experienced by Tamil Brahmins mentioned in Part II of this study. There is nevertheless a clear division between the cultural and political contexts in north and south India, leading to varied attitudes to the issue of fragmentation.

Brahmins form a strong cultural group in Tamil Nadu whose distinctive traits stand out in the competitive professional environment. However, Brahmins in the north generally have a more ambiguous attitude and it is only recently that they have attempted to crystallize their identity as an interest group, in the present context where other communities have started asserting themselves. References to this theme emerge at two levels: firstly, with reference to the Hindu community and, secondly, in a narrower context, with reference to the Brahmin community itself.

According to the Hindu Nationalist ideology, caste-based distinctions are considered to be harmful to the cause of Hindu unity.

The political persons and to a good extent, the distortions which later came have divided the society, have fragmented the Hindus. But otherwise, with the original caste system, the Hindus together could make a strong society. Because, the caste system was to bring order according to professions. Widening the gap between castes and using caste for political reasons has put India twenty to twenty-five years back, because of this political thing. For a strong Hindu society, all castes should come together.[65]

The BJP's plan of forging Hindu unity against communities like Muslims and Christians considered to be non-Indian runs counter to the political trend developed during the 1990s of using social rifts, particularly between castes, to garner votes. The examples of the pro-Dalit Bahujan Samaj Party and the pro-OBC, particularly pro-Yadav, Samajvadi Party, are totally in keeping with this trend inimical to the *Hindutva* doctrine.

The situation that emerged after the implementation of the Mandal Commission Report gave birth to a trend that was extremely dangerous for the long-term plans of the Hindu nationalist movement. The campaign launched in December 1992 for the demolition of Babur's mosque (Babri Masjid) supposed to have been built on the site where Ram was born in Ayodhya, was actually a strategic response of the Hindu nationalist movement to the Mandalization of Indian society. In brief, it was a matter of 'Mandir versus Mandal'.[66]

The issue of fragmentation is central to the *Hindutva* ideology. Using the Hindu procession (*yatra*) as an instrument of political mobilization appears to be a perfect solution to this problem. Setting aside social and caste differences, the procession becomes an expression of the common reaction of the Hindu community to the Muslim 'other'.[67]

In an interview published in the *Frontline* magazine, Arvind Rajagopal, author of *Politics after Television: Hindu Nationalism and the Reshaping of the Indian Public*, explains the scenario that favoured this procession towards Ayodhya. He focuses on the serial based on the *Ramayana* telecast from January 1987. This serial, though launched on the initiative of the Congress government under Rajiv Gandhi, turned out to be an ideal ideological base for BJP's plans. In an effort to further the nation's cultural unity, the audio-visual medium promoted the themes and symbols borrowed by the Hindu nationalist movement for its own benefit at a time when there was just one television channel in the country. References to a Golden Age in India's remote past and the justification of virtues of the champions of Hinduism were accompanied by more explicit tactics. An episode showing Ram's desire to find back his land, though not to be found in the versions of the *Ramayana* by either Valmiki or Tulsidas, was shown in the television serial, hinting at the Ayodhya controversy. Finally, this led to the emergence of a common iconography seen in the television serial as well as in the politico-religious processions (*yatra*) organized by the Hindu nationalist movement.[68]

This movement was prompted by a keen desire to revive Brahminism within the fold of BJP's militant Hinduism. It was also the result of the strong need felt by upper caste Hindus to redefine the main and vital issues affecting Indian society in the face of threats posed by Muslims, Christians, Dalits and OBCs.[69]

Ayodhya continues to be the most important weapon for mobilizing the public in the arsenal of the Hindu nationalist movement, especially organizations such as the RSS (Rashtriya Swayamsevak Sangh) and the VHP (Vishwa Hindu Parishad). These organizations belonging to the Parivar, the Hindu nationalist family, translate the BJP's intentions into action by playing on different images for electoral purposes. There is no place for moderation in the *Hindutva* ideology. But the BJP, which needs allies to remain in power, is not always very comfortable with the extremist stances of its sister organizations.[70] There are nevertheless numerous symbolic links and declarations by BJP leaders referring to a common cultural and ideological platform with the RSS. During an official visit to the United States, Prime Minister A.B. Vajpayee, head of the BJP government, insisted that apart from his functions as Prime Minister, he was and would always be a *swayamsevak* and that nobody could deprive him of the right of being a *swayamsevak*.[71]

The *Hindutva* doctrine represents the longing to restore social justice according to the *varna* system, which means providing resources to each individual according to his status within the system. This amounts to justifying traditional hierarchical structures and integrating them in the contemporary economic and political context. The Hindu nationalist strategy tends to construct a pan-Indian hegemonic identity that is more united and extend the values and style of Brahminical functioning to a wider middle-class, that is becoming more uniform everyday.[72]

The issue of fragmentation was also broached in the context of the failure, not just of Hindus but of Brahmins in particular, to unite in order to face an unfavourable socio-economical and political situation from a position of strength. This new element of protest that has now emerged among the Brahmins is expressed in their awareness of their common interests, leading to the crystallization of the debate on identity and otherness.

This feeling of fragmentation is already perceptible even within various Brahmin *jatis*. Let us look at the Chaturvedis interviewed in Agra. This community of Brahmins belonging to Mathura in Uttar Pradesh is a typical example of a Brahmin caste having a high position in the socio-religious hierarchy. In fact, the name Chaturvedi indicates that their ancestors had mastered the knowledge of all the four Vedas. But today, in socio-economic terms most of them belong to the middle-class or even the lower middle-class category. The newsletters published by their caste association (*Mahasabha*) deal with various topics related to the present state of affairs. For example, there is opposition to marriages outside the Chaturvedi *jati* because they disturb the community's harmony and unity. This criticism of inter-caste marriages, which recurs frequently in their newsletters, is also accompanied by an appeal not to neglect the community's common interests.

Apart from marriage, the issue of employment is also of prime concern. In the present situation where upper castes, particularly Brahmins, are constantly denigrated, it is important to maintain the solidarity of the Chaturvedi community. So, in addition to a large number of advertisements of the enterprises run by members of the community, these newsletters make known the community's willingness to assist young Chaturvedi Brahmins in finding employment, by helping them financially or by giving them preference in the above-mentioned enterprises.[73]

The fear of fragmentation also exists at the higher level of the *varna*. Citing examples of the strong identity forged by other groups acts as a stimulant.

The Brahmins are basically foolish, they are stupid (...), because they don't understand their self interest, because it is perceived that there is a great fragmentation among the Brahmins, and two segments of Brahmins cannot get together to safeguard their common Brahminical cause against the perceived other, whether it is the Dalit or it is the OBC, or the Thakurs or the Jats or whoever. . . . The fragmentation among the Brahmins is so deep . . . and their corporate identity is very poor, is very poor.[74]

The existence of problems common to the Brahmin *varna* can assume an extreme form and give rise to violent identity expressions. The situation in Bihar is the most obvious example. This state, which was the scene of more that fifty-nine massacres causing six hundred deaths between 1971 and 1999, has witnessed the emergence of private armies for protecting the interests of the upper castes. These repeated massacres are directed mainly against the Dalits by private armies employed by the upper castes like the Bhoomi Sena, Brahmarshi Sena, Sunlight Sena, Savarna Liberation Army and Ranvir Sena. The atrocities are a result of the clash of economic and political interests. The landlords belonging to the Bhumiyar caste, sharing the same lineage as the Mohyals and whose Brahmin status is often disputed, do not want the lower castes to seize political power. They believe their socio-economic interests have been flouted in the contemporary political situation in Bihar. That is why the election of a Chief Minister from the underprivileged classes in 1977 and the rule of Laloo Prasad Yadav and his wife Rabri Devi who support the lower castes, from 1989 to 1999, were the most violent periods for the Dalit population of Bihar.[75]

The issue of fragmentation, which also expresses the need to pay attention to the common interests of the Brahmins, reveals that new identities are in the process of being formed. The fact that the underprivileged classes have started asserting their identity has acted as a stimulant for the Brahmins who now feel the need to define their own identity. It is particularly the assertion of groups that were initially divided at the cultural level, but who now form a single body in the political domain due to the legal classification into categories like Scheduled Castes and OBCs, that has prompted Brahmins to think more deeply about their own group identity.

The identity-otherness dynamics functions very effectively in this context. The recent attempt by Brahmins to strengthen their identity constitutes a process that is the exact opposite of the Sanskritization process defined by M.N. Srinivas. Sanskritization is based on mimicry and the appropriation of attributes considered to be Brahminical by classes situated lower in the social hierarchy and often at the very bottom of the social ladder, because they want to attain a respectable social status. But as

Owen M. Lynch has pointed out in his study of Agra in the 1960s, following the modernization and the consequent Westernization of the Brahmins, the lower castes have become aware of this change and have understood that imitation is now outdated and that questions related to hierarchy have to be treated differently.[76]

The contemporary political situation arising from the developments in the 1990s, has accentuated this change in the significance of Sanskritization to the point of a total reversal of the process. It appears that Brahmins, confronted today by the strong and united stand of various social groups opposed to their traditional reference system, would be quite happy to use the same strategy.

When Kalyan Singh was Chief Minister of Uttar Pradesh, Brahmin interests were very visible within the BJP. These interests were not officially recognized but they were the subject of informal meetings and discussions. This shows that the Brahmins were aware of the danger of stating the need to protect their interests, since it would amount to admitting the fears and weaknesses of their community.[77]

Brahmin political interests were perceptible only because of the pressure exerted by groups opposed to Kalyan Singh's pro-lower caste policies. A seminar was held in Kanpur on 31 January 1999 on 'Brahmins and adverse situations'. It was the feeling of being neglected and the admission that there was a general apathy towards Brahmins, in view of several assassinations and the dismissal of several Brahmins from the Government in the state, that led to this political manifestation of a strong Brahmin identity within the BJP.[78] Reacting to criticism of this meeting, a Brahmin leader is said to have retorted, 'What is wrong if Brahmins meet and discuss their political importance and their peculiar social problems when all others are doing the same?'[79]

The creation of the Savarna Samaj Party by the upper castes in 1997 was a manifestation of this trend. Basing its name on the pattern of the Bahujan Samaj Party, the SSP was the Brahmin response to the formation of caste-based movements by the underprivileged classes. The forming of a party without any particular ideological import was an act of pure mimicry lending weight to the theory that Brahmins are not willing to overtly institutionalize specific political interests, for strategic reasons.

Referring to the inauguration on 9 August 1997 of the Madhya Pradesh branch of this party under the leadership of a Brahmin, the satirical magazine *Dalit Voice* commented that it was a rational move. This approach is perceived as more forthright than that of the BJP, nicknamed *Brahman Jati Party* (the Brahmin Caste Party) by the magazine, which covertly works for the promotion of the upper castes, while devising strategies and discourses that are overtly meant to cover the entire population.[80] The appointment of Bangaru Laxman, an Untouchable, as its national president in August 2000 was for example seen as a part of this BJP's electoral strategy.[81]

Evidently, the Brahmins are finding it necessary to forge a group identity. Celebrations of Parashuram Jayanti, the birth anniversary of the mythical Brahmin warrior Parashuram, are a step in this direction. Parashuram is the archetypal Brahmin believed to be the ancestor of all Brahmins who, according to the Dalits, symbolizes the crystallization of violent Brahmin domination. Further, by stressing the importance of this day, 28 April, Brahmins express their desire to set-up an exclusively Brahmin pantheon, a specific cultural and symbolic heritage.

NOTES

1. A. Sen, *Inequality reexamined*, Oxford: Oxford University Press, 1992, pp. 12-14.
2. G. Sharma, *Human rights and social justice—fundamental rights vis-a-vis directive principles*, Delhi: Deep & Deep Publications, 1997, pp. 401-2.
3. I have already explained in Chapter 4 the context in which Clause 4 was incorporated into Article 15 as a result of the first amendment to the Constitution.
4. *Reservation for Backward Classes, Mandal Commission report of the Backward Classes Commission*, Delhi: Akalank Publications, 1980, Chapters VI and VII.
5. S. Navlakha, *Elite and Social Change—A study of Elite Formation in India*, Delhi: Sage Publications, 1989, pp. 64-6.
6. C. Jaffrelot, *La démocratie en Inde*, Paris: Fayard, 1998, p. 219.
7. P. Radhakrishnan, 'Caste, Politics and the Reservation Issue', in *Illfare in India: Essays on India's Social Sector in Honour of S. Guhan*, ed. B. Harriss-White and S. Subramaniam, Delhi: Sage Publications, 1999,

pp. 171-2. S. Bayly, *Caste, Society and Politics in India from the eighteenth to the modern age*, the New Cambridge History of India, IV(3), Cambridge: Cambridge University Press, 1999, p. 301.

8. J. Mishra, *Equality versus justice—the problem of reservations for backward classes*, Delhi: Deep & Deep Publications, 1996, p. 63.
9. C. Jaffrelot, *La démocratie en Inde*, Paris: Fayard, 1998, pp. 179-81.
10. S. Bayly, *Caste, Society and Politics in India from the eighteenth to the modern age*, the New Cambridge History of India, IV(3), Cambridge: Cambridge University Press, 1999, pp. 293, 322-6.
11. We have already mentioned this process in Chapter 3 in relation to caste identities built around military ethic, as in the case of the Jats and Mohyal Brahmins.
12. N. Datta, 'Jats: Trading caste Status for Empowerment', *Economic and Political Weekly*, Mumbai, 06/11/99, p. 3172.
13. The Kolis of Gujarat claim the status of a martial peasant community culturally linked to the Kshatriyas, but different from the rich peasants of the Kanbi-Patidar community, so that they can claim access to OBC quotas: S. Bayly, *Caste, Society and Politics in India from the eighteenth to the modern age*, the New Cambridge History of India, IV(3), Cambridge: Cambridge University Press, 1999, pp. 329-31.
14. C. Jaffrelot and J. Zerenini-Brotel, 'La montée des basses castes dans la politique nord-indienne', *Pouvoirs* (90), Paris: Seuil, 1999, pp. 70-3.
15. 'Logic of Fragmentation', *The Hindustan Times*, 29/09/96.
16. C.P. Bhambri, 'The Cacophony of Reservation Politics', *The Hindustan Times*, 17/10/94; 'Folly of Reservations', *The Hindustan Times*, 23/05/97.
17. A. Beteille, *Backward classes in contemporary India*, Delhi: Oxford University Press, 1992, pp. 45-69.
18. D. Gupta, *Interrogating caste—Understanding hierarchy & difference in Indian society*, Delhi: Penguin Books, 2000, pp. 96-115.
19. N.B. Dirks, 'Différence et discrimination—La politique des castes dans l'Inde post-coloniale', *Annales—Histoire, Sciences Sociales*, Paris, 52(3), May-June 1997, pp. 611-12.
20. S. Patil, 'Should "Class" be the basis for recognising backwardness?', *Economic and Political Weekly*, Mumbai, 25(50), pp. 2733-44. These socio-political issues peculiar to each community have been taken up by some Brahmins, as we shall see later.
21. R. Kothari, ed., *Caste in Indian Politics*, Delhi: Orient Longman, 1989, pp. 4-5.
22. 'Democracy and Identities', *The Hindu*, 12/12/97.
23. H.A. Gould, *The Hindu Caste System : Politics and caste*, vol. 3, Delhi: Chanakya Publications, 1990, p. 3.
24. S. Pai, 'The BSP in Uttar Pradesh', *Seminar*, Delhi, no. 471, November 1998, pp. 39-40.

25. J. Alam, 'Is caste appeal casteism? Oppressed castes in politics', *Economic and Political Weekly*, Mumbai, vol. 34(13), p. 759.
26. R. Kothari, *Communalism in Indian Politics*, Delhi: Rainbow Publishers, 1998, pp. 171-6.
27. R.C. Heredia, 'Subaltern alternatives on caste, class and ethnicity', *Contribution to Indian Sociology*, Delhi, 34(1), pp. 39-49.
28. See Satish Deshpande, 'Counting on caste for social justice', *The Times of India*, 20/08/99.
29. 9.
30. A2.
31. 1.
32. 9.
33. A5. Even though this interviewee belongs to the impersonal Brahmin category, he is relevant in this context because he refers to the 'genetic superiority' of Brahmins in his capacity as a doctor. Also see the report on a study conducted in north-eastern Andhra Pradesh in collaboration with the American university of Utah on the genetic variations observed between the upper and lower castes, in *The Indian Express*, 18/01/98.
34. A19.
35. A9.
36. 8.
37. N.B. Dirks, 'Différence et discrimination—La politique des castes dans l'Inde post-coloniale', *Annales—Histoire, Sciences Sociales*, Paris, 52(3), May-June 1997, p. 604.
38. *Reservation for Backward Classes, Mandal Commission report of the Backward Classes Commission*, Delhi: Akalank Publications, 1980, p. 28.
39. *India Today*, 15/10/90, p. 15.
40. See the survey conducted by *India Today* in the 31/10/90 issue of the magazine.
41. M.S.A. Rao, *Social Movements and Social Transformation*, Delhi: Manohar, 1987, p. 210.
42. P. Kolenda, 'How should we think about inequality or no tears for losers', *Man in India*, Ranchi, 1991, 71(1), p. 106.
43. See the example of tribes in Bihar in the article by Rajalaxmi Rath. The author points out the positive social impact of reservations in terms of lifestyle, status and social acceptability and access to government jobs: R. Rath, 'Job reservation and social mobility—Case study of Tribal Bihar', *Man in India*, 1991, 71(4), pp. 639-46.
44. 11.
45. J. Mishra, *Equality versus justice—the problem of reservations for backward classes*, Delhi: Deep & Deep Publications, 1996, p. 3.
46. A1.

47. D. Gupta, *Interrogating caste—Understanding hierarchy & difference in Indian society*, Delhi: Penguin Books, 2000, p. 130.
48. A1.
49. Interview with Jagpal Singh, Delhi, 13/02/2001.
50. A1.
51. A13.
52. A13.
53. M. Galanter, *Competing equalities, Law and the Backward classes in India*, Delhi: Oxford University Press, 1984, pp. 154-80.
54. *Reservation for Backward Classes, Mandal Commission report of the Backward Classes Commission*, Delhi: Akalank Publications, 1980, p. 23.
55. Ibid., pp. 42-7.
56. Ibid., pp. 48-54.
57. Ibid., pp. 19-22.
58. See 'The Reservation Muddle', in *The Hindu*, Delhi, 29/01/97.
59. In this particular case, it appears that considerations of socio-economic backwardness were given priority over considerations of caste status (*Newstime*, Hyderabad, 05/09/2000).
60. See article by P. Radhakirshnan on the history of the Supreme Court's judgements on reservation policies for Backward Classes at the centre and in Tamil Nadu in *The Hindu*, 26/07/2000.
61. Also see the article 'The shifting sites of reservation', in *The Hindu* dated 21/02/97 which talks about the upper castes' shift to the private sector for both education and employment, due to internal competition and reservation policies and also as a result of globalization.
62. The Brahmins were actually overrepresented in government jobs, as observed by the British rulers when the non-Brahmin movement was being launched. K.S. Singh advances a figure of 91.4 per cent for involvement in government service. This figure refers to the pre-Mandal era and does not correspond to individuals but to Brahmin communities some of whose members were associated with government service. The figure of 91.4 per cent is compared with the national average of 66 per cent: K.S. Singh, *People of India, India's Communities,* National Series, vol. IV, Delhi: Oxford University Press, 1998, p. 542.
63. A15.
64. See 'In India, businessmen are seen as villains', in *The Times of India*, Delhi, 20/12/98.
65. A8.
66. S. Bayly, *Caste, Society and Politics in India from the eighteenth to the modern age*, the New Cambridge History of India, IV(3), Cambridge: Cambridge University Press, 1999, pp. 296-7.

67. See article by Christophe Jaffrelot: 'Processions hindoues, stratégies politiques et émeutes entre Hindous et Musulmans', in *Violences et non-violences en Inde*, ed. D. Vidal et al., Paris: Editions de l'EHESS, Purusartha, 1994, pp. 261-87.
68. See the interview by Darryl D'Monte published in *Frontline*, 18/08/2000, pp. 76-9.
69. R. Kothari, *Communalism in Indian Politics*, Delhi: Rainbow Publishers, 1998, pp. 126-33.
70. See *Frontline*, 07/07/2000, pp. 4-17.
71. *The Times of India*, 11/09/2000.
72. R. Desai, 'Culturalism and Contemporary Right—Indian bourgeoisie and Political Hindutva', *Economic and Political Weekly*, Mumbai, 20/03/99, p. 705.
73. Newsletters of the Chaturvedi *Mahasabha*, July 1993 (p. 4), March 1995 (p. 3), June 1995 (p. 8), January-February 1996 (pp. 12-14), May 1996 (p. 46).
74. A1.
75. *Frontline*, vol. 16, no. 5, p. 30.
76. O.M. Lynch, 'The Politics of Untouchability : a case from Agra, India', in *Structure and change in Indian society*, ed. M. Singer and B. Cohn, Chicago: Aldine Press, 1968, pp. 209-39.
77. Interview with the journalist David Devadas, Delhi, 30/06/2000.
78. *The Asian Age*, 02/02/99; *The Telegraph*, 03/02/99.
79. *The Hindu*, 27/01/99.
80. *Dalit Voice*, Bangalore, vol. 16, no. 20, p. 2.
81. *Frontline*, 29/09/2000, pp. 4-7. Bangaru Laxman had to resign in March 2001 following allegations of corruption.

Conclusion

In his study of the priestly functions of the Brahmins of Ayodhya entitled *Gods on Earth*, Peter van der Veer explains the diverse attitudes of the various Brahmin communities and the difference in their status, although they all practise the same type of profession. Simultaneously, he draws attention to the tendency of many writers to compare these Brahmin priests to the ideal of the renouncer defined in the Sanskrit texts of the Great Hindu Tradition. He then goes on to explain how he has adopted a more historical approach to get at the root of the attitudes of these different groups.[1]

My study of contemporary Brahmin identity has revealed the same three points, viz., the differences in attitude and status, social positioning with reference to the Brahmin ideal, and the importance of history. I have developed these three points from three complementary angles: profession, geographical origin and attitude towards policies of positive discrimination.

Brahmins in the army, though faced with a theoretical conflict between the contradictory values of *ahimsa* and military activity, have a long historical background replete with references and emblematic figures constituting their distinctive culture. It is this context that has given rise to the debate on the present position of Brahmins as compared to the ideal Brahmin. Even today, this group's distinctive traits are expressed through the definition of critical political issues such as secularism, a principle cherished by the military as an institution, and the relationship between military and civilian personnel, rather than any aspect related to the caste hierarchy.

Tamil Brahmins, on the other hand, base their identity on the caste hierarchy which has had a strong political connotation in south India since the late nineteenth century. Since then, Brahmins and non-Brahmins have become two separate categories with well-defined political attitudes and activities, giving rise to a situation peculiar to this region. Consequently, Tamil Brahmins present distinct identities, very different from the identities of the 'other' such as north Indian Brahmins or the lower castes, expressed through a range of attitudes, evincing pride or bitterness in relation to ideal Brahminical qualities.

A study of the attitudes of Brahmins towards positive discrimination policies revealed a whole range of viewpoints focused on the concept of social justice. As a reaction to the growing strength of other socio-political classes like the Dalits and OBCs, contemporary Brahmins have developed a variety of attitudes in the context of the politicization of caste in the 1990s. The image of the good Brahmin, who is talented and deserving, is central to such identities.

By adopting these three approaches, we have defined various types of identities betraying the pluralism of contemporary Brahmin identities. The Brahmin identity is not absolute and has to be understood in various peculiar contexts.

I should also emphasize the psychological dimension of this study arising from the very nature of the basic material of my research, viz., interviews during which the Brahmin interviewees explained their identity. There is nothing new about the relation between psychology and politics. The studies undertaken in the 1930s by the Frankfurt School and by Adorno in particular laid stress on the influence of economic and social conditions on attitudes and opinions, especially political opinion. As pointed out by this school of thought, an individual's beliefs, whether political, economic or social, form a comprehensive pattern whose coherence depends on the person's 'spirit' or 'mentality' expressing deep-seated personality trends.[2] This theoretical approach is centred around the two poles representing conservatism and protest. In the course of my study, it became evident that different types of 'Brahmin personalities' are moulded by different economic, social and political conditions.

Brahmins in the army seem to be simultaneously conservative and eager to protest. They are more conservative in respect of caste hierarchy. Since they are not directly affected by issues like caste-based politics, they are mainly concerned about the widening gap between military and civil personnel with respect to economic and official status.

As for Tamil Brahmins, their personality can be classified as anti-establishment and this trait becomes more evident when you move further down the socio-economic scale, as in the case of the Tambras.

A study of the attitude of Brahmins to the assertion of the Dalits and OBCs in the political field revealed a wide variety of attitudes between these two poles of conservatism and protest. Conservative Brahmins of contemporary India lay claim to an unquestionable superiority, while others, in a protesting mould, may simultaneously work towards the strengthening of their group identity and express fears about their socio-economic weaknesses.

This psychological dimension, in relation to the two poles of conservatism and protest, is determined by both caste and class relationships. Being a Brahmin today has different connotations depending on the person's socio-economic level. The link between the notions of caste and class seems natural when we take into account the strong link between socio-economic class and profession. In fact, the *varna* system, as pointed out in Part I of this study, was a division of society based on occupation. Social and professional classification have been inseparable from the very beginning as indicated by the adage, 'You are what you do or what you aspire to become'.

With the development of modern social structures in the economic and political spheres, caste and class became closely linked, though in a random manner, according to the different regional, historical and social traits of Indian society.[3] These social changes have defined the contours of the modern Indian élite at the junction of two hierarchies, the caste hierarchy in respect of religious and ritualistic matters and the class hierarchy on the basis of socio-economic status.

During the colonial period and the first few decades immediately after Independence, the upper castes were predominant in the fields of land ownership and education and stood at the top of both hierarchies. But the lower castes, as we have seen, managed to overcome this situation. In the late 1960s, the intermediate castes gained economic importance following agrarian reforms that put an end to the *zamindari* system and the advent of the Green Revolution.[4] Small landowners belonging to specific groups, who had benefited by these reforms, made socio-economic demands for access to education and government jobs leading to the appointment of the Mandal Commission, and also for political representation. The awareness of their common interests led to the formation of an 'OBC bloc' which clamoured for reservation policies in its favour.[5]

We have seen how this assertion of identity on the part of OBCs and untouchables incited Brahmins to consolidate their own identity. But the latter realized that there were too many internal differences that prevented them from forming a united front. Today, only the economically well off Brahmins are full-fledged members of the élite.

This phenomenon is the result of a more far-reaching change, viz., the emergence of a new middle-class in India. With the secularization of caste, through processes of growing indifference to rituals and politicization, there has been a radical change in the political system giving the intermediate castes a chance to move up the social scale. The old criteria like Sanskritization and high religious status needed for gaining access to the middle-class (consisting essentially of the upper castes) have had to make way for new criteria like a modern lifestyle, consumerism, economic assets and the awareness of belonging to this very group.[6]

In this context, we must take note of the differences that we observed in the strategic way south Indian and north Indian Brahmins responded to reservation policies. Positive discrimination policies are actually a means of providing more opportunities to the marginal classes to join the middle-class. This leads to the elimination of some other classes due to a decline in their status. In such a situation, Tamil Brahmins have found individual solutions by opting for promising careers in the private sector where there are no quotas. North Indian Brahmins, because they are more numerous, tend to react by defending the political interests of their group, especially within the Hindu nationalist movement.

The formation of a new middle-class has nevertheless permitted the free use of resources from the caste system in strategies related to social status. The low and intermediate castes use government policies in their favour to improve their social status. The upper castes, on the other hand, continue to cling to their traditional status: the reference to purely Brahminical values is particularly evident in difficult times.

In the case of economical disadvantaged Brahmin groups, the

reference to Brahminical values amounts to the glorification of their *varna* and its prestige in times gone by to justify the introduction of policies in their favour. Going back to the classification in Chapter 1, the attitude of the closed élitist type based on the perception of a threatened superiority is a typical example. Reference to Brahminical values and qualities seems to be a way out for Brahmins suffering from an identity crisis.

In the case of well-to-do Brahmins, Brahminical values are upheld to sustain a strong feeling of pride or to assuage a feeling of guilt. The feeling of a strengthened pride actually conceals a vague feeling of threat experienced in specific social scenarios. The implementation of the Mandal Commission Report is one of these. In Brahmins belonging to the 'responsible' type the feeling of guilt is an expression of the need to make up for centuries of abuse of the lower castes and adopt an altruistic attitude at a time when Brahmin élitism is being disparaged.

This trend of focusing on Brahmin identity in critical times can be seen in the attitude of one of the Brahmin lady interviewed who tries to justify her son's choice of an unusual profession. The latter works in a cotton textile mill, something that is quite alien to the Brahmin tradition. So she offers the excuse that her son is very knowledgeable in his field and is willing to increase his knowledge and share it with others, which is a sign of professionalism, tenacity and discipline. Beyond professional considerations, what really matters is that he is totally Brahmin in his attitude.[7]

Apart from the association with such psychological values, the reference to non-violence is also quite widespread. As we have seen in the case of Brahmins in the army or with reference to vegetarianism, moderation and forbearance, non-violence is the prime value of the ideal Brahmin model. The representative of the political organization of Kashmiri Pandits in exile, who are a typical example of Brahmins going through an identity crisis, describes his community's situation in the following words:

We have rejected violence despite being provoked to reciprocate (...). We were threatened, abducted, killed, tortured—despite being a non-violent, peace-loving community.[8]

The reference to these Brahminical values is a part of the quest for an ideal referent providing a meaningful base for identity, in a strategy that is essentially a reaction to socio-economic weaknesses or to the assertion of other communities. As Marc Augé explains, every person takes a stand in relation to others on the basis of one or the other of these two principles, belonging or identity. These principles define the relationship between the individual and the group through different class identities and the axis of relationship or difference that brings into play more abstract and relative categories to elucidate the relationship between the self and the other.[9]

I must finally point out that these Brahminical values can be dissociated from individuals who were simply born Brahmins. 'Who is a Brahmin?' is the crucial question that we asked ourselves all through this study. But one of the first reactions we came across in the course of our inquiry was 'What Brahmins are you talking about—those who are born Brahmins or others?' This comment takes us back to the original *varna* system according to which a person's *varna* was defined by his aptitudes and aspirations and not by his birth.[10] Further, this observation was made by non-Brahmin teachers or intellectuals who claimed to possess the essence of the Brahmin identity.

It was also pointed out in different places and at different times that non-Brahmin communities had appropriated the Brahmin status to overcome the limitations imposed by their social low status. The Lingayats of Mysore and the Chamars of Uttar Pradesh are known to have trained priests from their own communities in order to get around the refusal of Brahmin priests to officiate at their functions.[11]

I can also quote the example of the socio-religious reform movement launched in Gujarat by Pandurang Shastri Athawale who is trying to redefine the identity of the local fishermen. He has renamed them *Sagarputra* or 'sons of the ocean' and persuaded them to stop eating meat and give up their vices and old social dogmas in an effort to Sanskritize them. The more gifted among them have even been trained as priests after undergoing a three-year course followed by an initiation ceremony after which they can wear the sacred thread and perform rituals. One of them has expressed the following view about the Brahmin category:

I am a Brahmin by Karma (...). Most Brahmins don't know much about the Vedas but I do.[12]

Some Brahmins too share this view:

In those days we were supposed to know the Vedas . . . there are lots of Brahmins today who do not know what exactly is Veda and all . . . Men are supposed to wear the white thread, lots of them don't wear. . . . They are supposed to say those mantras, Gayatri mantra everyday, lots of them . . . they don't even say it a single time . . . . It makes absolutely no difference.[13]

In the same spirit, an academic has developed the theory that today a Brahmin by birth does not behave in accordance with the principles of the Brahmin *varna* at every moment of his life. In fact, according to him, most of them have become 'degenerate' and non-Brahmin in essence. The Brahminical qualities of purity and honesty and the quest for truth should now be adopted by all those who have the will to do so, irrespective of their origins, even if they are Dalits, so as to contribute to the harmonious development of society and the furtherance of democracy.[14]

So the question, 'Who is the real Brahmin?', is at the crossroads of the main ideological debates between religion and politics, caste and class, nationalism and democracy in India today. In addition to name and way of dressing and living, profession, regional traits and political attitude undoubtedly define the multiple identities that make India, in addition to being the world's largest democracy, a country of unique diversity.

NOTES

1. P. van der Veer, *Gods on Earth*, Delhi: Oxford University Press, 1989.
2. M. Grawitz and J. Leca, eds., *Traité de Science Politique*, Paris: PUF, vol. 1, 1985, pp. 24-5.
3. J. Pouchepadass, ed., *Caste et classe en Asie du sud*, Paris: Editions de l'EHESS, Purusartha, 1982, pp. 12-14.
4. T. Roy, *The politics of a popular uprising—Bundelkand in 1857*, Delhi: Oxford University Press, 1994, pp. 76-8.
5. C. Jaffrelot and J. Zerenini-Brotel, 'La montée des basses castes dans la politique nord-indienne', *Pouvoirs* (90), Paris: Seuil, 1999, pp. 69-73.
6. D.L. Sheth, 'Secularisation of caste and making of new middle class', *Economic and Political Weekly*, Bombay, 34 (34 and 35), 1999, pp. 2508-9.
7. Interview in Wardha, 09/06/2000.
8. 'Pandits in Exile', *The Times of India*, 21/08/2000.

9. M. Augé, *Le sens des autres—Actualité de l'anthropologie*, Paris: Fayard, 1994, pp. 50-1.
10. This approach is akin to the differentiation in the spiritual sphere of pure ritualism, which requires technical expertise, from wisdom, in connection with the divine.
11. Examples cited by Dipankar Gupta in his analysis of 'the Brahmin as a fiction', in D. Gupta, *Interrogating caste—Understanding hierarchy & difference in Indian society*, Delhi: Penguin Books, 2000, p. 117.
12. *Indian Express*, 09/12/2000. To be a Brahmin by *karma* means that he was not born a Brahmin but he has become one because of his actions, thus going back to the original theory of *varna* according to which such a change was possible before the caste system became rigid.
13. M18.
14. Bharat Jhunjhunwala, *Varna vyavastha—governance through caste system*, Jaipur: Rawat Publications, 1999.

APPENDIX

Information Related to the Brahmin Interviewees

- marriage within the *jati*: marriage with a Brahmin of the same subcaste
- marriage out of the *jati*: marriage with a Brahmin of a different subcaste
- marriage out of the *varna*: marriage with a non-Brahmin Hindu

DELHI

	Sex	Subcaste	State of origin	Place of birth	Date of arrival in the city where the interview was conducted	Age	Marital status	Profession	Father's profession	Mother's profession	Language used for the interview
1.	M	Iyer	Tamil Nadu	Parithiyur	1957	64	Marriage within the *jati*	Retired IAS officer	IAS officer	Teacher	English
2.	M	Non-identified	Punjab	Lahore (Pakistan)	1947	77	Marriage out of the *jati*	Engineer in the Army then in industry	Doctor	House-wife	English
3.	F	Iyer	Tamil Nadu	Kalakad	1988	31	Marriage out of the *varna*	Adminis-tration	Banking	House-wife	English
4.	F	Non-identified	Punjab	Non-identified	1989	30	Marriage out of the *varna*	Civil servant	Civil servant	House-wife	English

(contd.)

DELHI (contd.)

	Sex	Subcaste	State of origin	Place of birth	Date of arrival in the city where the interview was conducted	Age	Marital status	Profession	Father's profession	Mother's profession	Language used for the interview
5.	M	Iyer	Tamil Nadu	Madras	1982	43	Marriage out of the *jati*	Company Director	Chartered Accountant	House-wife	English
6.	F	Iyer	Tamil Nadu	Madras	1981	44	Marriage within the *jati*	Researcher in law	Engineer	Music teacher	English
7.	F	Barendra	West Bengal	Shantipur	1988	30	Single	Student	IAS officer	House-wife	English
8.	F	Velanati	Andhra Pradesh	Visakha-patnam	1995	27	Single	Student	Professor	House-wife	English
9.	M	Chatur-vedi	Uttar Pradesh	Orai	1946	60	Marriage within the *jati* United Nations	Consultant for the	Journalist	House-wife	English
10.	M	Munda	Rajasthan	Delhi birth	Since	25	Single Assistant	Production	**Professor** wife	House-	English
11.	M	Bharadwaj Pradesh	Uttar	Almora	1988	38	Single in political science	Researcher	Researcher wife	House-	English

12.	M	Iyangar	Tamil Nadu	Madras	1987	40	Marriage out of the *jati*	Lawyer	Engineer	Specialist in Sanskrit	English
13.	M	Niyogi	Andhra Pradesh	Ongole	1990	36	Marriage within the *jati*	Advocate	Judge	House-wife	English
14.	M	Iyer	Tamil Nadu	Kumba-konam	Since birth	31	Single	Administra-tion	Software Engineer	House-wife	English
15.	F	Non-identified	Kashmir	Srinagar	1971	63	Marriage within the *jati*	Teacher	Doctor	House-wife	English
16.	M	Non-identified	Kashmir	Srinagar	1971	65	Marriage within the *jati*	Engineer in the Army	Teacher	House-wife	English
17.	M	Non-identified	Uttar Pradesh	Nainital	1977	62	Marriage within the *jati*	Retired Army officer ; today involved in politics	Business-man	House-wife	English
18.	M	Iyer	Tamil Nadu	Penan-natykam (Kerala)	1992	34	Single	Fashion designer	Mana-gement	House-wife	English
19.	M	Non-identified	West Bengal	Varanasi	1991	64	Marriage within the *jati*	Metallur-gist	Teacher	House-wife	English
20.	M	Non-identified	West Bengal	Calcutta	1956	85	Marriage out of the *jati*	Economist	Civil servant	House-wife	English
21.	M	Smartha	Karnataka	Mysore	1965	67	Marriage out of the *jati*	Scholar	Professor	Professor	English

(contd.)

AGRA

	Sex	Subcaste	State of origin	Place of birth	Date of arrival in the city where the interview was conducted	Age	Marital status	Profession	Father's profession	Mother's profession	Language used for the interview
A1	M	Chaturvedi	Uttar Pradesh	Agra	Since birth	59	Marriage out of the *jati*	Professor	Businessman	Housewife	English
A2	F	Non-identified	Uttar Pradesh	Agra	Since birth	41	Single	Professor	Civil servant	Housewife	Hindi
A3	M	Chaturvedi	Uttar Pradesh	Bulandashahr	1936	81	Marriage within the *jati*	Teacher	Civil servant	Housewife	English
A4	M	Non-identified	Uttar Pradesh	Agra	Since birth	32	Marriage planned out of the *jati*	Professor	Civil servant	Housewife	English
A5	M	Kanyakubj	Uttar Pradesh	Agra	Since birth	47	Marriage out of the *jati*	Doctor	Doctor	Housewife	Hindi
A6	F	Chaturvedi	Uttar Pradesh	Agra	Since birth	22	Single	Student	Professor	Professor	English
A7	M	Non-identified	Uttar Pradesh	Nadholi	1984	38	Marriage within the *jati*	Professor	Agriculture	Housewife	Hindi
A8	M	Kanyakubj	Uttar Pradesh	Agra	Since birth	53	Marriage within the *jati*	Professor-Researcher	Professor-Researcher	Housewife	English

A9	M	Sanadhya	Uttar Pradesh	Agra	Since birth	59	Marriage within the *jati*	Professor	*Pandit*	House-wife	Hindi
A10	M	Chatur-vedi	Uttar Pradesh	Mathura	1940	74	Marriage within the *jati*	Teacher	Journalist	House-wife	English
A11	M	Sanadhya	Uttar Pradesh	Aligarh	1958	51	Marriage out of the *jati*	Teacher	Civil servant	House-wife	English
A12	M	Parashar	Uttar Pradesh	Karkoli	1955	73	Marriage out of the *jati*	Professor	Agriculture	House-wife	Hindi
A13	M	Tiwari	Uttar Pradesh	Bibauli	1987	61	Marriage within the *jati*	Civil servant	Agriculture	House-wife	English and Hindi
A14	M	Tiwari	Uttar Pradesh	Bibauli	1978	39	Marriage within the *jati*	Business-man	Civil servant	House-wife	English and Hindi
A15	F	Tiwari	Uttar Pradesh	Agra	Since birth	36	Marriage within the *jati*	Housewife	Civil servant	Teacher	Hindi
A16	F	Nagar	Gujarat	Meerut	1963	55	Single	Professor	Civil servant	House-wife	Hindi
A17	F	Chatur-vedi	West Bengal	Calcutta	1958	45	Marriage out of the *varna*	Professor	Civil servant	House-wife	English
A18	M	Pandey	Madhya Pradesh	Chari	1982	47	Marriage within the *jati*	*Pandit*	*Pandit*	House-wife	Hindi
A19	F	Chatur-vedi	Uttar Pradesh	Allahabad	1968	47	Marriage within the *jati*	Professor	Engineer	House-wife	English

(contd.)

MADRAS (CHENNAI)

	Sex	Subcaste	State of origin	Place of birth	Date of arrival in the city where the interview was conducted	Age	Marital status	Profession	Father's profession	Mother's profession	Language used for the interview
M1	M	Iyer	Tamil Nadu	Madras	Since birth	63	Marriage within the *jati*	Business-man	Advocate	House-wife	English
M2	M	Iyer	Tamil Nadu	Kalakad	1988	52	Marriage within the *jati*	Employee in a nation-alized company	*Pandit*	House-wife	English
M3	M	Iyer	Tamil Nadu	Tanjavore	1928	90	Marriage within the *jati*	Professor of English	Engineer	House-wife	English
M4	M	Non-identified	Tamil Nadu	Madras	Since birth	65	Marriage within the *jati*	Journalist	Advocate	House-wife	English
M5	M	Iyangar	Tamil Nadu	Madras	Since birth	72	Marriage with a Christian foreigner	Business-man	Business-man	House-wife	English
M6	F	Iyer	Tamil Nadu	Bombay	1974	50	Marriage out of the *jati*	Art historian	Engineer	Civil servant	English
M7	F	Iyangar	Tamil Nadu	Madras	Since birth	48	Marriage within the *jati*	Executive	Business-man	House-wife	English

M8	F	Telugu Brahmin	Tamil Nadu	Kumbakonam	1987	34	Marriage within the *jati*	Accountant	Teacher	Housewife	English
M9	M	Iyer	Tamil Nadu	Madras	Since birth	69	Marriage within the *jati*	Health sector	Civil servant	Housewife	English
M10	M	Iyer	Tamil Nadu	Madras	Since birth	67	Marriage within the *jati*	Finance executive	Businessman	Housewife	English
M11	M	Iyer	Tamil Nadu	Madras	Since birth	59	Marriage within the *jati*	Bank employee	Civil servant	Housewife	English
M12	M	Iyangar	Tamil Nadu	Madras	Since birth	77	Marriage within the *jati*	Lawyer	Civil servant	Housewife	English
M13	M	Iyer	Tamil Nadu	Kumbakonam	1969	57	Marriage within the *jati*	Businessman	Agriculture	Housewife	English
M14	F	Iyangar	Tamil Nadu	Madras	Since birth	60	Marriage within the *jati*	School director	Civil servant	Housewife	English
M15	M	Iyer	Tamil Nadu	Panmpet	1964	52	Marriage within the *jati*	Chartered Accountant	Agriculture	Housewife	English
M16	M	Iyer	Tamil Nadu	Kochi (Kerala)	1977	60	Marriage within the *jati*	Professor	Advocate	Housewife	English
M17	M	Iyer	Tamil Nadu	Palghat (Kerala)	1982	77	Marriage within the *jati*	Civil servant	Doctor	Housewife	English
M18	F	Iyer	Tamil Nadu	Madras	Since birth	31	Marriage within the *jati*	Marketing	Advocate	Housewife	English
M19	F	Iyer	Tamil Nadu	Coimbatore	1995	22	Single	Agent (arts)	Finance executive	Housewife	English
M20	M	Iyangar	Tamil Nadu	Srirangan	1979	44	Marriage within the *jati*	Marketing	Advocate	Housewife	English

(contd.)

MADRAS (CHENNAI) (contd.)

	Sex	Subcaste	State of origin	Place of birth	Date of arrival in the city where the interview was conducted	Age	Marital status	Profession	Father's profession	Mother's profession	Language used for the interview
M21	M	Iyer	Tamil Nadu	Madras	Since birth	25	Single	Finance executive	Marketing	House-wife	English
M22	M	Iyer	Tamil Nadu	Madras	Since birth	29	Marriage within the *jati*	Software Engineer	Business-man	Civil servant	English
M23	M	Iyer	Tamil Nadu	Madras	Since birth	26	Single	Software Engineer	Engineer	House-wife	English
M24	F	Iyangar	Tamil Nadu	Madras	Since birth	21	Single	Student (engineer-ing)	Marketing Manager	House-wife	English
M25	M	Iyer	Tamil Nadu	Madras	Since birth	29	Marriage within the *jati*	Software Engineer	Civil servant	House-wife	English
M26	M	Iyangar	Tamil Nadu	Mayilad-uthurai	1955	61	Marriage within the *jati*	Engineer	School teacher	House-wife	English
M27	F	Iyangar	Tamil Nadu	Madras	Since birth	37	Marriage within the *jati*	Journalist	Engineer	House-wife	English
M28	M	Iyangar	Tamil Nadu	Madras	Since birth	43	Marriage within the *jati*	Professor-engineer	Civil servant	House-wife	English
M29	M	Iyer	Tamil Nadu	Madras	Since birth	71	Marriage within the *jati*	Teacher	Civil servant	House-wife	English

Bibliography

GENERAL BOOKS AND ARTICLES

Augé, M., *Le sens des autres—Actualité de l'anthropologie*, Paris: Fayard, 1994.

Bourdieu, P., *La Distinction: critique sociale du jugement*, Paris: Les Edition de Minuit, 1979.

Boudon, R. and F. Bourricaud, *Dictionnaire critique de la sociologie*, Paris: PUF, 1994

Breckenridge, C.A. and P. van der Veer, *Orientalism and the postcolonial predicament*, Delhi: Oxford University Press, 1990.

Donegani, J.M., *La liberté de choisir, pluralisme religieux et pluralisme politique dans le catholicisme français contemporain*, Paris: Presses de la FNSP, 1993.

Durkheim, E., *Les formes élémentaires de la vie religieuse*, Paris: Le livre de poche, 1991.

Frederic, L., *Dictionnaire de la civilisation indienne*, Paris: Robert Laffont, 1987.

Geertz, C., *The interpretation of cultures*, London: Fontana Press, 1993.

Grawitz, M. and J. Leca, eds., *Traité de Science Politique*, Paris: PUF, 4 vols., 1985.

(de) Heusch, L., 'L'ethnie: les vicissitudes d'un concept', *Archives Européennes de Sociologie*, Cambridge: Cambridge University Press, XXXVIII, 2, 1997.

Hobsbawm, E. and T. Ranger, eds., *The invention of tradition*, Cambridge: Cambridge University Press, 1983.

Institut Français d'Etudes sur l'Asie Centrale (IFEAC), *Inde—Asie centrale, routes du commerce et des idées*, Cahiers d'Asie Centrale, nos. 1-2, Aix-en-Provence: Editions Edisud, 1996.

Kabra, K.N., *Political economy of brain drain—reverse transfer of technology*, New Delhi: Arnold Heinemann, 1976.

Lacoste, Y., ed., *Dictionnaire géopolitique des Etats 1998*, Paris: Flammarion, 1997.

Livre blanc de l'orientalisme, Paris: Société Asiatique, 1993.

Lévi Strauss, C., ed., *L'identité*, Paris: PUF, 1995.

Martin, D.C., ed., *Cartes d'identité—Comment dit-on'nous' en politique?*, Paris: Presses de la FNSP, 1994.

Mauss, M., *Sociologie et Anthropologie*, Paris: PUF, 1993.
Nora, P., 'Entre Mémoire et Histoire', in *Les lieux de mémoire*, ed. P. Nora, Paris: Gallimard, 1993, vol. 1.
Ricoeur, P., *Soi-même comme un autre*, Paris: Seuil, 1990.
Said, E.W., *Orientalism, western conception of the Orient*, London: Penguin Books, 1995.
Schemeil, Y., 'Les cultures politiques' , in *Traité de Science Politique*, ed. M. Grawitz and J. Leca, vol. 3, Paris: PUF, 1985, pp. 237-307.
Sciences Humaines, Identité—Identités, Paris, special issue no. 15.
Serres, M., *Esthétiques sur Carpaccio*, Paris: Hermann, 1975.
Sharma, G., *Human rights and social justice—fundamental rights vis-a-vis directive principles*, Delhi: Deep & Deep Publications, 1997.

BOOKS AND ARTICLES RELATED TO ANCIENT INDIAN CIVILISATION AND TRADITIONAL SOCIAL STRUCTURES

Berreman, G.D., 'The brahmanical view of caste', in *Social stratification*, ed. D. Gupta, Delhi: Oxford University Press, 1991, pp. 84-92.
Bhagavata Purana, tr. G.V. Tagare, Ancient Indian Tradition & Mythology series, vols. 7 to 11, Delhi: Motilal Banarsidass, 1976.
Bhattacharya, J.N., *Hindu castes and sects: an exposition of the origin of the Hindu caste system and the bearing of the sects towards each other and towards other religious systems*, Delhi: Munshiram Manoharlal, 1995.
Biardeau, M., 'Brahmanes combattants dans un mythe du Sud de l'Inde', *The Adyar Library Bulletin*: Madras, 1967-8, pp. 519-30.
———, *L'hindouisme—anthropologie d'une civilisation*, Paris: Flammarion, 1981.
———, 'Le Brahmanisme ancien, ou la non-violence impossible', in *Violences et non-violences en Inde*, ed. D. Vidal et al., Paris: Editions de l'EHESS, Purusartha, 1994, pp. 125-39.
Biardeau, M. and C. Malamoud, *Le sacrifice dans l'Inde ancienne*, Paris: PUF, 1976.
Bouillier, V., 'La violence des non-violents, ou les ascètes au combat', in *Violences et non-violences en Inde*, ed. D. Vidal et al., Paris: Editions de l'EHESS, Purusartha, 1994, pp. 213-43.
Brahma Purana, Ancient Indian Tradition and Mythology Series, vols. 33 to 36, Delhi: Motilal Banarsidass, 1985-6.
Chaudhuri, N.C., *Hinduism—a religion to live by*, Delhi: Oxford University Press, 1996.
Conlon, F.F., *A caste in a changing world—the Chitrapur Saraswat Brahmans, 1700-1935*, Delhi: Thomson Press, 1977.
Crooke, W., *The Tribes and Castes of the North-Western India*, Delhi: Cosmo Publications, 1974 (1st edn. 1896), 4 vols.

Das, V., *Structure and Cognition—Aspects of Hindu Caste and Ritual*, Delhi: Oxford University Press, 1982.

Datta, S., *Migrant Brahmanas in northern India*, Delhi: Motilal Banarsidass, 1989.

Dumont, L., *La civilisation indienne et nous*, Paris: Armand Colin, 1975.

———, *Homo Hierarchicus*, Paris: Gallimard, 1992.

Fuller, C.J., *Servants of the Goddess, the priests of a south Indian temple*, Cambridge: Cambridge University Press, 1984.

Gupta, D., ed., *Social stratification*, Delhi: Oxford University Press, 1991.

Hiebert, P.G., 'India: the politicization of a sacred society', in *Religions and Societies: Asia and the Middle East*, ed. C. Caldarola: Mouton Publishers, 1982, pp. 289-331.

Hymnes spéculatifs du Véda, tr. L. Renou, Paris: Gallimard, 1956.

Karve, I., *Hindu society: an interpretation*, Poona: Deccan College, 1991.

Kolenda, P., 'How should we think about inequality or no tears for losers', *Man in India*, Ranchi, 1991, 71 (1), pp. 103-14.

Lévi, S., *La doctrine du sacrifice dans les Brahmanas*, Paris: PUF, 1966.

Le Mahabharata, comm. M. Biardeau, Paris: Flammarion, 1985, 2 vols.

Malamoud, C., 'Remarques sur la dissuasion dans l'Inde ancienne' in *Violences et non-violences en Inde*, ed. D. Vidal et al., Paris: Editions de l'EHESS, Purusartha, 1994, pp. 53-60.

Marriott, M., ed., *India through Hindu categories*, Delhi: Sage Publications, 1990.

Naudou, J., 'L'analyse ternaire de la nature dans la pensée indienne', *Revue de l'Histoire des Religions*, Paris, 1980, pp. 7-26.

———, 'Polymorphisme du divin et monothéisme en Inde', *Les Grandes Figures Religieuses, Lire les Polythéismes 1*, Annales littéraires de l'Université de Besançon, Paris: Les Belles Lettres, 1986, pp. 12-33.

Oguibénine, B., 'De la rhétorique de la violence', in *Violences et non-violences en Inde*, ed. D. Vidal et al., Paris: Editions de l'EHESS, Purusartha, 1994, pp. 81-95.

Ordinances of Manu (the), tr. A.C. Burnell, Delhi: Oriental Reprint, 1971.

Quigley, D., *The interpretation of caste*, Oxford: Clarendon Press, 1993.

Renou, L., *La civilisation indienne d'après les textes sanskrits*, Paris: Flammarion, 1950.

———, *L'Inde fondamentale*, Paris: Hermann, 1978.

Renou, L. and J. Filliozat, *L'Inde classique. Manuel des Etudes indiennes*, Paris: Librairie d'Amérique et d'Orient, Jean Maisonneuve, 1985, vol. 1.

Rocher, L., *Puranas*, History of Indian Literature, vol. 2, no. 3, Wiesbaden: Otto Harrassowitz, 1986.

Rose, H.A., *Glossary of the tribes and castes of the north-west frontier and the protected territories of the north-west frontier provinces*, Delhi: Amar Prakashan, 1919 (reed. 1979), 3 vols.

Schmidt, H.P., 'The origin of Ahimsa', in *Mélanges d'indianisme à la mémoire de Louis Renou,* Paris: E. de Boccard, 1968.

Sharma, L.P., *Ancient History of India*, Delhi: Vikas Publishing House, 1981.

Sharma, K.L., ed., *Social Stratification in India*, Delhi: Manohar, 1992.

Shrirama and I. Deva, 'Crystallisation of the Traditional Pattern of Stratification in India', in *Social Stratification in India*, ed. K.L. Sharma, Delhi: Manohar, 1992, pp. 1-28.

Singh, K.S., *People of India, India's Communities,* National Series, vol. IV, Delhi: Oxford University Press, 1998.

Singh, Y., *Social stratification and change in India*, Delhi: Manohar, 1977.

Tahtinen, U., *Ahimsa—Non-Violence in Indian Tradition*, London: Rider and Company, 1976.

Thapar, R., *Ancient Indian Social History—Some Interpretations*, Delhi: Sangam Books, 1984.

van der Veer, P., *Gods on Earth—The Management of Religious Experience and Identity in a North Indian Pilgrimage Centre,* Delhi: Oxford University Press, 1989.

———, 'The concept of the ideal Brahman as an indological construct', in *Hinduism reconsidered*, ed. H. Kulke et al., Delhi: Manohar, 1991.

Walker, B., *Hindu world: an encyclopedic survey of Hinduism*, Delhi: Munshiram Manoharlal, 1983, 2 vols.

BOOKS AND ARTICLES RELATED TO THE INDIAN ARMY

Alavi, S., *The Sepoys and the Company: Tradition and Transition in Northern Indian Military Culture 1770-1830*, Delhi: Oxford University Press, 1995.

Bali, P.N., *The History of the Mohyals—A Legendary People*, Mumbai: published by the author at Popular Press, 1986.

Barua, T.K., 'The role of the military in South Asia with special reference to India and Pakịstan', *VIth European Conference on Modern South Asian Studies*, Paris: CNRS, 1978.

Maj. Bhatia, P.S., 'Army, politics and national integration', *Sainik Samachar*, Mumbai, vol. 42, no. 1223, 15/01/95, pp. 72-3.

Capt. Bingley, A.H., *Caste Handbooks for the Indian army—Brahmans,* Calcutta: Government of India, rpt., 1918.

Bonarjee, P.D., *A handbook of the fighting races of India*, Delhi: Asian Publication Services, 1899, rpt., 1975.

Chibber, Lt. Gen. M.L., *Soldier's role in national integration*, Delhi: Manohar, 1986.

Cohen, S.P., 'The Untouchable Soldier: Caste, Politics and the Indian Army', in *Journal of Asian Studies,* Association for Asian Studies: Ann Arbor (Michigan), 1969, 28 (3), pp. 454-8.

Cohen, S.P., *The Indian Army—Its contribution to the development of a Nation*, Berkeley: University of California Press, 1971.

———, *The Indian Army—Its contribution to the development of a Nation*, Delhi: Oxford University Press, revd. edn., 1990.

———, 'The Military and Indian Democracy', in *India's democracy: an analysis of changing State-society relations*, ed. A. Kohli, New Jersey: Orient Longman, 1991, pp. 99-143.

Cunnningham, Lt. Col. W.B., *Handbooks for the Indian army—Dogras*, Calcutta: Government of India, rpt., 1918 and 1932.

Das, Maj. Gen. C.N., *Traditions and Customs of the Indian Armed Forces*, Delhi: Vision Books, 1984.

Gaylor, J., *Sons of John Company—The Indian and Pakistan Armies 1903-1991*, Delhi: Lancer International, 1993.

Jaggi, Lt. J., 'Military values', *Sainik Samachar*, Mumbai, vol. 42, no. 1223, 15/01/95, pp. 72-3.

Kadian, R., *India and its army*, Delhi: Vision Books, 1990.

Khanduri, Brig. C.B., *Field Marshal K.M. Cariappa—his life and times*, Delhi: Lancer Publishers, 1995.

Khanna, Brig. B.K., 'Ancient military heritage in India and current relevance', *Strategic Analysis*, Delhi, August 1995, pp. 677-92.

Kundu, A., 'The Indian Army's Continued Overdependence on Martial Races' Officers', *Indian Defence Review*, Delhi, July 1991.

Longer, V., *Forefront for Ever—The History of the Mahar Regiment*, Saugor: The Mahar Regimental Centre, 1981.

Mason, P., *A Matter of Honour—an account of the Indian army, its officers and men*, London: Jonathan Cape, 1974.

Menezes, Lt. Gen. S.L., *Fidelity and Honour—The Indian army from the seventeenth to the twenty first century*, Delhi: Viking, 1993.

Mac Munn, Lt. Gen. G., *The Martial Races of India*, London: Sampson Low, Marston & Co., 1932.

Omissi, D., *The Sepoy and the Raj—the Indian Army, 1860-1940*, London: Macmillan Press, 1994.

Parmar, L., *Society, Culture and Military System*, Jaipur: Rawat Publications, 1994.

Prasad, B., *Official history of the Indian armed forces in the second world war 1939-1945, India and the war*, Delhi: Government of India, 1966.

Prasad, S.N., *A survey of work done on the military history of India*, Calcutta: K.P. Bachi & Co., 1976.

Rosen, S.P., *Societies and military power: India and its armies*, Delhi: Oxford University Press, 1996.

Roy, T., *The politics of a popular uprising—Bundelkand in 1857*, Delhi: Oxford University Press, 1994.

Sainik Samachar, Mumbai, vol. 42, no. 1223, 15/01/95.

Sardeshpande, S.C., 'The Army: Perspective of a "Holy Cow"', *USI Journal*, Delhi, 1992.

Saxena, K.L.M., *The military system of India (1850-1900)*, Delhi: Sterling Publishers, 1974.

Sharma, Lt. Col. G., *Indian army through the ages*, Delhi: Allied Publishers, 1979.

———, *Valour and sacrifice: famous regiments of the Indian army*, Delhi: Allied Publishers, 1990.

———, *Nationalisation of the Indian army—1885-1947*, Delhi: Allied Publishers, 1996.

Singh, Brig. K.K., *Overcoming crisis in leadership, Indian army*, Delhi: Manas Publications, 1998.

BOOKS AND ARTICLES RELATED TO THE HISTORY OF SOUTH INDIA

Baker, C.J., *The Politics of South India, 1920-1937*, Cambridge: Cambridge University Press, 1976.

Barnett, M.R., 'Cultural Nationalist Electoral Politics in Tamil Nadu', in *Electoral Politics in the Indian States—Party systems and cleavages*, ed. M.R. Barnett et al., *Studies in Electoral Politics in the Indian States*, vol. 4, Delhi: Manohar, 1975.

———, *The Politics of Cultural Nationalism in South India*, Princeton: Princeton University Press, 1976.

Béteille, A., *Caste, Class and Power: Changing Patterns of Stratification in a Tanjore Village*, Delhi: Oxford University Press, 1996.

Cederlof, G., *Bonds lost—subordination, conflict and mobilisation in rural south India, 1900-1970*, Delhi: Manohar, 1997.

Dirks, N.B., 'The Politics of Caste and Race in Contemporary Southern India', in *Caste Today*, ed. C.J. Fuller, Delhi: Oxford University Press, 1996, pp. 263-95.

Frankel, F.R., 'Middle Classes and Castes in India's Politics prospects for political accomodation', in *India's democracy: an analysis of changing state-society relations*, ed. A. Kohli, New Jersey: Orient Longman, 1991, pp. 225-61.

Fuller, C.J., 'The Brahmins and Brahmanical Values in Modern Tamil Nadu', in *Institutions and Inequalities—Essays in honour of André Béteille*, ed. R. Guha and J.P. Parry, Delhi: Oxford University Press, 1999.

Gabriel, S., 'Social background to politics in Tamil Nadu', in *Encyclopaedia of India and her states*, vol. 8: *Karnataka, Kerala and Tamil Nadu*, Delhi: Deep & Deep Publications, 1998, pp. 334-40.

Geetha, V. and V. Rajadurai, *Towards a non-brahmin millenium*, Calcutta: Samya, 1998.

Grover, V. and R. Arora, eds., *Encyclopaedia of India and her states*, vol. 8:

Karnataka, Kerala and Tamil Nadu, Delhi: Deep & Deep Publications, 1998.

Hardgrave, R.L., *Essays in the political sociology of south India*, Delhi: Manohar, 1993.

Irschick, E.F., *Politics and Social Conflict in South India—The Non-Brahmin Movement and Tamil Separatism, 1916-1929*, Berkeley and Los Angeles: University of California Press, 1969.

———, *Dialogue and History, Constructing South India, 1795-1895*, Delhi: Oxford University Press, 1994.

Kapur, A.C., *Constitutional history of India, 1765-1984*, Delhi: S. Chand & Company, 1985.

Nair, B.N., *The dynamic brahmin*, Mumbai: Popular Book Depot, 1959.

Palanithurai, G., ed., *Caste, Politics and Society in Tamil Nadu*, Delhi: Kanishka, 1994.

Pandian, S.S., 'Crisis in DMK', *Economic and Political Weekly*, Mumbai, 29(5), pp. 221-3.

Radhakrishnan, P., 'Backward Classes in Tamil Nadu: 1872-1988', *Economic and Political Weekly*, Mumbai, 10/03/90, pp. 509-20.

———, 'Communal Representation in Tamil Nadu, 1850-1916', *Economic and Political Weekly*, Mumbai, 21/07/93, 23(31), pp. 1585-97.

———, 'Backward class movements in Tamil Nadu', in *Caste—its twentieth century avatar*, ed. M.N. Srinivas, Delhi: Viking, 1996, pp. 110-34.

———, 'Caste, Politics and the Reservation Issue', in *Illfare in India: Essays on India's Social Sector in Honour of S. Guhan*, ed. B. Harriss-White and S. Subramaniam, Delhi: Sage Publications, 1999, pp. 163-95.

Ramaswamy, V., 'Tamil Separatism and Cultural Negociations: Gender Politics and Literature in Tamil Nadu', *Social Scientist*, vol. 26 (5-6), Delhi, May-June 1998.

Samuel, G.J., *Tamil identity and resistance to sanskrit*, Chennai: Institute of Asian Studies, 1998.

Singer, M., *When a great tradition modernizes—an anthropological approach to Indian civilization*, New York: Praeger Publishers, 1972.

———, 'Tradition and modernity in Madras and in Yankee City', *Man in India*, 1991 (Special), 71 (1), pp. 31-46.

Srinivas, M.N., *Village, Caste, Gender and Method—Essays in Indian Social Anthropology*, Delhi: Oxford University Press, 1998.

Subramanian, N., *The brahmin in the Tamil country*, Madurai: Ennes Publications, 1989.

———, *Ethnicity and populist mobilization—political parties, citizens and democracy in south Indian*, Delhi: Oxford University Press, 1999.

Viswanathan, V.N., 'Dravidian movement: an epiphenomenal study', in *Caste, Politics and Society in Tamil Nadu*, ed. G. Palanithurai, Delhi: Kanishka, 1994, pp. 87-95.

Washbrook, D.A., 'Caste, class and dominance in modern Tamil Nadu—

non brahmanism, dravidianism and Tamil nationalism', in *Dominance and state power in modern India: Decline of a social order*, ed. F.R. Frankel and M.S.A. Rao, Delhi: Oxford University Press, 1989, vol. 1, pp. 204-64.

BOOKS AND ARTICLES RELATED TO UNTOUCHABLES

Ambedkar, B.R., *Babasaheb Ambedkar writings and speeches*, comp. V. Moon, Mumbai: Education Department, Government of Maharashtra, vol. 1 (1989), vol. 5 (1989), vol. 7 (1990), vol. 9 (1991).

Dube, S., *Words like freedom: the memoirs of an impoverished family, 1947-1997*, Delhi: Harper Collins India, 1998.

Gavaskar, M., 'Colonialism within Colonialism: Phule's Critique of Brahmin Power', in *Dalits in Modern India—Vision and Values*, ed. S.M. Michael, Delhi: Vistaar Publications, 1999, pp. 80-98.

Gupta, S.K., *Scheduled castes in modern Indian politics: their emergence as a political power*, Delhi: Munshiram Manoharlal, 1985.

Guru, G., 'The politics of naming', *Seminar*, Delhi, no. 471, November 1998, pp. 14-18.

Ilaiah, K., *Why I am not a Hindu—a Sudra critique of Hindutva philosophy, culture and political economy*, Calcutta: Samya, 1996 .

———, 'In search of the roots of anti-caste stuggle: a dalitist reading of the buddhist reading', *Research-in-Progress Papers, History and Society*, Nehru Memorial Museum & Library, Third Series, no. 1, Delhi, March 1996.

Jaffrelot, C., *Dr. Ambedkar, Leader intouchable et père de la Constitution indienne*, Paris: Presses de Sciences Po, 2000.

Joshi, B.R., ed., *Untouchable!: voices of the Dalit liberation movement*, Delhi: Selectbook Service Syndicate, 1986.

Kamble, R., 'Dalit interpretations of society', *Seminar*, Delhi, no. 471, November 1998, pp. 19-23.

Kannan, M., 'les *dalit* tamouls en quête d'une littérature', *Bulletin de l'Ecole Française d'Extrême Orient*, Paris, 1996, vol. 83, pp. 125-53.

Khare, R.S., *Untouchable as himself: ideology, identity, and pragmatism among the Lucknow Chamars*, Cambridge: Cambridge University Press, 1984.

Lynch, O.M., 'The Politics of Untouchability: a case from Agra, India', in *Structure and change in Indian society*, ed. M. Singer and B. Cohn, Chicago: Aldine Press, 1968, pp. 209-39.

Michael, S.M., 'Dalit Vision of a Just Society in India', in *Dalits in Modern India—Vision and Values*, ed. S.M. Michael, Delhi: Vistaar Publications, 1999, pp. 99-117.

Michael, S.M., ed., *Dalits in Modern India—Vision and Values*, Delhi: Vistaar Publications, 1999.

Mohapatra, B.N., 'Understanding indignities', *Seminar*, Delhi, no. 471, November 1998, pp. 43-6.

Omvedt, G., *Dalits and the democratic revolution: Dr. Ambedkar and the Dalit movement in colonial India*, Delhi: Sage Publications, 1994.

———, *Dalit Visions: the anti-caste movement and the construction of an Indian identity*, Hyderabad: Orient Longman, Tracts for the Times (8), 1995.

Pai, S., 'The BSP in Uttar Pradesh', *Seminar*, Delhi, no. 471, November 1998, pp. 38-42.

Poitevin, G., tr. and comp., *Maharashtra: paysans et intouchables de l'Inde occidentale*, Paris: Lieu Commun, 1987.

Poitevin, G. and Rairkar, H., *Stonemill and bhakti: from the devotion of peasant women to the philosophy of swamis*, Delhi: D.K. Printworld, 1996.

Poitevin, G., *The Voice and the Will, Subaltern Agency: Forms and Motives*, Delhi: CSH–Manohar, 2002.

Pushpendra, 'Dalit assertion through electoral politics', *Economic and Political Weekly*, Mumbai, 34 (36), 1999, pp. 2609-18.

Rai, V.K., 'In search of a new balance—caste, region and community in Uttar Pradesh', *Economic and Political Weekly*, Mumbai, 34 (34 and 35), 1999, pp. 2400-8.

Ram, K., 'Why is Bahujan Samaj dependent in Independent India?', Delhi: Bahujan Samaj Party, 1997.

Singh, J., 'Ambedkarisation and assertion of Dalit identity, socio-cultural protest in Meerut district of western Uttar Pradesh', *Economic and Political Weekly*, Mumbai, 03/10/1998, pp. 2611-18.

Webster, J.C.B., 'Who is a Dalit?', in *Dalits in Modern India—Vision and Values*, ed. S.M. Michael, Delhi: Vistaar Publications, 1999, pp. 68-79.

Yadav, K.C., ed., *From periphery to centre stage—Ambedkar, Ambedkarism and Dalit future*, Delhi: Manohar, 2000.

Yadav, Y., 'Electoral Politics in the Time of Change—India's Third Electoral System, 1989-1999', *Economic and Political Weekly*, Mumbai, 34 (34 and 35), 1999, pp. 2393-9.

Zelliot, E., *From Untouchable to Dalit: Essays on the Ambedkar Movement*, Delhi: Manohar, 1992.

———, 'The roots of Dalit consciousness', *Seminar*, Delhi, no. 471, November 1998, pp. 28-32.

BOOKS AND ARTICLES RELATED TO THE POLITICAL HISTORY OF INDIA FROM COLONIAL TIMES

Ahmad, A., 'Between Orientalism and Historicism: Anthropological Knowledge of India', *Studies in History*, Delhi: Sage Publications, 7 (1), n.s. (1991).

Akinchan, S., *Caste, Class and Politics, Emerging Horizons of Political Sociology*, Delhi: Gyan Publishing House, 1995.

Alam, J., 'Is caste appeal casteism? Oppressed castes in politics', *Economic and Political Weekly*, Mumbai, vol. 34 (13), pp. 757-61.

Arora, B. and B. Radin, eds., *The changing role of the all-India services, an assessment and agenda for future research on federalism and the all-India services*, Delhi: CASI/UPIASI-CPR, 2000.

Appadurai, A., 'Number in the colonial imagination', in *Orientalism and the postcolonial predicament*, ed. C.A. Breckenridge and P. van der Veer, Delhi: Oxford University Press, 1990, pp. 314-39.

Assayag, J., R. Lardinois and D. Vidal, *Orientalism and anthropology: From Max Müller to Louis Dumont*, Pondy Papers in Social Sciences, no. 24, Institut Français de Pondichéry, 1997.

Bailey, F.G., 'For a sociology of India', *Contributions to Indian Sociology*, III, Delhi, 1959.

Bayly, S., *Caste, Society and Politics in India from the eighteenth to the modern age*, The New Cambridge History of India, IV (3), Cambridge: Cambridge University Press, 1999.

Béteille, A., 'Caste in contemporary India', in *Caste Today*, ed. C.J. Fuller, Delhi: Oxford University Press, 1996, pp. 150-79.

———, *Society and politics in India—essays in a comparative perspective*, Delhi: Oxford University Press, 1992.

———, *Backward classes in contemporary India*, Delhi: Oxford University Press, 1992.

Bhambhri, C.P., *Indian Politics since Independence*, Delhi: Shipra Publications, 1999.

Bhatia, B.M., *India's middle class: role in nation building*, Delhi: Konark Publishers, 1994.

Brass, P.R., *The Politics of India since Independence*, The New Cambridge History of India, Cambridge: Cambridge University Press, 1990.

Chalam, K.S., 'Caste and economic reforms', *Seminar*, Delhi, no. 471, November 1998, pp. 33-7.

Chatterjee, P., 'The Manifold Uses of Jati', in *Region, Religion, Caste, Gender and Culture in Contemporary India*, ed. T.V. Sathyamurthy, Social Change and Political Discourse in India: Structures of Power, Movements of Resistance, vol. 3, Delhi: Oxford University Press, 1996, pp. 281-92.

Chaturvedi, G. and J. Chaturvedi 'The construction of Saraswati—Formation and transformation of Saffron identity in contemporary Uttar Pradesh', in *Education and Society in India*, Seminar organized by the International Centre and the Centre de Sciences Humaines, Delhi, India International Centre, 29-31 March 2000.

Cohn, B.S., *An anthropologist among the historians and others essays*, Delhi: Oxford University Press, 1990.

The Constitution of India, Government of India, 1991.

Dalmia, V. and H. Stietencron (von), *Representing Hinduism—The construction of religious traditions and national identities*, Delhi: Sage Publications, 1995.

Datta, N., 'Arya Samaj and the making of Jat identity', *Studies in History*, Delhi: Sage Publications, 13 (1), n.s., 1997, pp. 97-119.

Datta, N., 'Jats: Trading caste Status for Empowerment', *Economic and Political Weekly*, Mumbai, 06/11/99, p. 3172.

Desai, R., 'Culturalism and Contemporary Right—Indian bourgeoisie and Political Hindutva', *Economic and Political Weekly*, Mumbai, 20/03/99, pp. 695-712.

Dirks, N.B., 'Différence et discrimination—La politique des castes dans l'Inde post-coloniale', *Annales—Histoire, Sciences Sociales*, Paris, 52(3), May-June 1997, pp. 593-619.

Dodwell, H.H., ed., *Cambridge History of India: the Indian Empire, 1858-1919*, Delhi: S. Chand & Co., vol. 6, 1932.

Dorin, B. et al., eds., *Le Patronat en Inde*, Delhi: Centre de Sciences Humaines, June 2000.

Elst, K., *Dr Ambedkar—a true aryan*, Delhi: Voice of India, 1993.

Farooqui, A., 'Some Comments on Louis Dumont and the Orientalist Understanding of Caste', *Trends in Social Science research*, Delhi: Cambridge Press, vol. 3, no. 2, December 1996.

Frankel, F.R. and M.S.A. Rao, eds., *Dominance and state power in modern India, Decline of a social order*, Delhi: Oxford University Press, vol. 1 (1989) and vol. 2 (1990).

Fuller, C.J., ed., *Caste Today*, Delhi: Oxford University Press, 1996.

Galanter, M., *Competing equalities, Law and the Backward classes in India*, Delhi: Oxford University Press, 1984.

Galanter, M., *Law and society in modern India*, Delhi: Oxford University Press, 1989.

Gandhi, M.K., *Expériences de vérité ou autobiographie*, Paris: PUF, Quadrige, 1994.

Ghosh, P.S., *BJP and the Evolution of Hindu Nationalism—From Periphery to Centre*, Delhi: Manohar, 2000.

Gould, H.A., *The Hindu Caste System: Politics and Caste*, vol. 3, Delhi: Chanakya, 1990.

Gupta, D., *Interrogating caste—Understanding hierarchy & difference in Indian society*, Delhi: Penguin Books, 2000.

Halbfass, W., *India and Europe—an essay in philosophical understanding*, Delhi: Motilal Banarsidass, 1990.

Hasan, Z., 'Communal Mobilization and Changing Majority in Uttar Pradesh', in *Making India Hindu*, ed. D. Ludden, Delhi: Oxford University Press, 1996, pp. 81-97.

Heath, O. and Y. Yadav, 'The United Colours of Congress, social profile of

Congress voters, 1996 and 1998', *Economic and Political Weekly*, Mumbai, 34 (34 and 35), 1999, pp. 2518-28.

Heath, O., 'Anatomy of BJP's rise to power—social, regional and political expansion in 1990s', *Economic and Political Weekly*, Mumbai, 34 (34 and 35), 1999, pp. 2511-17.

Heidrich, J., ed., *Changing Identities: The transformation of Asian and African societies under colonialism*, Berlin: Verlag Das Arabische Buch, 1994.

Heredia, R.C., 'Subaltern alternatives on caste, class and ethnicity', *Contributions to Indian Sociology*, Delhi, 34 (1), pp. 37-62.

Hooda, S.P., *Contesting reservations, the Indian experiment on affirmative action*, Jaipur: Rawat Publications, 2001.

Inden, R.B., *Imagining India*, Oxford: Basil Blackwell, 1990.

Irschick, E.F., 'Gandhian non-violent protest: rituals of avoidance or rituals of confrontation?', *Economic and Political Weekly*, Mumbai, 21 (29), 1986, pp. 1279-83.

Jaffrelot, C., 'L'émergence des nationalismes en Inde—Perspectives théoriques', *Revue Française de Science Politique*, Paris, August 1988, pp. 555-75.

———, 'Des nationalistes en quête d'une nation: des partis nationalistes hindous au vingtième siècle', Ph.D. thesis, Paris, 1991, 3 vols.

———, *Les nationalistes hindous, idéologie, implantation et mobilisation des années 1920 aux années 1990*, Paris: Presses de la FNSP, 1993.

———, *Hindu nationalist movement and Indian politics, 1925 to the 1990s: strategies of identity building implantation and mobilisation*, Delhi: Penguin Books, 1996.

———, *La démocratie en Inde*, Paris: Fayard, 1998.

———, 'La stratégie de bienfaisance des nationalistes hindous—conjurer l'aspiration égalitaire des basses castes', *Critique Internationale* (4), Paris: Presses de Sciences Po, Summer 1999.

Jaffrelot, C. and J. Zérénini-Brotel, 'La montée des basses castes dans la politique nord-indienne', *Pouvoirs* (90), Paris: Seuil, 1999.

Jayaram, N., 'Caste and Hinduism: changing protean relationship', in *Caste—its twentieth century avatar*, ed. M.N. Srinivas, Delhi: Viking, 1996, pp. 69-86.

Jhunjhunwala, B., *Varna vyavastha—governance through caste system*, Jaipur: Rawat Publications, 1999.

Karve, D.D., *The new brahmins, five maharashtrian families*, Berkeley and Los Angeles: University of California Press, 1963.

Khilnani, S., *The idea of India*, London: Hamish Hamilton, 1997.

King, R.D., *Nehru and the language politics of India*, Delhi: Oxford University Press, 1997.

Klass, M., *Caste, the emergence of the south Asian social system*, Delhi: Manohar, 1998.

Kohli, A., *India's democracy: an analysis of changing state-society relations*, New Jersey: Orient Longman, 1991.

Kothari, R., *Politics in India*, Delhi: Orient Longman, 1989.

Kothari, R., ed., *Caste in Indian Politics*, Delhi: Orient Longman, 1991.

Kothari, R., *Communalism in Indian Politics*, Delhi: Rainbow Publishers, 1998.

Kurian, G. and R.P. Srivastava, *Overseas Indians—a study in adaptation*, Delhi: Vikas, 1983.

Lal, S.K., *The urban élite*, Delhi: Thomson Press, 1974.

Lardinois, R., 'Louis Dumont et la science indigène', *Actes de la Recherche en Sciences Sociales*, Paris: Seuil, nos. 106-7, March 1995.

Leach, E.R., 'What we should mean by caste', in *Aspects of Caste in South India, Ceylon and North-West Pakistan*, ed. E.R. Leach, Cambridge: Cambridge University Press, 1960.

Livre blanc de l'orientalisme, Paris: Société Asiatique, 1993.

Madan, T.N., *A l'opposé du renoncement*, Paris: Editions de la Maison des Sciences de l'Homme, 1990.

———, 'Whither Indian Secularism?', *Modern Asian Studies*, Cambridge: Cambridge University Press, 1993, 27 (3), pp. 667-97.

Mahajan, G., ed., *Democracy, difference and social justice*, Delhi: Oxford University Press, 1998.

Majeed, J., *Ungoverned imaginings—James Mill's The History of British India and Orientalism*, New York: Clarendon Press-Oxford, 1992.

Markovits, C., ed., *Histoire de l'Inde moderne: 1480-1950*, Paris: Fayard, 1994.

Mathur, K. and J.W. Bjorkman, *Top policy makers in India—Cabinet ministers and their Civil Service advisors*, Delhi: Concept Publishing Company, 1994.

Menon, D.M., 'Being a brahmin the marxist way: E.M.S. Nambudiripad and the pasts of Kerala', *Research-in-Progress Papers, History and Society*, Nehru Memorial Museum & Library, Third Series, Delhi, January 1998.

Mishra, J., *Equality versus justice—the problem of reservations for backward classes*, Delhi: Deep & Deep Publications, 1996.

Moller, J., 'Anti-reservation protests and the Uttarakhand pro-autonomy movement: caste and regional identities in the Indian Himalayas', *South Asia Research*, Delhi: Sage Publications, 20 (2), 2000.

Naipaul, V.S., *L'Inde: un million de révoltes*, Paris: Plon, 1992.

Nandy, A., 'Rencontre ultime: la dimension politique de l'assassinat de Gandhi', in *Miroir de l'Inde: études indiennes en sciences sociales*, ed. L. Lardinois, Paris: Maison des Sciences de l'Homme, 1988, pp. 269-99.

———, *At the Edge of Psychology, Essays in Politics and Culture*, Delhi: Oxford University Press, 1990.

Navlakha, S., *Elite and Social Change—A study of Elite Formation in India*, Delhi: Sage Publications, 1989.

Patel, S., 'On the discourse of communalism', in *Region, Religion, Caste, Gender and Culture in Contemporary India*, ed. T.V. Sathyamurthy, Social Change and Political Discourse in India: Structures of Power, Movements of Resistance, vol. 3, Delhi: Oxford University Press, 1996, pp. 145-79.

Pinto, A., 'Education and democracy in India: contribution of the Christian missions', in *Education and Society in India*, seminar organized by the India International Centre and the Centre de Sciences Humaines, Delhi, India International Centre, 29-31 March 2000.

Pouchepadass, J., ed., *Caste et classe en Asie du sud*, Paris: Editions de l'EHESS, Purusartha, 1982.

Rai, V.N., *Combating Communal Conflicts (Perception of police neutrality during Hindu-Muslim riots in India)*, Delhi: Renaissance Publishing House, 1999.

Rath, R., 'Job reservation and social mobility—Case study of Tribal Bihar', *Man in India*, Ranchi, 1991, 71 (4), pp. 639-46.

Rao, M.S.A., *Social Movements in India*, Delhi: Manohar, 1984.

———, *Social Movements and Social Transformation*, Delhi: Manohar, 1987.

Reservation for Backward Classes, Mandal Commission report of the Backward Classes Commission, Delhi: Akalank, 1980.

Rudolph, L.I. and S.H. Rudolph, 'The Political Role of India's Caste Associations', *Pacific Affairs*, 33 (1), March 1960.

———, *In pursuit of Lakshmi, the political economy of the Indian state*, Delhi: Orient Longman, 1987.

Sathyamurthy, T.V., ed., *Region, Religion, Caste, Gender and Culture in Contemporary India*, Social Change and Political Discourse in India: Structures of Power, Movements of Resistance, vol. 3, Delhi: Oxford University Press, 1996.

Sen, A., *Inequality reexamined*, Oxford: Oxford University Press, 1992.

Sheth, D.L., 'Secularisation of caste and making of new middle class', *Economic and Political Weekly*, Mumbai, 34 (34 and 35), 1999, pp. 2502-10.

Srinivas, M.N., *On living in a revolution and other essays*, Delhi: Oxford University Press, 1992.

Srinivas, M.N., ed., *Caste—its twentieth century avatar*, Delhi: Viking, 1996.

Varma, P. K., *The great Indian middle class*, Delhi: Viking, 1998.

van der Veer, P., *Religious nationalism: Muslims and Hindus in India*, Delhi: Oxford University Press, 1996.

Vidal, D., 'Max Müller and the theosophists, or the other half of Victorian Orientalism', *Pondy Papers in Social Sciences*, no. 24, Institut Français de Pondichéry, 1997.

Zins, M.J., *Histoire politique de l'Inde indépendante*, Paris: PUF, 1992.

Index

Adi-Dravidas, 119
ahimsa, 64-5, 71, 95, 103, 199-200, 259. *See also* non-violence
Ahirs, 81
Ahmad, Aijaz, 13
Ahura Mazda, 10
AIADMK, *see* All India Dravida Munnetra Kazhagam
All India Dravida Munnetra Kazhagam, 127, 131
alterity, notion of, 23-4, 27-8
Ambedkar, B.R., 44, 128, 177, 191, 198-207, 209, 213-14, 216-18, 228
Anna University, 151
Annadurai, C.N., 127, 137
anti-Brahminism, 137, 147, 149, 171, 195, 198, 217
anti-Hindi agitation, 137
anti-Hindu agitation, 218
Appadurai, Arjun, 16
Arya Samaj, 99, 233
Aryans, 68, 82, 132-6, 193, 213
Athawale, Pandurang Shastri, 264
Augé, Marc, 264
Ayachaks, 75
Ayodhya controversy, 212, 215, 249-50, 259

Babri Masjid demolition, 249
Backward Classes Commission, 131, 233
Backward Classes, 129-32, 149-51, 154, 173, 233
Bahishkrut Hitakarini Sabha, 204
Bahujan Samaj Party, 210, 215-18, 220, 237, 249, 253
Bailey, F.G., 18
battle of Karbala, 74
Baviskar, B.S., 236
Bengal Army, 73, 77-8
Béteille, André, 18, 20-1, 235-6, 241
Bhagavad Gita, 94-5, 175
Bhagavata Purana, 67, 69
Bharati, C. Subramania, 135
Bharatiya Janata Party, 49, 207, 209-17, 219-20, 249-50, 253-4
Bhoomi Sena, 252
Bhumihars, 73-5
Bhumiyar, 252
Biardeau, Madeleine, 71
BJP, *see* Bharatiya Janata Party
Bombay Presidency, 77
Bouglé, Célestin, 14, 17
Brahma Purana, 68
brahman, 66
Brahmanas, 64-5, 103
'brahmanocentrism', 14
Brahmarshi Sena, 252
Brahmin ethics, 37
Brahmin identity, 9, 17, 21, 24, 26-8, 33-4, 36-9, 46, 48, 55, 61-3, 99, 111, 119, 146-8, 151, 163, 167-8, 175, 179, 190, 207, 220, 248, 253, 259-60, 263-4
Brahminical values, 14-15, 21-2, 36-7, 39-40, 43, 46, 48, 68, 72, 94, 9697, 103-4, 120, 159, 163, 165, 168, 179, 192, 195-6, 198, 200-3, 206, 211-12,

214, 216, 239, 246, 250-2, 260, 262-5
Brahminism, 24, 43, 48, 121, 125, 132, 137, 147, 164, 172, 175, 179, 189, 193, 199, 201-2, 204, 213, 217, 250. *See also* neo-Brahminism
Brahmins and politics, 33
Brahmins and the military, 61, 99
Brahmins in Indian army, 28, 42, 56, 61-3, 72-4, 76-86, 93-108, 110-11, 155, 189, 233, 259-60, 263. *See also* Indian army, 'Punjabization' of Brahmins of Awadh, 83
Brahmins of Tamil Nadu, 111, 155, 158. *See also* South Indian Brahmins
Brahmins, as an élite group, 35, 51, 162, 240
Brahmins, classification of
  'closed élitist' Brahmins, 50, 56, 161, 239, 263
  'natural' Brahmins, 35, 37, 43, 46-50, 99, 167, 246
  'responsible' Brahmins, 43
  contemporary Brahmin, 24
  impersonal Brahmins, 34
  Kashmiri Brahmin, 160
  middle-class Brahmins, 93, 154-5, 169-70, 240
  Nayee Brahmins, 247
  open elitist Brahmins, 43
  See also non-Brahmins
British Raj, 78
BSP, *see* Bahujan Samaj Party
Buddhism, 66-7, 72, 199-200, 203, 206

Caldwell, Robert, 133
Caste Handbooks for the Indian Army, 72, 81, 84
Caste in Indian Politics, 236
caste, 9, 11-12, 14-22, 25-6, 28, 33, 35-7, 39, 40-3, 47, 50-6, 62, 66, 73, 77-8, 80, 83-4, 86, 94, 98-103, 105, 110-11, 119, 122, 124-5, 127-31, 133, 135, 137, 139-40, 146, 149, 154, 160, 169, 173-4, 180, 192-5, 199, 201-13, 215-16, 220, 228-30, 234-8, 242-3, 246-53, 259-62, 265
caste-based reservation, 235
  ethnicization of, 20
  institution of, 17, 202, 235, 238
  nature of caste, 17
  casteism, 19, 39-40, 44, 49, 139, 237-38, 246
  notion of, 9, 15, 17
Catholics, 176-79
Chamars, 98, 192-3, 264
Chatterjee, Partha, 19
Chavan, Y.B., 101
Chitpavans, 75
Christians, 37, 100, 125, 161, 175, 249-50
civilisation indienne et nous, La, 14
Cohen, S.P., 101, 106
Cohn, B.S., 16
Congress, *see* Indian National Congress
Crooke, W., 17
culture, 18, 20, 23-5, 28, 44, 87, 96, 107, 120, 126, 133-7, 139, 159-60, 165-8, 194, 196, 220, 259

Dalit empowerment, 220
Dalit identity, 206, 218
Dalit politics, 189, 228
Dalitbahujans. *See also* Scheduled Castes
Dalits, 55, 180, 189-90, 194-5, 197-9, 206-7, 209, 213-20, 228-9, 234, 237-9, 244-5, 249-52, 254, 260-1, 265
Desai, Morarji, 232
Devi Lal, 232

Dharmashastras, 68
Dirks, Nicholas B., 133
divide and rule policy, 16, 93, 214, 236
DMK, *see* Dravida Munnetra Kazhagam
Dogras, 74, 81, 86, 93, 100
Donégani, J.M., 176-7, 179
Dravida Kazhagam, 127
Dravida Munnetra Kazhagam, 127, 136-8, 140
Dravidianism, 132
Dravidians, 119, 125-7, 132-40, 147, 149, 160, 195, 198, 228, 232
Dravidian movement, 119, 125-7, 132, 134-40, 147
Dumont, Louis, 12, 14-15, 18, 20, 243
Durkheim, Emile, 14-15

East India Company, 15, 76, 98
Economic and Political Weekly, 43, 211
Edda, 10
Engineer, Asghar Ali, 237
Eurocentricism, 13

forward community, 148, 152, 166, 172
Frontline, 168, 249

Gandhi, 75, 108, 175, 192, 195, 199-201, 203-4, 206, 208-9, 216, 232, 244, 249
  and emotional blackmail, 200-1
Gandhi, Indira, 108
Gandhi, Rajiv, 216
Garhwalis, 81
Gaudras, 73-4
Gauds, 73-4, 77, 81
Geertz, Clifford, 23
Ghurye, 16, 242
Gita, see Bhagavad Gita
Gods on Earth, 259
Godse, Nathuram, 75
Goswami, Rajiv, 243
gotra, 73-4
Gould, Harold A., 237
Government of India Act of 1919, 85, 125
Great Hindu Tradition, the, 192, 195-6, 199-200, 202, 212, 214, 219, 235, 259
Green Revolution, 210, 233, 261
Guénon, René, 14
Gujars, 81
gunas, 11
Gupta, Dipankar, 245
Gurkhas, 81-2, 100

Harijan, 54, 195, 197, 246. *See also* Untouchables
Hervey, Albert, 81
Heusch, Luc de, 20
Hinduism, 9, 13, 21, 36, 65, 72, 75, 124, 133-4, 161, 175, 180, 192, 201-3, 206, 213-14, 249-50
Hindu-Muslim conflicts, 106, 161
Hindutva, 214-15, 219, 249-50
Hocart, A.M., 17
Homo Hierarchicus, 14-15, 18
Hutton, J.H., 17, 128
hymn to *Purusa*, 10

Ibbetson, D., 17
IMA, *see* Indian Military Academy
Inden, Ronald, 12, 13
India Today, 105
Indian Administrative Service, 109, 174, 231
Indian Army, 98, 100-3, 106, 108
  'Punjabization' of, 80
Indian Military Academy, 86, 95, 108, 110
Indian National Congress, 50, 84, 108, 124-6, 131, 136-8, 160, 189, 194, 203-4, 206-212,

216-17, 220, 232, 234-5, 239, 249
ipse, 23

Janata Dal, 232
Janata Party, 232
jatis, 11, 21, 35-6, 73-4, 99, 237, 251
Jats, 55, 81, 99, 233-4, 244, 247, 251
Jayalalitha, J., 131, 138
Justice Party, 125-6, 134, 136

Kalelkar Commission, 130-1
Kalyan Singh, 215, 253
Kammas, 125
Kanaujiyas, 73-4
Kancha Ilaiah, 192, 194-5, 203, 218-19
Kanshi Ram, 216-18
Kanyakubjas, 73
karma, 35, 65
Kashmiri Pandits, 152, 173, 263
Kayasths, 16, 68
Khatris, 119
Kondvilkar, Madhav, 198
Kothari, Rajni, 19, 55, 195, 236-8, 246
Kshatriyas, 11, 16, 34, 49, 63-4, 66, 68, 70-3, 75, 95, 99, 101-2, 119, 193, 203, 233-4
Kumaonis, 81

Lardinois, Roland, 15
Laws of Manu, 17, 69. *See also* *Manusmriti*
Laxman, Bangaru, 254
Leach, E.R., 18
Lévi-Strauss, 24
Lingayats, 264
'logic of fragmentation', 235
Lord Chelmsford, 85
Lord Macaulay, 122, 124
lower castes, 27, 55-6, 77, 105, 151, 163, 177, 194, 203, 208, 214-15, 220, 229, 252, 253, 260-1, 263

Mac Munn, 82-3
Madras Presidency, 122, 124, 126
Madras University, 150, 155
Mahabharata, 71, 74, 100, 193
Mahars, 196, 204
Mahasabha, 98, 251
Mahatma, *see* Gandhi
Mandal Commission, 39, 43, 105, 130-2, 148, 150, 152, 155, 158, 173, 176, 179, 189-90, 212, 215, 228-34, 236-8, 242-4, 246, 248-9, 262-3
Mandal Report, 179
Mandalization, 232-3, 239, 249
Mandir *versus* Mandal, 249
Manu, 67, 69, 194, 202. *See also* Laws of Manu
Manusmriti, 202-4
Marxist ideology, 194-5
military, 28, 40, 61, 63, 72-6, 78-81, 83-7, 93-7, 99-110, 230, 259-60
Mill, James, 13, 29, 287
Mohapatra, Bishnu N., 192
Mohyal Brahmins, 81, 93, 110
Mohyal Mahasabha, 110
Mohyals, 74-5, 99, 100, 103, 105, 110, 252
Montagu-Chelmsford Report, 85
Mueller, Max, 12
Muslims, 37, 45, 71, 75, 77, 79, 81-2, 100, 105-6, 123, 125, 133, 161, 178, 189, 206, 208, 213, 249-50

Naicker, E.V. Ramaswamy, 126, 135
Nairs, 125, 195
Narayanan, K.R., 105
Narayanan, N., 170

National Front, 232
National Minorities Commission, 173
nationalization of banks, 153
Nehru, Jawaharlal, 108, 155, 192, 205, 208
neo-Brahminism, 43, 46, 176
  and non-Brahmins, 25, 121, 123, 125-6, 132-3, 135-6, 138, 140, 146, 150-1, 161, 166-7, 171-2, 174, 189, 259
non-violence, 64-5, 75, 95, 199, 200, 263. *See also ahimsa*

OBCs, *see* Other Backward Classes
Ordinances of Manu, *see* Laws of Manu
Orientalism, 12-13
Orientalist approach, 12, 14, 22
Orientalists, 12-14, 18, 22, 133-4, 192, 235
Other Backward Castes, 229
Other Backward Classes, 39-40, 49, 52, 54-5, 127-31, 148, 180, 210, 215, 217, 219, 229-34, 237, 239, 241, 244-7, 249-52, 260-2

Panikkar, K.N., 189
peasant movements, rise of, 210, 232
Phule, Jyotiba, 192, 202
Poona Pact, 201-2
pramrta, 67
Probus Club, 171
Puranas, 67, 69-70
Purusa, 10, 63

Quit India movement, 124

Radhakrishnan, P., 154
Rajagopal, Arvind, 249
Rajagopalachari, C., 136-8
rajas, 11
Rajputs, 74, 77, 80, 83
Ramachandran, M.G., 127
Ramayana, 134, 193, 196, 249-50
Ranvir Sena, 252
Rao, M.S.A., 243
Rao, Narasimha, 216
Rashtriya Swayamsevak Sangh, 35-6, 219, 250
Reddys, 125
Republican Party, 206, 209
Ricoeur, Paul, 23
Rigveda, 10, 61, 64
Roberts, F.S., 81-2
RSS, *see* Rashtriya Swayamsevak Sangh

Sagarputra, 264
Said, Edward, 12-13
Saiva Siddhanta, 135
samskar, 38
Sandhurst Committee, 85-6
Sanskritization, 193, 214, 233, 252-3, 262
Sarasvat Brahmins, 74, 81
Sarasvats, 73-4
sattva, 11
Savarna Liberation Army, 252
Scheduled Castes, 40, 45, 54, 105, 127-8, 130-1, 147-8, 151, 154, 173, 178, 197, 205, 213, 218-19, 228-9, 240, 244-5, 252
Scheduled Tribes, 40, 105, 127-8, 130-1, 148, 151, 154, 173, 218, 228
Second World War, 102
Sen, Amartya, 230
Sepoy Mutiny, 76, 78, 80, 86
Serres, Michel, 24
Shah, A.M., 236
Shastras, 135, 159, 202
Shiv Sena, 219
Shourie, Arun, 214

Shudras, 11, 34, 39, 68, 101, 119, 123, 127, 133, 192, 217, 228
Sikhs, 79, 81, 82, 98, 100-1
Singer, Milton, 179
Singh, Jagpal, 245
Singh, V.P., 131, 232
Singh, Yogendra, 152
Society for Promotion of Indian Classical Music and Culture, 167
South Indian Brahmins, 119, 152, 154, 159, 163, 180, 190, 232. *Also see* Brahmins of Tamil Nadu
Srinivas, M.N., 16, 20-1, 193, 236, 252
Sundaram Iyengar, T.V., 153
Sunlight Sena, 252
Swami Dayananda, 99

tamas, 11
Tambras, 170-4, 179-80, 240, 246-7, 261
Tamil Brahmins, 28, 48, 56, 111, 132, 140, 146, 156, 158, 161, 163, 174-5, 189, 240, 247, 259, 262
Tamil Isai Sangam, 134
Tani Tamizh Iyakham, 134
The Hindu, 36, 108, 138, 192, 212-14, 250
The Sacred Books of the East, 12

untouchability, 44, 128, 172, 192, 201-2, 204-5, 217, 230
Untouchables, 126, 191-3, 170-1, 191-220, 228, 254, 228, 230, 233-44. *See also Harijans*
upper castes, 77, 79, 83, 104, 119, 123, 125, 128, 131-2, 180, 190, 192-5, 201, 204, 208-12, 215, 218, 220, 243-4, 246-7, 251-4, 261-2

Vaishyas, 11, 16, 49, 66, 68, 101
Vajpayee, A.B., 250
Valmiki, 193, 214, 250
van der Veer, Peter, 259
varna, 11-12, 17, 21, 26, 36, 39, 43, 61, 63-4, 66-8, 70-1, 73, 83, 95, 99, 101-2, 104, 110, 119, 135, 149, 151, 169, 176, 201, 235, 237, 243-4, 250-2, 261, 263-5
varnashrama dharma, 123, 135
Vedas, 9, 17, 37, 47, 63-4, 66, 202, 251, 264-5
Velamas, 125
Vellalas, 123, 125-6, 135
Vishva Hindu Parishad, 161, 214, 250

Weber, Max, 20
Weekend, 157
World War I, 84-5

Yadav, Laloo Prasad, 252
Yadavs, 98, 211, 212, 217, 249
Ymir, 10-11

Zelliot, Eleanor, 193, 196